HUTCHINS' UNIVERSITY

1891–1991

A CENTENNIAL PUBLICATION OF THE
UNIVERSITY OF CHICAGO PRESS

WILLIAM H. McNEILL

HUTCHINS' UNIVERSITY

A MEMOIR OF THE
UNIVERSITY OF CHICAGO
1929–1950

THE UNIVERSITY OF CHICAGO PRESS
CHICAGO AND LONDON

William H. McNeill is the Robert A. Millikan Distinguished Service Professor Emeritus at the University of Chicago. His many books include *Plagues and Peoples; Venice: The Hinge of Europe, 1081–1797; The Rise of the West: A History of the Human Community; The Pursuit of Power: Technology, Armed Force, and Society since A.D. 1000;* and *Mythistory and Other Essays.*

All photos in the gallery are from the University of Chicago Archives, unless otherwise noted.

The University of Chicago Press, Chicago 60637
The University of Chicago Press, Ltd., London
© 1991 by The University of Chicago
All rights reserved. Published 1991
Printed in the United States of America

00 99 98 97 96 95 94 93 92 91   5 4 3 2 1

Library of Congress Cataloging-in-Publication Data

McNeill, William Hardy, 1917–
    Hutchins' university: A memoir of the University of Chicago,
1929–1950 / William H. McNeill.
        p.   cm.
    "A Centennial publication of the University of Chicago Press"—
Half t.p.
    Includes bibliographical references and index.
    ISBN 0–226–56170–4
    1. University of Chicago—History.   I. Title.
LD929.M36   1991
378.773′11—dc20   91–9322
                                                            CIP

CONTENTS

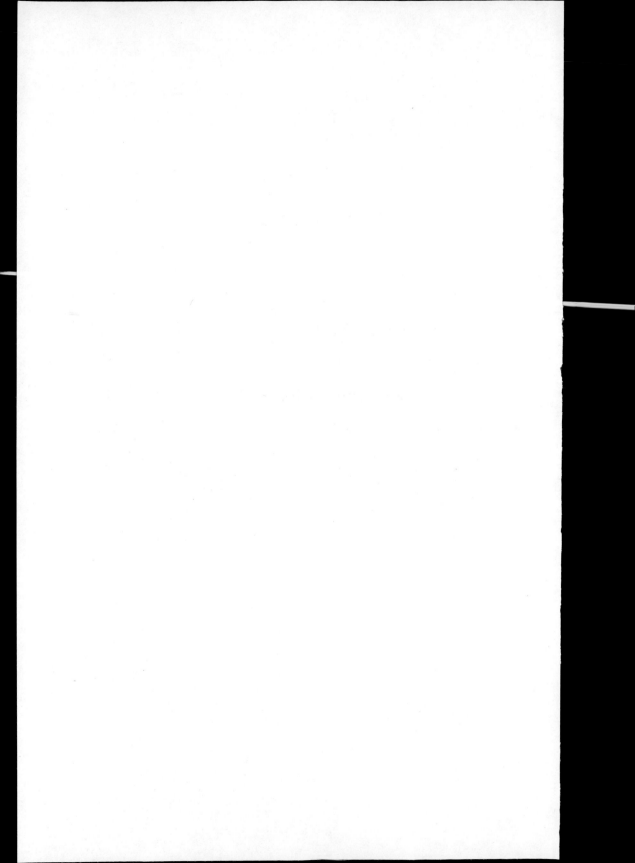

PREFACE

On 19 November 1929 a splendid, anachronistic academic procession walked down the aisle of the brand-new Rockefeller Chapel on the campus of the University of Chicago. Hundreds of academics had gathered from far and wide to celebrate the installation of a young man named Robert Maynard Hutchins as fifth president of the University of Chicago. The stock market crash, inaugurating the Great Depression, had occurred three weeks before; so the Hutchins era at the university coincided with a drastically changed social and economic climate in the United States and, indeed, throughout the world.

During the next twenty-one years Hutchins remained in charge of the university's administration, and turmoil continued to reign on the world scene. Recovery from the depression remained incomplete until the approach of World War II provoked armament programs that mopped up America's troublesome unemployment. In the early 1940s, wartime mobilization substituted shortages for the surpluses that had clogged the economy in the 1930s. Then, when the war was over, a new, relatively prosperous, peacetime balance for American society (and the world) was just emerging at the time Hutchins announced his resignation on 19 December 1950.

Depression, war, and demobilization dictated a series of drastic adjustments within the university; but what happened on the Midway was more than a response to external events, because Hutchins developed ideas of his own about what the university ought to be and tried hard to induce those around him to act on his convictions. Other university presidents of the era were content with maneuvering to minimize friction among the diverse groups affecting the institutions entrusted to their care—faculty, students, the general public, trustees, alumni, and potential donors. But Hutchins became more and more impatient as the years passed, and his policies met with increasing opposition. By posing fundamental questions about the aims of education and the purposes of the university, he kept the campus in turmoil, and this differentiated Hutchins' University, 1929–50, from other institutions of higher learning more sharply than has since been the case.

Within the university community, debate on educational and philosophic questions reached an extraordinary intensity. Students, faculty, and trustees were all caught up in the controversies Hutchins provoked. Convinced of the universal importance of the issues so heatedly discussed (and sometimes decided in faculty meetings), members of the University of Chicago often seemed both provincial and smug. Many believed that they, and they alone, were wrestling with basic questions about education and the pursuit of truth. Though after the passage of fifty years and more, some of the phrases fought over at Chicago seem quaintly archaic, I still feel that Hutchins, and the professors and students who responded to him, were entirely right in trying so hard to make the goals of higher education explicit. Serious debates on such questions were weak and anemic elsewhere, whereas at Chicago almost the entire faculty and a substantial portion of the student body—especially among undergraduates—took part.

It was marvelous to be young in such a time and place. Freshmen and sophomores boldly set out to explore the great questions of human life and society, arguing incessantly, both within the classrooms and outside of them. Hutchins soon convinced most of Chicago's undergraduates that they were indeed the hope of the world because they were getting such a good education. As a result, adolescent rebellion never separated the students of the university from the president. After all, Hutchins himself remained stubbornly sophomoric, seeking truth, scorning compromise, and, every so often, impugning established authority with his characteristic barbed wit. Witty self-deprecation was also part of Hutchins' rhetorical armory, partially disarming those who thought his program for the university was outrageous, or merely irrelevant to their careers.

My aim in this essay is to set forth the convergence of institutional and sociological circumstances with intellectual and personal aspirations that made the University of Chicago such a special place in the 1930s and 1940s. Times have changed since then, but memory of what the campus was like in those days can fumble toward a portrait of that vanished age. Recollection is deceptive, of course, even when checked by what others remember. Nevertheless, I am convinced that it can be a useful supplement to written records, whose bulk and heterogeneous character make reconstruction of the spirit of the place very difficult. I was a student at Chicago from 1933 to 1939 and returned as a young faculty member in 1947. Accordingly, much of what follows derives from personal experience, supplemented by some rather cursory investigation of university records deposited in the Special Collections of Regenstein Library and by conversations with others who still remembered the Hutchins era when I talked over old times with them in the winter of 1990.

The manuscript benefited from criticism by Mortimer Adler, Wayne Booth, Donald Levine, Edward Levi, Douglas Mitchell, and Milton Singer. None will be entirely satisfied by the changes made in response to their observations, even though I corrected some errors, modulated some judgments, and improved a great many sentences under their tutelage. I am therefore very grateful for their help, but since this is merely a memoir of Hutchins' University, I felt no compunction at persisting in opinions that they do not share and, in some instances, vehemently reject.

1

THE UNIVERSITY OF CHICAGO

IN 1929

As Chicago entered the last decade of the nineteenth century, the booming city gave birth to a remarkable pair of twins: the World's Columbian Exposition, which opened a year late in 1893, and the University of Chicago, which opened, according to plan, in 1892. Both met with instant success. A "White City" of vast exposition halls, classical in style, whose plaster mimicked marble, suddenly sprouted by Lake Michigan on the swampy land of the city's south side. There it abutted directly on a more enduring "City Gray" of Gothic limestone designed to mimic Oxford and Cambridge.

Although a brush with economic depression put off the opening day until a year after the anniversary it purported to celebrate, the World's Columbian Exposition of 1893 turned out to be the most successful world's fair ever held. A nationwide rail net allowed visitors to come from all across the country; and the innumerable wonders on display, some of which had never been seen on earth before, attracted more than 21 million paid admissions. Electric floodlights, for example, made the fair's white plaster buildings shine dazzlingly at night. It was nothing less than a preview of heaven for people accustomed to the flickering flames of gas and kerosene lighting, most of whom had never before seen an electric bulb, much less a world of incandescent light.

Other attractions were thrilling, like the giant ferris wheel on the Midway, or shocking, like Little Egypt's belly dance, or alarming, like Frederick Jackson Turner's lament over the disappearing influence of frontier freedom upon American history. Sessions of the World's Parliament of Religions managed to be thrilling, shocking, and alarming all at once. Small wonder,

1

then, that the exposition actually made money and closed its accounts with a handsome surplus.

The World's Columbian Exposition of 1893 signified a sort of coming of age for Chicago and for the Middle West. Chicago had just surpassed Philadelphia as the second city of the nation. Most of the city's population had been born in central and eastern European villages and were Catholic, but the city's businesses were almost entirely in the hands of native-born Protestants, and so were most farms and small towns of the Middle West. In this environment, where traditional religious identities were wearing thin as they mixed and clashed, it was entirely appropriate that one of the highlights of the Columbian Exposition was a speech by an Indian holy man who called himself Vivekananda. As spokesman for Hinduism at the World's Parliament of Religion, he challenged the religious prejudices of his audience by asserting that Christianity and all the other leading faiths of the earth shared the same divine message, with the difference that Hinduism expressed that message most clearly. Such an exotic idea shocked and titillated the minds of Vivekananda's audiences in exactly the same way that Little Egypt's belly dance shocked and titillated the animal senses of hers.

After such experiences, rural and small-town mid-America could never be the same, and Chicago's claim to be a seat of culture as well as of commerce and industry seemed assured. Intimations of heaven and a new familiarity with the wonders and variety of the world had enlarged the consciousness of millions who visited the fair. Provincial isolation may not have disappeared, but it was surely shaken both by the brilliance of electric light and by exposure to new ideas.

As for Chicago, the seat of the fair, it was no longer a raw frontier town, but a place where visions of the future turned into reality faster than anywhere else. Dreams, hurriedly acted upon, had turned the Columbian Exposition into a triumph; and when the temporary buildings were removed, the fairgrounds became handsome parks, all according to plan. Indeed, the planners were not content with that achievement, but went on to design parks for the entire waterfront, giving Chicago a spectacular and glorious front yard along Lake Michigan the like of which no other city yet can boast. Enduring cultural institutions also emerged from the fair, most notably the Field Museum of Natural History, which was created to house some of the exhibits.

The university that rose beside the Midway (and, after the temporary structures of 1893 had been destroyed, bestrode it) was also a great success and quickly developed a range of appeals to mind and body comparable to those that made the Columbian Exposition so important for popular consciousness. On the intellectual side, the new university proclaimed itself to be a center of graduate study where research and the discovery of new knowledge, rather than mere teaching and the transmission of established truths, was to be the central aspiration of professors and students alike.

In the university's early days, biblical criticism was by far the most controversial aspect of this exotic ideal. The university's first president, William Rainey Harper (d. 1906), was an Old Testament scholar and a champion of German methods of textual criticism. He, and other biblical scholars whom he appointed to the new university, believed that the words of the Bible had been written down by human beings who were quite capable of error and who, even if inspired by God, were nonetheless also influenced by the ideas of their day—ideas which were far removed from those of nineteenth-century American Protestants.

Some Christians and Jews agreed with these radical ideas, but most Baptists took strong exception to the notion that the text of the Bible as transmitted to them was susceptible to error. This meant that an intended link between the new University of Chicago and the Baptist denomination shattered very quickly. Even though the Divinity School retained a legal connection with Baptists, the rest of the university lost its initial sectarian religious ties. Cast forth on the secular world, President Harper and his successors had to find a different basis of support for the new university from anything that had hitherto prevailed in the United States.

Harper was in fact strikingly successful in doing so. On the one hand, he persuaded John D. Rockefeller to follow up his initial founding gift with subsequent donations that helped the university to keep on growing as fast as students poured in. Other donors, too, were attracted by Harper's vision of how newly discovered truth could be counted on to improve human life. The university's motto, "Crescat Scientia, Vita Excolatur," expressed Harper's creed concisely, but only for those who could penetrate the obscurity of passive verbs and Latin subjunctives. For others, less learned, the English translation "Let knowledge increase, life be enriched" is too harshly materialistic to do justice to the Latin, for *excolatur* derives from the Latin word for tillage and, to quote my Latin-English dictionary, means "to cultivate, improve, ennoble, refine, perfect" as well as to enrich through better harvests.

But Harper did not rely solely on the claim that intellectual work, if properly funded and freed from the trammels of outworn authority, would improve, and might even ennoble, refine, and perfect human life. Bodies, bigger and even more mobile than Little Egypt's exposed midriff, also entered into the new university's public image and popular appeal. For Harper brought Amos Alonzo Stagg from Yale as head professor with full academic status of something previously unheard of—a Department of Physical Culture and Athletics—and then lent the weight of the president's office to developing football at the university into a popular spectacle. Downtown businessmen and civic boosters soon began to imitate undergraduates by identifying the university's and the city's prowess with the success Stagg expected from his teams. Chicago, Carl Sandburg's "city of big shoulders," found much to admire in Chicago's Maroons, whose strength and agility usually outclassed their opponents on the football field before and for a short while after World War I.

A university that combined the role of research institution, whence new truths and technological wonders might be expected to emerge, with the maintenance of athletic teams that provided popular entertainment was a completely new phenomenon in the 1890s. Harper's University was therefore unique. To be sure, there were flourishing state universities in the Middle West which served their constituencies by preparing teachers and training the young for a variety of other professional occupations. But research in pursuit of new truths seemed like a wild goose chase to most state legislators. They therefore grudged funds for professors whose prospective contributions to knowledge were difficult to assess and whose efforts to improve upon received ideas at a time when both Darwinism and biblical criticism still shocked most Americans were sure to arouse politically embarrassing religious controversy.

And, except for Michigan, midwestern state universities were slow to go in for big-time football. Encouraging young men to bump into one other on a grassy field looked like an extreme case of urban frivolity to ordinary farmers, who got more exercise than they wanted by working in their fields. Moreover, the state universities were located in small towns, where limited transportation prohibited the assemblage of large football crowds. This meant that gate receipts could not sustain an athletic program on anything like Chicago's scale.

In the east, where state universities were puny, two private institutions, Johns Hopkins and Clark, antedated Chicago as graduate research universities by a few years. But they commanded less money than Chicago was able to acquire, thanks, largely, to John D. Rockefeller's continued support; and these pioneer graduate schools never developed links with their surrounding communities in the form of big-time football. In the 1890s, Harvard, Yale, Columbia, and Princeton were only beginning to emerge from their collegiate status. Sectarian connections were still real—Unitarian, Congregational, Anglican, and Presbyterian respectively. But religious training and preparation for the ministry had already shrunk toward marginality for these institutions. Instead, a new role had emerged—that of initiating young men of the upper classes into the arts of life as gracefully as possible. Teachers at Harvard, Yale, Columbia, and Princeton embraced this task gladly enough, without aspiring to compete with German universities in research, and without wishing to emulate the athletic spectacle offered by professional baseball. Most certainly, football had begun to attract much attention at the Ivy League schools, both as a test of individual manliness and as a proof of institutional prowess. But the upper-class character of those who played the game meant that crowds were smaller and popular following far weaker than at Chicago.

Subsequently, the growth of research and of graduate training began to alter the balance of university life in the east, especially at Harvard and Columbia. But the central importance of initiating young men of the upper classes into adult and professional roles remained unchallenged. The private universities, in fact, subsidized their expanding graduate studies from undergraduate tuition; and wealthy college alumni could be counted on to help out with gifts as well. Only at Columbia did the growth of graduate and professional schools under its famous president, Nicholas Murray Butler (1901–45), threaten to overshadow the undergraduate college—a development that both pleased and bothered Butler, since it made the university's financial base more precarious.

World War I brought changes in the circumstances of the University of Chicago and of its various sister institutions of higher learning. For one thing, a national elite began to emerge as young men experienced the displacement of war service and came to know sections of the country other than those in which they happened to grow up. As far as Chicago was concerned, this made it increasingly difficult for the university to attract the upper classes of its immediate hinterland as undergraduates. Before 1914, civic pride and the convenience of going to college close to home meant that some of the richest families of the city sent their children to the new university. Thus, for example, Harold Swift, scion of the meat packing family, graduated in 1907 and then turned into an enthusiastic alumnus and, ere long, a trustee. His attachment to the university was lifelong, for after his election to the Board of Trustees in 1914, he served as a very active Chairman of the Board from 1922 until his retirement at age 65 in 1949.

In the 1920s, Swift's localized career and resulting attachments became more exceptional than was the case before the Great War. Local boosterism, which had reached extremes in Chicago, became the prerogative of populist politicians, nicely illustrated by Mayor "Big Bill" Thompson's boast that Chicago would "make culture hum." But the mayor's bumbling enthusiasm turned off the young of the upper classes, whose fathers shared the local pride that Thompson had reduced to a caricature. Instead of accepting the city's "I Will" spirit, they began to harbor the sneaking suspicion that Chicago and the whole Midwest lacked the authentic polish appropriate to upper-class life.

Accordingly, a wish to leave home and secure the advantages of association with old money and with the emerging national elites of the east gained ground after World War I, with the result that fewer of the city's rich and well born now chose to become undergraduate students at Chicago. Simultaneously, in the 1920s, Ivy League schools began deliberately to recruit students from upper-class families of the whole country and established quotas for Jews from the eastern cities in order to assure a more "representative" student body.[1]

But Chicago's College could not really afford to be snooty. Most undergraduates lived at home and commuted to campus; and since the university looked like a seat of godlessness and corruption to the immigrant Catholic population of the city, in practice the College drew most of its students from among middle- and lower-middle-class Protestants who could not afford to send their children away to college. A Jewish quota was never attempted, partly, perhaps, because of a residual philo-Semitism inherited from President Harper's evangelical Baptist faith, but also because extra tuition income was always welcome.

Chicago's undergraduate college found itself under another pressure as the boom of the 1920s headed toward the depression of the 1930s. A potent rival for the city's allegiance arose in the form of the University of Notre Dame, whose football team, although based a hundred miles away in South Bend, Indiana, began to play "home games" in a vast new civic stadium on the lakefront—Soldier Field. When Notre Dame proved capable of defeating the topmost teams recruited from the Protestant ascendancy of the United States, the predominantly Catholic working-class public of Chicago rejoiced; and the fact that Stagg's old-fashioned, almost gentlemanly methods of recruitment failed to assemble a championship team after 1924 meant that the Maroons began to fade from the city's affections. Thus one of the pillars upon which Harper's University had relied, both for local support and for national publicity, was showing serious signs of decay in the late 1920s. But what, if anything, to do about it was tied up in a much wider debate that turned on what the College should teach, how it should be staffed, and what sort of students it should try to attract.

The graduate departments, where research was prized above all else, had never approved of the undergraduates' preoccupation with riotous living and rah-rah athletics. Graduate students gravitated to Chicago on the strength of its high reputation for research. They came from every part of the country and mingled with others who came from Canada and other foreign countries. But Chicago's undergraduates were nearly all local, and, in the 1920s, more and more of the cream—both social and intellectual—was being skimmed off by Ivy League recruiters. Consequently, those who came to Chicago were often attracted more by its athletic reputation than by anything else.

The result was mixed. Some earnest souls were intent on using the College as a social escalator, knowing that a good academic performance might raise them to professional status; but the majority, whose interest in academic study was dim to begin with, merely had their expectations confirmed by casual or inept teaching. Many of the College courses were taught by graduate students assigned to the task by their departments in lieu of fellowship support. And since the best graduate students had fellowships, the morale and dedication of those who had to delay their graduate careers by taking time to teach was often questionable.

On the other hand, Chicago's undergraduates did put enormous energy into extracurricular activities. Some were puerile, such as the disciplined freshmen cheering sections at football games and the ritual springtime dunkings in Botany Pond. Others were substantial business enterprises. The *Daily Maroon,* for example, was a profit-making organization run on quasi-professional lines. At the end of each year, the senior members of the Board of Control divided up the year's accumulation among themselves, and, in a good year, their collective reward exceeded a professorial salary. Similarly, the Order of Blackfriars, devoted to staging an all-male review each spring, spent large sums on publicity, coaching, and the like; and, in some years, it approached a professional standard of production.

On a more purely social level, fraternities and women's clubs created a tightly bonded microstructure within the undergraduate body, for each such group had its place in a carefully graded pecking order of prestige. For undergraduates who could not afford or refused to join fraternities and clubs, all-campus dances, concerts, religious associations, and a handful of political causes gave varied outlet to extracurricular energies. In addition, innumerable public lectures brought all sorts of famous personalities to campus.

But to a remarkable degree, football dominated undergraduate life every fall. Then, with the turn of the seasons, other sports hogged headlines in the student newspaper until spring football practice returned, competing with, and half-obscuring, baseball. Chicago's undergraduates, clearly, identified themselves, individually and collectively, with the Maroon teams, and the worth of the university, in their eyes and in those of most of the citizens of Chicago, was measured mainly by athletic success.

This inversion of values offended many professors. The radical response to the long-standing discrepancy between the outstanding graduate enterprise at Chicago and the questionable intellectual quality of the College was to abolish undergraduate education entirely. This had been repeatedly proposed by impatient professors who saw undergraduate antics as a silly distraction from the proper pursuits of the university. On the other hand, the College subsidized the graduate enterprise. College tuition income amounted to about twice the direct costs of instruction,[2] and how could the departments support all their deserving graduate students if there were no College teaching for them to do?

A contrary plan was to upgrade the College so as to compete directly with the Ivy League schools. That meant going national and trying to attract an upper-class student body from far and wide that would be more nearly worthy of the graduate departments. The cost of that strategy was, however, substantial. Apart from staff costs for better teachers, it presupposed the construction of dormitories in which an appropriate atmosphere could only be assured by assigning carefully chosen resident heads. Such an investment made the plan controversial, since it threatened to deflect university funds away from the graduate departments.

On the other hand, a successful undergraduate college, attracting its share of the country's rich and well born, might give the graduate enterprise a more secure financial base than anything the university had yet attained. This, after all, was what Harvard was doing with conspicuous success, for its rise to the status of the premier university of the country had become apparent by the 1920s. Chicago's precocious graduate enterprise depended instead on grants from individuals and, increasingly, from philanthropic foundations. Individual professors and heads of department were in the habit of approaching donors and foundation executives personally in order to persuade them to fund whatever new research enterprise the professor in question wished to pursue. This was a very precarious base for an ongoing institution, since everything depended on the energy and persuasiveness of individual professors and on the readiness of donors to allow themselves to be persuaded.

Moreover, as graduate teaching and research ideals spread to other institutions, including state universities of the Midwest and California, competition for grants became acute. Chicago's early lead was harder and harder to sustain. Foundation executives, many of whom had Chicago connections to begin with, were shy of awarding too much money to a single institution and tended to spread the wealth at their disposal by offering everybody a little. A favorite tactic was to give "seed money" to start some sort of new activity, expecting the host institution to find funds from other sources if the undertaking turned out well.

In this increasingly competitive environment, Chicago's professorial entrepreneurs were sometimes able to secure endowments to perpetuate at least some aspects of their research. James Henry Breasted, for example, built the Oriental Institute on the strength of his enthusiasm for finding the dawn of conscience and the origins of monotheism among the ancient Egyptians and by persuading various members of the Rockefeller family of the importance of continuing archaeological and literary investigations in the ancient Near East. In much the same fashion, Charles Merriam, professor of political science, set out to assure permanent improvement of local and state government in the United States by soliciting funds for the erection of the Public Administration Clearing House.

A more ambitious effort to institutionalize research was embodied in a new medical school erected, with appropriate hospitals, on the Midway in 1927. Significantly, the idea for such a medical school did not originate within the Chicago faculty. In its early days, instead of setting up a school of its own, the university decided to affiliate with Rush Medical School, located on the city's West Side. This was a reputable, thoroughly traditional institution, staffed by doctors immersed in the private practice of medicine. But the apprentice system that prevailed at Rush, and all other American medical schools, came under devastating attack in a report written by Abraham Flexner in 1910. The Rockefellers then appointed him secretary of their General Education Board, one of whose missions became the reform of medical training.

The University of Chicago was quite ready to respond to Flexner's idea of making medical training more scientific and systematic, but the established and respected professionals at Rush resisted outside efforts at changing their ways. A new start at a new site, immediately adjacent to the campus, seemed the quickest way to achieve a thoroughgoing reform of medical education. The result was a brand new University of Chicago Medical School that opened its doors in 1927, more as an embodiment of Flexner's ideas and of Rockefeller funds than of initiatives arising from anywhere within the university. Nevertheless, all concerned hoped that close association between researchers in the graduate departments of the biological sciences and doctors in the reformed Medical School would discover new cures and help to make American medicine thoroughly scientific, leaving old sectarian quarrels between homeopaths, osteopaths, and all the other apprenticeship traditions of medicine behind.

Doctors appointed to Chicago's new Medical School were required to abandon the time-honored practice of charging fees for attending the sick. Patient fees were collected by the hospital administration instead. In theory, this meant that salaried doctors could concentrate on research and on transmitting their art to aspiring students of medicine, while the treatment of patients became, as it were, merely incidental. But in practice, patients could not be treated like guinea pigs, and the need to keep fees coming in to meet hospital costs meant that clinical rounds and services became a heavy burden. Even though a professor in the new Department of Medicine no longer got his income directly from the fees he collected from patients, the enterprise as a whole still depended on what patients paid for hospitalization, supplemented, as in other parts of the university, by grants for specific programs of medical research coming from foundations and other outside sources.

Rockefeller initiatives also lay behind a major effort at institutionalizing and improving research and graduate training in the social sciences. In the first three decades of the twentieth century, a Chicago school of sociology arose around two key figures, William I. Thomas and Robert E. Park. They began as individual entrepreneurs, raising money from philanthropic individuals by convincing them that the social ills of Chicago were only susceptible to cure if what was actually happening in the immigrant communities of the city were carefully observed and thoroughly understood. Study of the strains and stresses created by migrating from tight-knit European village communities into the turbulent anonymity of a city like Chicago provoked Thomas to theorizing about general psychological and cultural conditions of human life, but he had to leave the university before his great work on *The Polish Peasant in Europe and America* (five volumes, 1918–20) was completed. (A hotel detective discovered him in bed with a young Polish woman, and the resulting scandal drove him to take refuge in New York.)

Park was less theoretically inclined than Thomas, but it was he who remained to become the catalytic figure around whom self-consciously "scientific" study of contemporary American society became an academic profession. The central concern was always moral, even though Thomas and Park both rejected the customary Protestant reliance on preaching against sin and depravity as the way to bring about reform. They argued that blind and righteous indignation was futile in the absence of an accurate understanding of the facts of city life. Only with knowledge of those facts could efficacious remedies be prescribed. And the way to find the facts was to go into the streets, seek out ordinary people, administer questionnaires, and keep careful records that might then be transmuted into statistics.[3]

Behind the whole effort at direct observation and quantification lay the assumption that small-town and rural Protestant mores were normative. Assimilation to that norm was the task facing immigrant (and black) populations. When the process faltered, social malady ensued. From such a viewpoint, Chicago (a place where Al Capone made a business of defying the law and gave the city a gangster image that still endures) was the best laboratory in the country for the study of what was going wrong in American cities. Accordingly, the Chicago school of sociology diligently set about making an accurate diagnosis, mobilizing scores of graduate students, and publishing dozens of books crammed with all sorts of relevant information.

Psychology, politics, and geography were intimately entwined in the task from the start, even though the main thrust remained with the Department of Sociology. In 1929, a new Department of Anthropology chimed in, expanding the range of human behavior that needed to be studied to embrace remote Indian communities of Latin America and other primitive societies.[4] Economists at Chicago remained apart, committed to generalized market theory and mathematical modeling. Historians, too, focused their attention on the national and European past and had little contact with the sociologists. Yet in their different ways, Chicago's economists and historians were also distinguished representatives of their respective fields.

The resulting cluster of what came to be called the social sciences therefore attained particular luster at Chicago, thanks to its early start and to the broad sympathies and alert curiosity that Thomas and Park exhibited in their relations with students and colleagues alike. Charles E. Merriam's concern with everyday, local politics made the Department of Political Science fit hand in glove with the Chicago school of sociology. His combination of political activism and reform (he ran unsuccessfully for mayor of Chicago in 1912) with more or less dispassionate analysis of who got what, why, when, and where from local politics was simply an application of the Chicago brand of sociology to public affairs.

During the 1920s, grants from philanthropic foundations had supported Chicago's entrepreneurial professors so as to make the university's separate social science departments into lodestars for the entire country. But, as Abraham Flexner's example showed, foundation executives were not entirely content to remain passive donors. In particular, a youthful Chicago Ph.D. in psychology named Beardsley Ruml, on becoming an officer of the Spelman Memorial Fund (a new Rockefeller foundation set up to remedy social ills in much the same way that Abraham Flexner was already using Rockefeller money to remedy bodily ills), decided that what the social sciences needed more than anything else was to break down departmental barriers.

Chicago's professors had already gone a long way in that direction and willingly fell in with Ruml's proposal for housing previously separate departments in a single Social Sciences Research Building. As a result, the new Medical School and hospital buildings that arose west of Ellis Avenue on the Midway in the late twenties were swiftly followed by the erection of a new Social Science Research Building facing the Midway near the corner of University Avenue. It was not completed until a few months after the crash of 1929; and soon after it opened, Beardsley Ruml arrived on campus as the first dean of a newly constituted Social Science Division.

Efforts to institutionalize research, whether in the Oriental Institute, the Medical School, or the Social Sciences Research Building, did not really assure continuity, for the university's endowment never caught up with the multitude of things its professors wanted to do. To sustain its activity, Chicago had to secure an unceasing flow of grants and gifts, nearly all of which were expendable and earmarked for some particular enterprise. The rise of philanthropic foundations meant that academic panhandling, initially very largely an affair between individual professors and individual donors, became a matter of negotiation between institutions. In that new game, the University of Chicago was a major player, but one which faced ever intensifying competition.

The intellectual eminence of the university had initially depended on what individual professors accomplished, working either by themselves or with only a few assistants and associates. This was true even in physics, for Chicago's first Nobel Prize winners, Albert A. Michelson (1907), Robert A. Millikan (1923), and Arthur H. Compton (1927), won their awards for ingenious personal experiments using quite modest equipment. In other fields, individual effort and acuity reigned supreme. For example, John M. Manly's edition of Chaucer depended only on his diligence in comparing manu-scripts and his skill in applying time-tested methods of philological scholar-ship for choosing among discrepant readings.

To be sure, rampant intellectual individualism was modified by the way schools of thought formed around particularly influential individuals. As we saw, this happened in sociology, where Thomas and Park were the catalytic figures. In philosophy, the same thing happened, for John Dewey (until he left for Columbia after a quarrel with Harper in 1904) and then George H. Mead made the Department of Philosophy into a stronghold of American pragmatism.

These and others like them did live up to Harper's claim by making im-portant contributions to knowledge; and their achievements placed the Uni-versity of Chicago at the cutting edge of academic research in a great many fields. Harvard was ahead of Chicago by 1929, according to such measures as the number of starred men of science listed in a standard biographical reference book. Other universities, notably Columbia and California, were close behind and catching up. But on the American academic scene and especially within the walls of the university itself, the graduate departments, where research was carried on, enjoyed undoubted prestige and were not shy about claiming the lion's share of the university's resources.

Five professional schools, an adult education program that conducted its classes downtown, and the Summer Quarter (which had a separate budget and administration of its own), together with a miscellany of associated en-terprises, such as the Laboratory Schools, and affiliated institutions such as Rush Medical School, constituted the rest of the university. Of these, the Summer Quarter was the most unusual, since when the university was first established, long tradition in the United States halted academic work in summertime to allow students to go home and help out on the farm until after the harvest. Harper realized that urbanization made such an academic calendar obsolete and decided that his university would function throughout the year, giving full academic credit for work done in summers. He therefore divided academic sessions into four quarters of eleven weeks, allowing a week of vacation time between quarters and the month of September off.

Keeping the university open through the summer accomplished two things. First of all, it created a new constituency among high school teachers, who swarmed to campus to improve their mastery of the subjects they were teaching in schools. Soon other institutions of higher learning imitated Chi-cago, and the initially powerful attraction to the Midway gradually faded away. But until the Great Depression of the 1930s hit, the Summer Quarter continued to draw large numbers of high school teachers, whose acquaintance with, and occasional affection for, the university constituted a very considerable asset in recruiting undergraduates, especially from the city and suburbs.

The other effect of staying open all summer was that professors, who were only asked to teach for three quarters each academic year, could add to their salaries, if they so wished, by taking on extra summer courses. But since many regular professors did not wish to teach all summer, the Dean of the Summer Quarter recruited professors from elsewhere to staff all the courses needed. This, too, brought a stable of visiting academics to the Midway each summer; and they, like their students, the high school teachers, became a significant constituency for the university, being strategically located on other campuses whence graduate students came.

The Law School enjoyed a high reputation on the strength of professors like James Parker Hall, Floyd Meachem, and Ernst Freund; but the undergraduate Business School attained no special eminence and was, in fact, a safe haven for athletes who needed to maintain academic eligibility while devoting their main effort to sport. Similarly, the School of Education had relaxed its academic standards to such a point as to lose the respect of professors in the graduate departments. On the other hand, the School of Social Service and the Graduate Library School were unique in their fields. Both were still new in 1929 and, being first in the field, were able to set standards for their respective professions.

The Divinity School, despite its continued connection with the Baptists, was the seat of a distinctive historical and ecumenical vision of Christianity. Its central tenet was that God's revelation to humankind had always come to fallible human beings, whose understanding of religious and other forms of truth was a historical product reflecting all the peculiarities of the time and place in which individuals happened to live. The Christian faith, from this point of view, was still evolving. Doctrinal definitions, no matter how securely enshrined in authoritative texts, captured only fragments of God's truth. It followed that doctrinal quarrels over what Christians should believe were sadly wrongheaded.

Addressed to a denominationally fragmented American Protestantism, this was powerful, healing doctrine. Church history became central. Instead of serving as a branch of apologetics showing how one sect alone held fast to the true doctrine, while, one by one, other denominations fell into error, it became an ecumenical exercise showing how persistently human beings had striven after holiness, stumbling slowly toward a better understanding of

God's will. And, according to Divinity School professors of the 1920s, what God willed was that Christians should help others. Accordingly, Christian churches were, or at least ought to be, devoted to social amelioration. Simultaneously, the Department of Sociology claimed that its researches would show them how.

The congruence was not accidental. In fact, almost all of the university faculty in 1929 had been shaped in their youth by Protestant forms of Christian teaching. Most fell away from the doctrines of whatever church they were born to; but this did not necessarily involve an open break with organized religion. Arthur Compton, for example, habitually attended the Hyde Park Baptist Church on Sunday; and Robert A. Millikan once preached in the University Chapel, explaining how science and religion were fully compatible when properly understood.

A strong evangelical residue remained. As most professors saw things, teaching was an improvement on preaching, since it gave reason its due and freed human minds from the bonds of outworn beliefs. In fact, for most of the faculty, that was their main mission as members of the university community, since only a few could ever expect to discover important new knowledge by their own researches. But the propagation of scientific truth was a secular ministry entirely analogous to the Christian ministry that had shaped the literate culture of rural and small-town America. Accordingly, the faculty of the University of Chicago devoted itself to this secular ministry with all the conviction one expects from the newly converted; and, as acolytes of reason, many professors retained the traditional Christian hope that anyone could be saved simply by hearing the truth. A populist, small-town spirit thus survived among the faculty at the University of Chicago. There they found themselves in uneasy symbiosis with the tumult of a city whose Catholic immigrant populations, fresh from Europe, were still making their own painful adjustment to urban living.

This, then, was the institution to which Robert Maynard Hutchins came as president in November 1929. The uproarious encounter that ensued will be the subject of this memoir.

2

HONEYMOON ON THE MIDWAY
1929–1931

Policy-making at the University of Chicago suffered abrupt interruption twice in the 1920s when two successive presidents, having barely begun to wrestle with the question of what to do about the discrepancy between graduate and undergraduate work on the campus, unexpectedly disappeared from the scene. President Ernest DeWitt Burton (1923–25) established a committee to look into reform of the College, but died before anything was decided. His successor, Max Mason (1925–28), persuaded a vigorous young historian, Chauncey Boucher, to become Dean of the College and entrusted him with the task of doing something about undergraduate education. By May 1928, after appropriate consultation with a variety of faculty committees, Boucher's recommendations were ready to come before the Senate, which comprised all the full professors of the university. The Senate was the university's ruling academic body and its approval was necessary before changes in curriculum and governance of the College could come into force. But just as a decision was expected, President Mason's resignation brought everything to a sudden standstill.[1]

Choice of a new president rested with the Board of Trustees, but several senior faculty members developed a lively interest in the matter. Some considered themselves to be presidential timber, and some distrusted the trustees and central administration, thinking that overly ambitious plans for the College would diminish the sovereign importance of the graduate departments. To allay such suspicions, the trustees asked the Senate to appoint a faculty committee to advise the board in looking for a new president.

The effect of this move was to block the presidential ambitions of everyone already on the scene. The leading spirits of the faculty committee were

16

vigorous champions of the ideal of a research university with full departmental autonomy. As such, they distrusted Max Mason's obvious heir, Frederic C. Woodward, who had unexpectedly become acting president. As vice president under Mason, Woodward had advocated College reform and before that he had been a professor of law. Thus he represented segments of the university that competed with the graduate departments for university funds. Being energetic champions of the graduate departments, the faculty committee therefore vetoed Woodward's candidacy and, by doing so, in effect vetoed other local candidates. For it soon became clear that anyone from within the university who would be acceptable to the faculty committee would be unsatisfactory to those who felt that structural and managerial reforms were in fact needed.[2]

The search therefore focused on outsiders. Scores of names came under consideration, and many were interviewed before the youthful dean of the Yale Law School was chosen. Courtship lasted a year, for Robert Maynard Hutchins' youth and panache were hard for his elders to accept, and his appointment obviously involved more than ordinary risk. But, as Edwin R. Embree of the Rosenwald Fund wrote in recommending him to the Board of Trustees: "A conventional leader may continue the University as a respectable institution. A brilliant choice may enable the University to return to its earlier role as a real leader in American education."[3]

In choosing Hutchins as fifth president of the university, both the faculty committee and the trustees were betting on a glorious future and simultaneously harking back, nostalgically, to the past. For Chicago's past was dominated in 1929 by living memories of how a brilliant young man, William Rainey Harper, had suddenly made the university into the bellwether of higher education throughout the United States. By 1929, the very success the university had met with during its first decades meant that many other schools had hurried to become seats of research (and of big time football), so that Chicago inevitably lost its initial preeminence. To regain preeminence, the university presumably required a new leader, one as brilliant, brash, and bold as Harper once had been.

In Robert Maynard Hutchins the Board of Trustees and the faculty committee that advised the board felt they had found such a man. Misgivings remained, but they were countered during the first two years of his presidency both by Hutchins' commanding presence and by some nimble footwork on his part, as he sidestepped the rifts and disagreements within the university community that had led to his selection. Though quarrels blew up, especially toward the end of the period, a two-year honeymoon resulted, during which brief time Hutchins resolved some major contentious issues with quite astonishing ease, thereby achieving his most enduring imprint on the governance of the university.

Who then was this young man who provoked such high hopes?

Hutchins, the second of three sons, was born in 1899 to a young Presbyterian minister and his wife in Brooklyn, New York. Brooklyn was the site of William J. Hutchins' first and only pastorate. Eight years later, after conspicuous success in building up his congregation, he accepted a call to Oberlin Theological Seminary as professor of homiletics. For the next ten years, therefore, the future president of the University of Chicago grew up in Ohio, where his father swiftly became a leading figure at Oberlin College as well as in the seminary attached to it. At Oberlin, the Hutchins family and the college community combined to create a supportive matrix that shaped the young man's habits and defined the high expectations that he set for himself and for everyone around him. To be sure, Hutchins experimented with rebelliousness by engaging in youthful japes; and in later life he turned away from the outward pieties and religious observances that played a central role in his childhood. But habits of work and a fundamental thirst for righteousness imbibed from his early surroundings never changed. Though he mimicked his father by becoming first a teacher and then an educational administrator, he remained very much a preacher at heart.

It is hard for those unfamiliar with Presbyterianism to imagine what it was like to be a successful minister's son. The first thing to understand is that Presbyterians considered the ministry the highest imaginable calling, so that a minister commanded universal respect and deference. He was, after all, the ordained vehicle by which the voice of God, recorded in the Bible, reached ordinary human beings. To perform that function adequately, a minister had to know enough Hebrew and Greek to consult God's word in the original tongues; and that, in turn, meant that training for the ministry was prolonged and rigorous. Moreover, a minister had to be eloquent as well as learned in order to explain the Bible's meaning in clear, logical, and convincing fashion every Sunday. That he should exemplify all the Christian virtues was taken for granted. What else would one expect from a man of God?

Presbyterians distrusted raw religious emotion. That was the mark of Methodists and Baptists, whose ministers were distinguished more by the warmth of their conviction than by the accuracy of their knowledge of the word of God. Being cool, clear-minded disciples of Calvin, Presbyterians understood that salvation depended on knowing what God willed and that this precious knowledge came from the Bible and nowhere else. Knowledge,

therefore, and truth, deriving from the correct interpretation of sacred scripture, were what mattered; and the minister's role in society was to provide
such knowledge and preach the saving truth Sunday after Sunday.

The Reverend William J. Hutchins conformed to these high expectations
with magnificent ease. He was a fine preacher—eloquent, logical, firm and
clear, and if he had any doubts about the adequacy of biblical guidance to all
the important questions of human life, he kept them very much to himself.
Within the bosom of the family, each day began and ended with prayer and
Bible reading. A father who knew so much, who commanded such respect,
and who personally communicated with God in prayer every day at family
meals as well as in public was a formidable figure for any young boy to get
used to having about the house.

Their father's sort of knowing, his sure sense of right and wrong, and his
lofty status *vis-à-vis* ordinary mortals—all this remained, I think, an ideal
norm for each of his sons.[4] But it was a norm that his middle son, Robert,
was never able to attain, despite his best efforts to do so. He quickly achieved
a lofty status *vis-à-vis* ordinary mortals and did so, as it were, effortlessly;
but all his outward success remained hollow because he fell short of really
knowing the truth. The trouble was that soon after leaving home in 1918,
Robert rejected his father's path to knowing all the most important truths
and spent the rest of his life trying to find a substitute for his father's Bible,
without ever quite succeeding. In this, as in other ways, his life was therefore
a tragedy.

All was not solemn seriousness in the Hutchins household. The father,
being thoroughly at ease with himself and with God, was also at ease with
his sons. Far more important was the fact that his wife had a strong sense of
the ridiculous. Her satiric witticisms and occasional irreverence were aimed,
among other things, at overt expression of the deep-seated family pride that
drove her sons to emulate their father's social leadership, moral earnestness,
and intellectual rigor. But to all appearances she remained well content with
her role as wife and mother and took pleasure in the successes that came to
her husband and sons. Presumably, she secretly shared the family pride,
whose outward signs she so strongly deprecated. Yet her witty sallies and
occasional irreverence introduced an astringent element into their daily discourse, obliging her husband and sons to see themselves from outside, so to
speak, and to scorn pomposity both within and beyond the family circle.[5]

Robert Maynard Hutchins' acerbic wit, which won him innumerable ad-
mirers as well as enemies in later life, clearly descended from his mother,
just as his eloquent, concise style of speaking descended from his father.

What made him different was his appearance. When he attained his full height of six feet, two and one-half inches, he towered over his father and brothers. An unusually erect carriage and spectacularly handsome face magnified the effect of his height. The resulting physical presence set him apart from ordinary mortals. In his prime, simply by walking into a roomful of people, he commanded instant attention; and when he began to talk, spouting witticisms and lavishing extravagant (semi-ironical?) compliments on those around him, his nimble tongue reinforced the extraordinary magnetism of his outward appearance.

Early in his career, Hutchins certainly profited from his extraordinary physical beauty. Without it he would not have risen as rapidly as he did. But there were costs as well. Men as well as women were attracted to him; and a sexual undertone, however rigorously he repressed it, could not be excluded from many, perhaps most, encounters with others. He learned to protect himself from the attractiveness of his physical presence by firing off witty remarks designed to shock most of those who crowded to him. He often seemed arrogant, and the result was to keep ordinary, casual acquaintances very much at arm's length. Some few were admitted to a distant sort of intimacy, but even they did not escape occasional thrusts of his self-protective wit. To hold one's own in his intimate company, it was almost necessary to respond in kind, resorting to raillery which sometimes became competitive as each egged the other on toward new heights of impudence.

Far more than most men, he kept a mask between himself and others. He never revealed himself fully, even to his closest friends and associates, and kept his emotions rigorously and emphatically to himself. He thus fell into the role of an antique tragic actor, commanding public attention through a magnificently eloquent voice that issued from behind a mask. This was a heavy price to pay for the genetic accident of his extraordinary physical attractiveness; and as he grew older, it continued to hamper him, whereas the advantages that he derived from his appearance when he was young inevitably evaporated as his physical vigor and freshness faded. Accordingly, like a great athlete, he outlived his fame, and this made Hutchins' life tragic in still another sense.

But when he left Oberlin in 1918 to join the army and see the world after two years of college in that secluded community of like-thinking seekers after truth and justice, the young Hutchins had yet to experience failure. He excelled in school, athletically and scholastically. His participation in the tight-knit college community did nothing to weaken his parents' imprint. On the contrary, the shared concerns and commonality of outlook that characterized Oberlin College before World War I reinforced everything he had learned at home. Being best in school and at anything else he chose to undertake simply conformed to family expectation.

Two years in the army therefore came as quite a shock. Hutchins volunteered as an ambulance corpsman and served as a private on the Italian front, but his actual exposure to combat was brief. For the most part he wasted time in the army, first waiting to get overseas and then waiting to get back home, while officers and sergeants devised silly tasks to keep Private Hutchins and his fellow heroes from complete idleness. Exquisite and prolonged fatuity was not what he expected when he volunteered, and for once in his life the young man did not excel. Being totally out of tune with the mores and folkways of army life, he simply could not fit in with what those around him expected. In later years, he therefore remembered his participation in World War I with unmitigated revulsion.

Nevertheless, military service marked him. For one thing, it began to erode the tight-laced, puritanical lifestyle he had grown up with. For example, he learned to smoke, drink, and swear, if not in the army, then immediately afterward at Yale, where he enrolled in 1919. His father was a Yale graduate, so in abandoning Oberlin for Yale he was conforming to paternal example. Moreover, William J. Hutchins was about to leave Oberlin to assume the presidency of Berea College, Kentucky, so there was no home to go back to in Oberlin, even if Robert had wished to return.

On a deeper level, too, Hutchins' exposure to the great world, as manifested in the boredom and brutality of war and the behavior of his fellow soldiers, presumably helped to provoke a parting of the ways with his father's religion. In later life, at any rate, Hutchins did not believe that the Bible, even when wisely interpreted, could lead humankind to salvation or to the knowledge of God's will. Another path toward truth was needed, and Hutchins always hoped that human reason might suffice as a substitute for his father's faith. Exactly when and how he rejected that faith is impossible to say. Such things were too important in the Hutchins family ever to be openly expressed in words, much less written down and recorded. There was no formal break between Robert and his father; and it is possible that William J. Hutchins shared enough of his son's reservations about the adequacy of old-time Calvinist reliance on the Bible to make him at least partially sympathetic with his son's views. And from the son's side, he did not completely abandon churchgoing until after he found, during his first years at Chicago, that the sermons in Rockefeller Chapel were no more than a weak and wavering echo of the eloquent exposition of Christian truth that had pervaded his youth.[6]

The tone of undergraduate life at Yale in the early 1920s was set by wealthy graduates of eastern prep schools. With all the ebullience of youth, they defied Prohibition, a monument to the provincialism of Bible Belt reformers, and embraced jazz, which was then emerging from the Negro underworld. "Anything goes," was the refrain of a popular song of the day, and Yale undergraduates were eager to find out just what that meant. Drinking illegal alcohol and clinging close to short-skirted, silk-stockinged girls on the dance floor was a big part of what they discovered. Few took school work seriously. Snap courses and a grade of C was quite enough for anyone to aspire to. Getting ready to get rich by getting to know the best people was what really mattered. Or so an outsider like Robert Maynard Hutchins, who had to work at menial tasks for as much as six hours a day to meet his living expenses, later declared to be the case.

At Yale, as in the army, he started as a misfit; but the difference at Yale was that he gained acceptance and then learned to excel in that alien environment, partly by academic brilliance, and partly by dint of his exceptional appearance and the aloof manner and verbal repartee that he perfected as an undergraduate. In his senior year, he was tapped for one of the prestigious secret societies that defined the social universe of Yale undergraduates and also entered the Yale Law School, where he found a kind of intellectual stimulus that had previously been missing from his formal education. That was because the prevailing "case method" for the study of law required close examination of how judges reasoned in deciding difficult points of law. This exactly fitted his aptitudes and predilictions. What his father had done with the words of the Bible, law students did with judicial opinions—first studying all the relevant texts to make sure of their meaning and then reconciling discrepancies as best they could.

The law, moreover, dealt with questions of right and justice and sought to answer them on the authority of a corpus of writings in quite the same way that Presbyterian ministers used the text of the Bible to answer the same questions. And even though judicial opinions did not claim to be inspired, and were not always expressed in elegant or logical prose, at least they were authoritative and therefore important for the conduct of everyday affairs. The study of law therefore fitted Hutchins' expectations of what really deserved his attention far better than the miscellaneous courses he sat through during his first years at Oberlin and Yale. Indeed, he later declared that his education began only when he entered law school at age twenty-one.[7] Affinity for law and aspiration to make an imprint upon the way American law intersected with society remained a powerful undercurrent of Hutchins' life even after he became, as it turned out, permanently committed to educational and then to philanthropic administration.

A much more baneful influence on his life also dated from his undergraduate days at Yale, for in his first year there he met Maude Phelps McVeigh and married her after his graduation from college in 1921. An only child, she was orphaned in infancy. An aunt brought her up on the fringes of Long Island high society. At age nineteen, when Maude became engaged to Hutchins, she had just completed finishing school and intended to win fame as an artist. Like her husband, she was tall and handsome, spirited in conversation, and supremely confident of her abilities. She was also very much accustomed to having her own way and expected to be admired, indeed, doted upon, as her aunt, presumably, had done after her parents' untimely deaths.

Another pronounced trait in Maude Phelps McVeigh was the pride she took in her descent from distinguished Long Island and Virginia ancestors— a pride only intensified by the fact that she inherited none of their wealth. Not surprisingly, young Hutchins was completely dazzled by her, for she was gifted, beautiful, and, having picked him for her own, was perfectly able to talk back to him, matching his barbed wit with wit of her own that often transgressed the boundaries of polite discourse to become downright rude. More intensely than he, she felt impelled to shock and repel persons whom she felt to be her inferiors. This included nearly the whole human race, since everyone who was not both witty and well born was, by definition, beneath her. And since Hutchins was merely witty, he, too, was an inferior. He accepted the status at first, being indeed an outsider to the upper-class circles of New York in which his wife had grown up.

Nevertheless, their initial attraction, strong and passionate though it was, proved to be a fragile basis for a life together, and the fact that the marriage began to fray soon after their arrival in Chicago turned out to be a dreadful handicap to Hutchins' presidency. Within a few months of their arrival in Chicago, his wife withdrew from almost all social contact with members of the faculty, trustees, and prospective donors and rebelled against all the polite rituals and usages of university life. The play of wit that enlivened their first years together soon degenerated into a running quarrel, making Hutchins' home life a bed of thorns.

All the same, roses rather than thorns predominated as long as they lived in the east. After graduation and marriage, Hutchins spent a year teaching at a prep school before returning to New Haven as secretary to the Yale Corporation. His appointment to such a post only a year after graduating was extraordinary, for it made him the principal administrative assistant to the president of Yale University, responsible for alumni relations in general and for raising money from the alumni in particular. It was a full-time job, yet Hutchins decided to resume his study of law, thus, in effect, taking on two jobs simultaneously just as he had done as an undergraduate when he had to work six hours a day to earn his living expenses. His wife, meanwhile, enrolled as a student at the Yale School of Fine Arts. In 1925, they both emerged winners: he ranking first in the graduating class of the law school and she gaining first prize in an art show. When, soon after, the first of their three daughters was born, the Hutchinses seemed perfectly positioned to launch themselves on promising yet compatible careers.

The strains that subsequently became so hobbling for them both remained trivial as long as Maude could indulge her bohemian impulses with impunity within a circle of admiring young academics and hangers-on. Her claim to distinction on the basis of ancestry meant something in New Haven, and Hutchins' responsibilities at the university made him a novice in her sort of social circle. She remained, as it were, his superior, even after he became first an instructor in the Yale Law School (specializing in "Evidence") and, amazingly, acting dean in 1927. Then, when he became dean of the Yale Law School in 1928 and, in the very next year, accepted the invitation from the Board of Trustees to preside over the University of Chicago, his meteoric career clearly threatened to outstrip hers. But Maude was not prepared to relinquish the upper hand she had hitherto enjoyed in their marriage. She therefore asserted herself by resorting to childish tantrums and refusing to perform the public roles of a president's wife. Eventually she blighted her own life and his by behaving like a spoiled child, but for many years Hutchins indulged her whims and continued to admire her despite all her bouts of unreasonableness.

It was while dean of the Yale Law School that Robert Maynard Hutchins emerged as a figure of national significance. His extreme youth was partly responsible; but so was the energy he put into reforming the study of law. Having to teach the rules of evidence, Hutchins, in effect, asked the same questions about them he had earlier asked about his father's biblical theology. He began to wonder whether the rules of evidence that lawyers had to conform to in court cases were really valid, or were they, perhaps, only based on antiquated judicial opinions? Consultation with psychologists and other social scientists, who presumably knew how human beings actually behaved, seemed a sensible first step; for only if the rules of evidence were logically deduced from an accurate knowledge of human conduct could they support the administration of real, as against a mere semblance of, justice in the courts. Logic, building on the empirical truths of social science, Hutchins surmised, might require reform of legal procedure and much else in the traditions of American law, and he set vigorously about using his position as dean to hurry the process along.

A few older men among the Yale Law School faculty supported this departure from professional tradition, and Hutchins rapidly recruited additional sympathizers to the faculty, including the future Supreme Court Justice William O. Douglas. Yale Law School thus quickly became (with Columbia) a stronghold of the notion that law did and should change to fit society, instead of being a set of unchanging rules and practices defined by antique judicial opinions and defended against ignorant outsiders by the prerogatives of the legal profession. "Our effort," he said "like that at Columbia, is focused on the facts." [8] Hutchins also took a leading role in persuading the Rockefeller Foundation to fund a new Institute of Human Relations at Yale which was intended to bring medicine as well as law into fructifying touch with all of the social sciences.

Such a record, supplemented by a series of personal encounters, disarmed doubts about Hutchins among the Chicago faculty committee. His demonstrated readiness to treat the results of social science research respectfully could be taken as proof of a suitably deferential attitude toward research in general; and this was what defenders of the graduate departments at Chicago wanted to hear. His demonstrated success as a fund-raiser pleased the trustees. A powerful personal charisma reinforced (and helped to explain) these remarkable achievements, for Hutchins' cool, patrician manner and his spectacular physical presence impressed all who approached him. In particular, the still youthful Harold H. Swift, chairman of the Board of Trustees, was completely bowled over and became a warm admirer and steadfast supporter of the man he formally inducted as president of the University of Chicago on 19 November 1929.

Between April 1929, when Hutchins accepted the invitation to Chicago, and his ceremonial installation as president, he spent some weeks as a guest at Swift's house in Chicago and at Swift's summer residence on the eastern shore of Lake Michigan. Swift introduced him to key figures on campus and was at pains to explain the university's problems to the young man who was going to have to cope with them. Hutchins was therefore well briefed for his inaugural address in Rockefeller Chapel and for subsequent speeches that he delivered to students and to leading citizens at a downtown banquet afterwards.

The inaugural address began by praising the devotion and ability of the faculty, and toward the end he declared that salaries must be raised, as Harper had done in his day, so as to be able to "attract the best men in competition with business and the professions." The severity and duration of the Great Depression was entirely unforeseen as he spoke, so that the enticing prospect Hutchins thus held up before the faculty seemed far more plausible than it became just a few months later. Such sentiments, together with praise for "productive scholarship" working "with and for Chicago" and exhibiting "an experimental attitude," were all designed to reassure the graduate faculty of Hutchins' goodwill and respect for their endeavors.

But there were also hints of changes which the young president thought were needed if the university were to continue its pioneering role. "We are studying and proposing to study problems that do not fit readily into the traditional departmental pattern of a University," he remarked. "We must regard the University as a whole, and consider the formulation of University programs rather than departmental or school policies." Rather more radical than this subdued assault upon departmental autonomy was Hutchins' further assertion that graduate training needed to be overhauled by distinguishing professional preparation of college teachers from the training of real researchers. He went on to suggest that distinct degrees should be awarded, "the Ph.D. remaining what it chiefly is today, a degree for college teachers," while another set of letters after a candidate's name should be used to signify aptitude in research.

Hutchins sought to resolve the long-standing friction within the university over the proper relation between graduate and undergraduate education by suggesting that if the Ph.D. program became explicitly what it already was in practice, namely, training for college-level teachers, then the College was needed as a laboratory for the graduate enterprise. "If the departments are to experiment with the education of teachers, they must work out their ideas in the College here. Nor does this apply to the Senior College alone: for the whole question of the relation of the first two years of college to the high school on the one hand and the senior college on the other is one of the most baffling that is before us. Instead of withdrawing from this field we should vigorously carry forward experiments in it." [9]

Having thus flattered and challenged the faculty in the morning, Hutchins proceeded to exercise his charm on leading citizens and friends of the university in the evening at a downtown banquet. "Nothing like the raising of Chicago from the mud or its recovery from the fire has been seen in modern times," he told them. "The people of Chicago are still dreaming and making their dreams come true. . . . Chicago is going ahead with its plan, its parks, its schools and its building. It dominates the West in industry, finance, the professions and the arts." The university and its professors, he argued, were essential to Chicago's continued success since "improvement in the life of the city is bound to emerge from their researches." After ticking off medical, industrial, social, and educational benefits to be expected from current university research undertakings, he concluded by pledging the university's support for the effort to "make Chicago the most cultivated as well as the greatest, the most intelligent as well as the most powerful city in the world." [10]

Such unabashed boosterism deliberately harked back to Harper's days when wonders were indeed commonplace in the city of Chicago as attested both by the Columbian Exposition and by the university's sudden rise. Invoking that past in the immediate wake of the October 1929 crash turned out to be empty incantation; but at the time no one could foresee how California and Texas would supplant Chicago and the Middle West as the principal seats of economic expansion when recovery from the depression of the 1930s came at long last. Hutchins' courtship of Chicago's business and political leaders therefore proved to be more of a swan song than a rallying cry; yet it remains indicative of the moment, when resumption of a triumphant, mutually supportive partnership between town and gown, such as had been at least fitfully attained in Harper's time, still seemed feasible.

Though Hutchins' initial courtship of Chicago's citizenry was destined to fall far short of his hopes, his appeal to students, and especially to undergraduates, proved solid and enduring. Outrageous flattery was his hallmark in speaking to students, and they lapped it up. On the day after his formal inauguration, he began his address to the student assembly by saying: "To become President of a University with a student body so numerous, so intelligent, and, I may add, so handsome would be gratifying to anyone in education." When it came to educational policy, his platform was simple: "I favor the best faculty that could be obtained, teaching the best students that could be found, with a curriculum intelligently adjusted to the needs of the individual." [11]

In practice, a curriculum "intelligently adjusted to the needs of the individual" had been waiting in the wings for more than a year, since the plan Dean Chauncey Boucher had devised for the College he headed was built around the notion that advancement toward a B.A. should turn upon individual competency to be demonstrated by passing examinations, rather than by accumulating class credits. Class attendance would become voluntary. When to take a particular exam would also be a matter for individual students to decide, subject only to the provision that to retain student status some exams would have to be passed within a reasonable time of initial registration. Examinations were to be designed and administered by a board of examiners, so individual teachers would no longer give grades for the courses they taught. Instead, teachers were to prepare a syllabus for every course, listing prescribed readings and setting forth essential skills and information, and then collaborate with professional examiners in devising ways to test whatever the syllabus prescribed.

Classes would still be offered to help students prepare for the examinations. They were supposed to bring the subject to life by going over the syllabus, explaining difficulties, and conducting simple scientific experiments. But individual study was an alternative. In principle, someone who entered the university with skills and knowledge sufficient to pass all prescribed examinations would be able to earn a B.A. by doing so the first time they were offered, that is, in a single year.

European university practice inspired this plan. Just as Chicago had pioneered the establishment of graduate research in the United States, Boucher and his committees of colleagues now proposed to make the College unambiguously into a seat of higher education, treating students as responsible adults who could be trusted to make their own decisions about how to spend their time. Yet the plan also involved new constraints. In the first two years, required survey courses were to supplant the miscellaneous array of electives that had arisen from the debris of the classical curriculum that American colleges had abandoned toward the end of the nineteenth century.

Colleges in the United States had always straddled the boundary that Europeans drew between secondary schooling (where a prescribed curriculum and close supervision of daily behavior was deemed necessary) and higher education (where adult autonomy for students, and specialized study prevailed). In the 1920s, American colleges retained the role *in loco parentis* that European secondary schools took for granted, but, like European universities, offered nearly complete freedom of choice as to the exact course of study. In effect, Boucher's new plan for the Junior College reversed this pattern. A prescribed curriculum would be offered to students free to live and study pretty much as they saw fit. Yet, surrendering the traditional supervision of undergraduates seemed risky, if only because American high schools sent students away to college aged seventeen to nineteen, whereas European students were usually about two years older when they matriculated into a university.

Moreover, it was far from clear whether the university faculty could or would agree on exactly what undergraduates ought to study in their first two years. Obviously enough, American high schools graduated students who lacked skills and knowledge imparted by the lengthier course of European secondary education. Boucher and his committee wished the university faculty to overcome this discrepancy and even improve on European models by inventing a better balance between arts and sciences than commonly prevailed in Europe. This meant agreeing on what undergraduates ought to know about things in general before trying to initiate students into the arcana of particular departmental specialities. Few disputed the principle, but even fewer among the faculty were willing to devote time and effort to its realization.

Despite these unresolved problems, Boucher's scheme appealed to President Hutchins. Accordingly, he endorsed the policy of implementing it as soon as possible. For the Senior College, where departmental courses prevailed, existing practices needed little modification. Preparing a course syllabus and helping to frame suitable examinations demanded extra effort from the faculty; but this involved no real departure from their accustomed routines.

It was otherwise in the Junior College, where new survey courses would have to be devised. Yet Boucher had a model for such surveys in the form of a very successful introductory course in natural science, entitled "The Nature of the World and of Man." Staffed mainly by biologists, this course had been offered to freshmen for almost a decade. Starting small, it soon attracted a large proportion of the entering class, and at graduation time seniors ranked it emphatically ahead of all the other courses they had taken at the university. Efforts to develop comparable courses in humanities and social science had not succeeded, though much exhortation, and some tentative efforts, had been directed toward that goal during the 1920s.

In view of the failure of Dean Boucher's efforts to persuade professors from the departments of the arts faculty to abandon, or at least interrupt, their professional careers in order to invent suitable survey courses, his proposal for making general examinations mandatory for the B.A. became a calculated device for compelling the faculty to take action. Everyone agreed that someone would have to develop courses to match each required examination. But that awkward choice could be postponed for the time being—and perhaps indefinitely—because agreement on what general examinations should be required of all students and on what capability in English composition and foreign language belonged in the undergraduate curriculum had not been attained when planning was interrupted by President Mason's unexpected resignation.

Obviously, Hutchins had an unusual opportunity in coming to office when he did. Boucher was convinced that his plans for reform were intellectually sound and would not cost more than the existing smorgasbord of departmental courses, taught, as many of them were, by underpaid graduate students. The archetypical general course on "The Nature of the World and of Man" showed how, for in that course a succession of senior professors lectured to several hundred freshmen, relying on a few graduate students to grade quizzes and prepare demonstration experiments. Such instruction was delightfully cost effective; and if the faculty could be induced to invent comparably popular and intellectually coherent courses in other fields, Boucher believed that the Junior College could become a model for other institutions to follow, just as the university's graduate teaching had been in Harper's time.

Hutchins concurred. His inaugural address contained a hint of how he proposed to restructure undergraduate work, for he went out of his way to commend large lecture courses aimed at students who were seeking a general introduction to the subject rather than preliminary training in their presumed future speciality. But Boucher's proposals had still to pass the University Senate, dominated, as it was, by elderly professors who were wholly attached to departmental interests and traditions. How to transcend departmental boundaries was anything but clear. It was on this obstacle that Boucher's advocacy of general courses in the arts and social sciences had foundered, since no senior professor was prepared to abandon professional respectability by lecturing on subjects beyond his departmentalized expertise.

Rescue came from outside when a team of management experts, summoned to look over the university's administration on the occasion of Hutchins' assumption of office, pointed out that more than fifty wholly autonomous bodies and agents reported directly to the president, whereas it was a recognized principle of business administration that a dozen subordinates was about as many as anyone could effectively supervise. Consolidation of all the offices and individuals who had previously handled student affairs under a single Dean of Students was easy and required no faculty action. Consolidation of the thirty-nine separate departments and five professional schools was a bit trickier. In the event, the professional schools retained their autonomy, each under a dean who reported to the president; but the graduate departments agreed to group themselves into four divisions, each headed by a dean who would report to the president.

On the face of it, this clearly threatened departmental autonomy, for the new divisions were to function as budgetary units, and the dean would have to decide exactly how divisional funds would be allocated among competing departments. But having such power in the hands of a dean was not different from having it lodged in a president; and a dean chosen from among the senior ranks of the graduate faculty, and whose research specialty was akin to those of the departments entrusted to his jurisdiction, probably seemed a good deal less threatening to the members of the University Senate than retention of their existing subordination to a president whose inaugural pronouncements and initial administrative actions had been a disturbing mix of deference to and defiance of their accustomed routines and professional practices.

At any rate, on 22 October 1930 a motion to establish four Graduate Divisions in Physical Science, Biological Science, Social Science, and Humanities passed the Senate with little or no controversy and was duly endorsed by the Board of Trustees. Simultaneously, the College was accorded equivalent standing; and a few weeks later a dean of students and a new office of university examiner were instituted. The result was a streamlined chain of command, whereby a coven of academic deans (four for the Graduate Divisions, five for the Professional Schools, one for the College, and one for University Extension) presided over the faculty; while the dean of students and the comptroller presided over student affairs and university finances. All reported to the president, who now had far fewer direct subordinates, even though the structure of the university still remained more diffuse than business practice prescribed.

By grouping departments into four divisions in this fashion, a new basis for defining appropriate College survey courses emerged as a by-product of the administrative reform. For each of the new divisions immediately staked a claim to an introductory general course of its own in the College, presumably because such a course seemed essential for attracting students into more advanced, departmental courses later on. This meant splitting "The Nature of the World and of Man" in two, for that course had bridged the physical and biological sciences. It also presented the miscellaneous departments of the new humanities and social sciences divisions with urgent need to define what they wanted students to know about their particular sorts of knowledge.

In practice the Humanities Division delegated the task to a senior historian, Ferdinand Schevill, while the Social Sciences Division sloughed the job off on three juniors: a sociologist, Louis Wirth, a political scientist, Jerome Kerwin, and an economist, Harry Gideonse, who had to be appointed for the purpose since none of the existing staff was willing to teach economics to beginners. The Biological Sciences Division called on a young botanist, Merle Coulter, to expand the biological portion of "The Nature of the World and of Man," while maintaining its integrated structure much as before, whereas the Physical Sciences Division simply allotted each department (except Military Science) a specific number of weeks in the introductory year to do with as it pleased.

Four such survey courses, required of all undergraduates, together with examinations in English composition and foreign language, left space for two electives in the first two years of college. That degree of flexibility seemed eminently desirable because the College was heavily dependent on an influx of students who had started college work elsewhere and then (usually for financial reasons) decided to live at home and earn a B.A. by commuting to the Midway, often on a part-time, on-again, off-again basis. Four general courses preparing for examinations that were not replicated elsewhere was a serious obstacle to place in the path of future transfer students; and, partly for that reason, Hutchins' emerging notions about what liberal education really ought to be—to wit, mandatory study of "the great books" for as much as four years—was slow to get off the ground.

But in 1930–31, when the so-called "New Plan" for the College took shape, Hutchins' ideas about education had not yet crystallized. He heartily agreed with the general aim of Dean Boucher's reforms even though he soon came to feel that the survey courses generated within each division fell far short of his ideal. But for the time being this made no difference. Reform was in the air, and Dean Boucher had the acquiescence (when he did not have the support) of senior faculty for his new syllabi, courses, and examinations. Accordingly, during the spring and summer of 1931 hastily assembled groups of faculty members drew up syllabi for four new division-wide general courses and the new Board of Examiners busied itself with drawing up examinations to match.

Everything had to be done in haste, for the New Plan was scheduled to begin in the autumn of 1931—less than a year after the administrative reorganization of the university had come into effect and long before the new divisional structure could much affect the separate departments. Indeed, the creation of survey courses was undoubtedly the most significant form of departmental cooperation that the new administrative structure of the university provoked, not merely in this, its first year, but subsequently also. Ever-increasing specialization of research persistently fragmented the academic community, and for that reason, fissiparousness continued to prevail. In the long run, and despite all the powers of his office, Hutchins' aspiration for unity and truth, heartfelt though it was, therefore failed to counter the trend toward academic specialization. But at the time no one could clearly foresee the upshot of his effort at synthesis.

Hutchins' name, of course, was immediately associated with the New Plan for the College, even though he had done little more than give Dean Boucher a green light.[12] His reservations about the character of the new survey courses and his agenda for further reform of liberal education had begun to emerge even before the first new-plan students arrived on campus. But for the time being, seeds of controversy generated by Hutchins' ideas remained buried in ineffective faculty committees, while the new survey courses and comprehensive examinations took on a vigor of their own, thanks in part to the vested interest of those who taught and examined in the new College, but mainly to the strong and positive student response that the New Plan of 1931 provoked.

Overall, therefore, Hutchins' first two years as president were a time of far-reaching change for the university. The four-fold divisional structure gave graduate study a new look, though the depth of its impact on departmental practices was yet to be explored. The first deans of Physical and Biological Science and of Humanities were elderly, respected members of the faculty who had no intention of using their new authority to alter the pattern of graduate training to which they were accustomed. In the Social Sciences Division, however, Hutchins appointed a new broom, Beardsley Ruml, as Dean. Instead of giving Rockefeller money to the university (and to others) for social science research, as he had previously done, Ruml saw the new deanship as a chance to forward interdisciplinary study of the sort he believed was required for real understanding of human society.

Once on campus, Ruml became one of Hutchins' tiny circle of (distant) intimates. Amidst private jest and badinage, they nurtured a serious hope of transforming the graduate enterprise by bringing the separate departments together and insisting on more theory, more logic, more meaning for the empirical facts of behavior which the Chicago school of sociology was, by and large, satisfied to record. Men like Fielding Ogburn, Ernest Burgess, and such younger associates as Louis Wirth felt it was not their business to decide what to do about the signs of social breakdown their statistical surveys of American society discovered. But the deepening depression that developed out of the October 1929 stock market crash showed all too clearly that American society was in serious trouble, and, under such circumstances, baldly descriptive social science began to seem empty and inadequate.[13] Hutchins' initial interest in social science therefore faded rapidly away, for he was above all a moralist and, like Ruml, a man of action.[14]

This shift in Hutchins' views was aided and abetted by another friend and associate, Mortimer J. Adler, whose influence on Hutchins and on the university quickly eclipsed Ruml's. Adler arrived on campus in the autumn of 1930 and started his stormy career at the university by telling Chicago's social scientists that they were guilty of logical ineptitude. Three years younger than Hutchins and far more indiscreet in public discourse, Adler showed up at Chicago with a fresh Ph.D. and the rank of associate professor, together with a salary that exceeded what most of the university's senior faculty received. This deeply offended scholars whose long years of service and accomplishments in research far outweighed anything Adler had yet achieved. But what made him an especially intense center of controversy was the fact that Hutchins' personal association with him made it unclear how far Adler's emphatic pronouncements carried Hutchins' endorsement.

Adler never claimed to speak for Hutchins. He was interested only in truth—plain and compelling logical truth as he had encountered it in the pages of the Great Books, and, in particular, in the pages of Aristotle and St. Thomas Aquinas's *Summa Theologica.* Hutchins, for his part, remained aloof and noncommittal, while seeming to relish the dismay Adler's pugnacious arguments aroused among the senior faculty. Moreover, Hutchins never disagreed with Adler in public and seemed ready to back him in practice when differences of opinion about appointments in philosophy became acute in 1931.

Hutchins' partnership with Adler dated back to 1927 when as acting dean of the Yale Law School he invited the young New Yorker to visit him in New Haven and explain what a psychologist and logician from Columbia had to say about legal rules of evidence. They hit it off from the start, and although Adler refused Hutchins' invitation to come to New Haven, he soon established a connection at the Columbia Law School and for the next three years directed his spare energies to the task of bringing logic and his knowledge of psychology to bear on the law of evidence. Only after completing a Ph.D. in psychology in 1929, and receiving Hutchins' offer of a salary of almost three times what he had been getting as instructor at Columbia, did their collaboration become close and enduring.[15]

Since Adler did more than anyone else to shape Hutchins' mature ideas about education, it is interesting to know something of how he came to embrace his controversial views. Son of a retail jeweler, who was part-owner of a modest store located in lower Manhattan, Adler descended from a German family whose Jewish identity had become a social rather than a religious reality. Judaism as a way of life lay far behind them, cast off with the German *Aufklärung*. A vague liberalism, and a vivid hope of overcoming anti-Semitic discrimination by thoroughgoing assimilation to an environing secularized society, pervaded the New York circles in which Mortimer Adler grew up.

Adler's parents expected him to start earning a living as soon as he could. Accordingly, he dropped out of high school and got a job as copy boy on the *New York Sun* before attaining the statutory school-leaving age of sixteen. But Adler's job allowed him to devote spare time to an ambitious program of reading, in the course of which he discovered philosophy and promptly fell in love with it. Adler had a quick and, above all, a tidy mind. He delighted in words and wanted them well arranged so as to order and classify truth in its totality. This, he discovered, was what philosophers did, or at least ought to do; and when he encountered discrepancies of doctrine, he passionately took the side of truth as the truth appeared to him.

Clarity, comprehensiveness, and logic appealed to Adler above all else; but there was also a streak of the show-off in his makeup. As a result, when he was admitted to Columbia (without graduating from high school) and began to pursue philosophy as an undergraduate, he quickly made himself obnoxious by repeated, emphatic private and public criticism of the views of John Dewey, the resident, reigning high priest of pragmatism. In due course, Adler failed to get a B.A., not because of his opinions, but because he refused to attend physical education classes, which were then required for graduation from Columbia. When, nevertheless, he sought a teaching job in philosophy so that he could continue graduate study, the department would not have him. Instead, he shifted to psychology and, as a graduate student, was appointed instructor, thereby becoming the third Jew on the Columbia faculty.

Three encounters during his time at Columbia shaped Adler's subsequent career. One was an honors course taught by John Erskine which introduced undergraduates to classics of Western thought by asking them to read a book a week and then to talk over in class whatever ideas the reading provoked. Adler delighted in such a concentrated exposure to abstract ideas and to the authentic words of famous authors, ancient and modern. He soon became correspondingly disdainful of courses that relied on textbooks and lectures to summarize the opinions of thinkers who could perfectly well speak for themselves if given a chance. Accordingly, when Hutchins invited him to Chicago and the philosophy department asked him to take over the introductory freshman course in which Will Durant's *Story of Philosophy* served as textbook, Adler flatly refused.

Instead, at Hutchins' suggestion, he collaborated with Hutchins in teaching a two-year course in Great Books to a select group of entering freshmen. This course did not fit into existing administrative patterns, since credit for the course was to wait two entire years, after which time an oral examination would test each of the students' capacity to talk sensibly about what they had read. It therefore rather embarrassed the College administrators, who, however, were in no position to refuse the new president the right to teach undergraduates in any way he saw fit. And he saw fit to follow his friend's lead by introducing himself together with a few selected students to the list of books that John Erskine had designated as "great."

From Hutchins' point of view, he was simply applying the case-study method of Yale Law School to different and rather more complicated texts than those the lawyers studied. And his aim was what it had been in law school: to understand the argument and then assess its validity by using simple logic and careful judgment. Unlike Adler, Hutchins' critical powers did not slumber when brought to bear on the teachings of Aristotle or any other philosopher, ancient or modern. Having abandoned the Bible as a reliable guide to truth and righteousness in his youth, and having found the law sadly confused about truth and justice in his twenties, he sought for the rest of his life to find other texts that could satisfy his yearning for metaphysical and moral truth. The quest proved vain.[16] But, of course, when he started, he did not know what he might find; and his close association with Adler certainly made it easy for outside observers to confuse Adler's pat answers with Hutchins' persistent questions.

Ultimate failure did not affect Hutchins' estimate of the value of his quest. The proposition that the core of a liberal education ought to rest in firsthand acquaintance with books that had shaped Western literary culture seemed completely convincing to Hutchins even before he made his own acquaintance with a suitable selection of such books through his classroom partnership with Adler. He never repented this judgment. This was Adler's principal and most enduring impact upon Hutchins and the university. Through the two of them, John Erskine's famous course therefore had a powerful afterburn at Chicago and, after 1937, at St. John's College in Annapolis, Maryland, as well.

Adler's second shaping experience during his time at Columbia was much more controversial, for his espousal of Aristotelian philosophy, and his agile defense of the version of Aristotelianism set forth in the bulky pages of Aquinas's *Summa Theologica,* seemed perverse and, indeed, incredible to almost everyone he encountered at Chicago.[17] Most Chicago professors, after all, had emancipated themselves from various forms of Protestant dogma in youth and were simply flabbergasted by the spectacle of a nonobservant Jew demanding that the official philosophy (since 1870) of the Roman Catholic Church be taken seriously and explored on its own terms. Yet this was the position Adler took when he showed up at Chicago; and his argumentative skill, combative temper, and connection with Hutchins soon made it impossible for others to overlook his surprising intellectual posture.

Adler's seriousness and conviction were straightforward, however odd they might seem to others. Aquinas's scholastic method of introducing every question with objections to his views, then spelling out the truth in crisp, logical form before refuting the initial objections with the same clear logic fitted Adler's habit of mind perfectly. Here he found reasoned answers to the most important questions a man could ask, as well as armor against a vast array of objections to the answers St. Thomas found convincing. Adler took real delight in retracing for himself the arabesques of philosophical argument developed across the generations of scholastic debate that lay behind Aquinas's magistral pages. This is what attracted him in the first place; plus the fact that Thomist doctrines were both startlingly new and delightfully old. For at Columbia, as later at Chicago, almost no one in university circles[18] had ever looked into the pages of the *Summa*—dismissing St. Thomas's great work out of hand as mere lumber from Europe's medieval attic. Adler's arrival at Chicago soon made that sort of cavalier dismissal impossible, even though he never persuaded anyone on the faculty to agree with him.

Adler's third important encounter in his student days at Columbia was with Helen Boynton. She was a student at Barnard College and daughter of a well-to-do Chicago family whom he secretly married just before her twentieth birthday. Because of their very different backgrounds, each was exotic and strange to the other; and this became a basis of mutual attraction. In addition, marriage across such a social gap meant for each a definitive break with parental authority, and for Adler it meant a connection with the gentile world that was usually closed to Jews. Attracted to men of unusual character and ability, Helen Boynton and Maude Hutchins had both married down the social scale. When Hutchins and Adler met in 1927, this parallelism of private circumstance may have helped to cement their early friendship.

Later, the fact that both marriages began to wear thin after the move to Chicago meant that shared domestic difficulties could become a more lasting link between them.

This, then, was the young man Hutchins appointed to the University of Chicago in 1930. Adler's initial appointment was to Philosophy, Psychology, and the Law School, with the understanding that he would devote one quarter of the year to teaching in each of the three. But rationalizing the law and philosophizing psychology were the least of Adler's ambitions in coming to Chicago. Instead, he entertained bright visions of what he could do with Hutchins' backing to straighten out professorial thinking in all branches of learning. As he explained to Hutchins, he wished "to do for science and culture in the twentieth century what Thomas did for that of the thirteenth. . . . It would mean cutting through all the departmental divisions, and 'dialecticizing' all the various subject matters, as I have already tried to do in psychology and evidence." [19] All that was needed, he felt, was to bring Aristotelian philosophy to bear on all the intellectual procedures professors were accustomed to follow in their various specialties.

As the lawyers at Yale and Columbia had (more or less) welcomed outside expertise in trying to bring their rules of evidence into logical harmony with existing knowledge about human behavior, so Adler hoped other disciplines might welcome or at least tolerate the same sort of critique. To accomplish this reform, he proposed that two of his friends should be brought to Chicago to help out: Richard P. McKeon from Columbia and Scott Buchanan from Virginia. Circumstances seemed propitious, for two senior members of Chicago's Department of Philosophy, including its doyen, George Mead, were about to retire. Hutchins saw this as an opportunity to alter philosophy at Chicago along the lines that Adler envisioned.[20] He therefore rejected a nominee the department suggested as Mead's successor and proposed Adler's two friends instead. The department was outraged. Mead and two of his colleagues resigned in protest, provoking campuswide controversy that came before the faculty Senate in March 1931.

Uncharacteristically, Hutchins backed down, perhaps because he was not sure of his ground,[21] and agreed to surrender his statutory power of making faculty appointments without prior concurrence from the department or school concerned. Conformity to this rule, in turn, compelled modification of Adler's initial appointment, for by now the Department of Philosophy rejected him emphatically. His position was therefore pruned back to an appointment in the Law School, where, largely by his own choice, he remained marginal.

Clearly, Adler's initial hope of provoking sweeping reform of higher learning at Chicago faced serious obstacles. For the time being, he would have to content himself with a more modest scale of operation and start the renovation by his own unaided effort. The obvious place to begin was the social sciences, where a friendly dean and his youthful accomplishments in rationalizing the law of evidence gave him a plausible claim to expertise. At the very start of his career in Chicago, in September 1930, Adler had addressed a meeting of the local Social Sciences Research Council on "The Social Scientist's Misconception of Science." As was his wont, he went out of his way to be provocative, declaring that without the principles and logic of true, that is, Aristotelian, philosophy "raw empiricism" became "bad science." [22] His audience, for the most part, simply gasped with puzzled amazement. Subsequently, after the quarrel of 1931 had echoed throughout the university, Dean Ruml invited Adler to explain his ideas about reform of the social sciences in a year-long seminar for faculty and graduate students. A few Chicago social scientists strove to argue back, but were completely incapable of meeting Adler on his chosen ground, since the Aristotelian vocabulary was rich and complex, and simply by using those terms, and arguing within them, Adler could overwhelm objections as easily and as logically as St. Thomas had done in his *Summa.* [23]

In his exposition of truth as the truth appeared to him, Adler did not flinch from exotica. In 1932, for example, he began a lecture on the position of psychology among the sciences with a definition of the soul lifted from Aristotle and then defended St. Thomas's elaboration of Aristotle's psychology by arguing that angelic knowledge was a mode of intellection to be distinguished from human and divine ways of knowing. [24]

Considerable anger and complete failure of communication ensued. Robert Redfield, a thoughtful young anthropologist who succeeded Ruml as dean of the Social Sciences Division, summed up the fiasco some years later, saying in a letter to Hutchins: "My difficulty centers on the two words 'metaphysics' and 'principles.' I do not know what you mean by either of them . . . Some time ago I had hopes that such a procedure would be helpful to social science. I then witnessed Mr. Adler's testing of this procedure during a seminar . . . held for this purpose. Mr. Adler was admirably clear and demonstrated to me the sterility of this approach for social science." Redfield reluctantly concluded that "hunches" were a better guide to thought and research in social science than metaphysics and principles. [25]

By the end of 1931, therefore, the initial enchantment of Hutchins' presidency was over. His agenda for the university was not the same as that of most faculty members, who wished merely to be left alone to do whatever they were doing already. All the same, a residue of the initial euphoria lingered. Six weeks after his inauguration, at the annual Trustees Dinner for the Faculty on 8 January 1930, Hutchins had said: "All of you have been so thoughtful, so considerate, so forgiving that I have at times had difficulty in recognizing you as a university group at all. You are the kindest as well as the finest I have ever known." [26]

He would never say that again, but initial disputes precipitated in the ensuing academic year by Adler's impolitic effort to convert men twice his age to a new way of thinking did nothing to hinder the take-off of the New Plan College on the one hand, nor to close off potential future developments that the new divisional structure of graduate study might permit. Hutchins had only begun to think through what he wanted in the way of educational reform. His efforts at implementation were still experimental, narrowly confined to a handful of students who took the course he co-taught with Adler. Being the man he was, his initial clashes with the faculty over his power of appointment in general, and over Adler's program of curricular reform in particular, merely made him more stubborn. He had just begun to fight for radical reforms of education, the outlines of which, though clear enough in the abstract, remained permanently blurred in detail. As a result, and as the following years attested, Hutchins' University was destined to be more intellectually serious and far more uproarious than other institutions of higher learning ever cared to be.

3

CHIAROSCURO OF
THE DEPRESSION YEARS
1931–1936

Hard times set in with a vengeance in the first years of Hutchins' presidency. Recovery, though Herbert Hoover declared it to be "just around the corner," stubbornly refrained from spontaneous generation of the sort that the nation's business leaders expected. No one knew what to do. Franklin D. Roosevelt, elected to succeed Hoover as president of the United States in 1932, relied on incantation ("We have nothing to fear but fear itself"), supplemented, after he took office in March 1933, by pell-mell action, modeled mainly on what the Democratic party had done when last in power during the emergency of World War I. Simultaneously, Germany came under the malign power of Adolf Hitler, who also set out, far more radically than Roosevelt, to resuscitate wartime methods of mobilizing German manpower and resources in order to undo the peace settlement of 1919 and restore his country's greatness.

For a while, events in Europe were only a distant, though engrossing spectacle for members of the university community. Events at home preoccupied everyone, for the depression brought massive unemployment to Chicago, and the university's income shrank precipitously. Gifts from all sources in 1929–30 had totaled $14.5 million; in 1933–34 they shrank to $2.0 million. Income from endowment and tuition shrank simultaneously, so that in 1933 Hutchins figured that "to balance the budget the average reduction in salaries and wages would have to be 33.33%."[1] He did cut his own salary and that of other administrative officers, but persuaded the trustees that it was better to run a deficit and, if need be, expend some of the university's en-

41

dowment rather than cut professorial salaries. In this backhanded way, Hutchins actually lived up to one part of the program of his inaugural speech, for as prices fell the university's tenured faculty members experienced a modest improvement in their standard of living. At a time when financial crisis threatened nearly everyone, the privileged professors on the university payroll had reason to be grateful.

Yet Hutchins paid a price for maintaining faculty salaries. For when jobs elsewhere almost disappeared, stable Chicago salaries tended to freeze everything and everyone in place, thus creating a massive human barrier to Hutchins' projects for reform. Personnel changes came to depend mainly on the chance arithmetic of retirements. Every such departure offered welcome relief for the overstrained budget, but only as long as there were no new appointments. In practice, some new appointments were made, for it was impossible to manage the university wholly on the basis of the random incidence of age. But in most cases, retirements brought lasting cutbacks.

The graduate departments and professional schools fared badly under these circumstances. Grants for research dwindled. Anything that cost money became difficult to maintain and it was doubly difficult to start up something new. Entrepreneurial energy survived in some departments, thanks to unusual circumstances. The astronomers, for example, had the good fortune to link up with the University of Texas, where a large bequest supplied funds for the construction of a new observatory at a time when the facilities at Yerkes Observatory had become so antiquated as to be of little use. But Texas had no astronomers when this unexpected gift was made.

Under these remarkable circumstances, Otto Struve, chairman of the Department of Astronomy, saw a chance for Chicago's astronomers to help out at Texas and get access to much needed new equipment. Struve's idea immediately attracted President Hutchins' warm support. He telephoned the president of the University of Texas, and the two agreed to cooperate. Struve subsequently negotiated a detailed contract which, in effect, gave Texas a first-rate department of astronomy without having to pay any salaries, while the Chicago astronomers got control of a brand-new, state-of-the-art observatory paid for by the University of Texas. Construction at the McDonald Observatory began in 1932 and took seven years; but throughout that period of time, when worldwide depression meant near complete halt elsewhere, the Chicago department had the privilege of working at the forefront of technical design and retained a buoyancy that other departments found it hard to equal.[2]

Enough funding continued to be available to allow a famous physicist like

Arthur Compton to organize expeditions to remote regions of the earth for the purpose of collecting data on cosmic rays, sometimes by sending balloons into the stratosphere. But an ordinary professor, like Samuel Allison, used a made-over classroom for his nuclear experiments and personally constructed a complex apparatus with the help of a few graduate students. Research in chemistry, biology, and other natural sciences was limited to what professors and students could do, with help from a very modest (though skilled) supporting staff of technicians.

During the early depression years, Chicago more or less held its own in the natural sciences. Other institutions suffered exactly the same financial constriction; and Chicago's heritage from Harper's time assured a high rank among research universities. In 1933, one respected reference book, titled *American Men of Science*, showed Chicago behind Harvard and Columbia in the number of scientists newly ranked as outstanding in their fields, while the 1938 edition of the same work made Chicago second only to Harvard in this category.[3] This, presumably, reflected informed opinion at the time and seems to be the best available index of how Chicago's research departments in the natural sciences fared during the depression years.

No comparable listing allows assessment of what happened to the humanities and social sciences, or in the professional schools. The graduate departments retained a high reputation, as was proven in 1934 when the American Council on Education rated them "distinguished" in twenty-one out of the twenty-six fields in which ratings were made. But such assessments inevitably lag behind reality, depending, as they must, on experts' impressions of particular departments, often formed years before. Even so, a close look at what happened between 1929 and 1936 reveals some bright spots. For example, the School of Social Service Administration flourished. All of a sudden, jobs in social service administration burgeoned as public and private relief programs multiplied; and the number of students grew correspondingly to make this the largest of Chicago's professional schools. Consequently, Sophonisba Breckinridge's retirement in 1933 (she was the school's founder and leading spirit) did not signify any reduction of activity. On the contrary, her friend and successor, Grace Abbott, extended the school's role in shaping an emergent profession, emancipating the management of public relief from the overtones of condescending, ladylike, and amateurish benevolence that had enveloped it at birth.

But the circumstances of the School for Social Service Administration were as exceptional as those of the Department of Astronomy. Elsewhere in the arts, penury and constriction prevailed, and the retirement of scholars like George Mead in philosophy (1931), John Manly in English (1932), James W. Thompson in history (1932), Charles Breasted in Egyptology (1933), Shailer Mathews in divinity (1933), Carl Buck in linguistics (1933), and Robert Park in sociology (1934) added up to a very substantial diminution of the level of Chicago scholarship, since replacements were few and far between.[4] Even when a new appointment proved possible—like that of John A. Wilson to succeed Breasted—it substituted a young and unproven scholar for a figure of world fame; and in fact Breasted's Oriental Institute had to cut back the scale of its operations drastically, abandoning all new archaeological digging and concentrating instead on publishing the results of what had already been done in Egypt, Iran, and Palestine. Similarly, Sir William Craigie's return to Scotland in 1933 (where he initiated work on a Scottish dictionary) meant that the work of compiling a dictionary of American English on historical principles, which he had launched, slowed down when it passed into the (quite competent) hands of an obscurely youthful assistant named Mitford Mathews.

The medical school that had been launched with such high hopes in 1927 became a serious problem. Salaries for medical professors had been set higher than for the rest of the university, and when hard times set in, Hutchins decided that cuts would have to be made. But this put salaries below what doctors could earn in private practice. Other medical schools, including the university's longtime affiliate on the west side, Rush Medical College, paid their teaching staffs of practicing doctors with prestige more than with cash; but on Chicago's South Side, a founding principle and raison d'être had been the divorce of private practice from medical teaching and research. A number of doctors stayed on under these circumstances, but many others left when it became evident that their academic salaries were not going to match what they could earn privately.

As a result, the Department of Medicine became a world apart from the rest of the university. Anything up to half a dozen new appointments had to be made each year to replace those who had departed, since the hospitals had to be staffed. The original ideal of combining teaching and research was difficult to sustain under these circumstances, for very few of each year's crop of new assistant professors did more than service patients, teach a few classes, and then depart for private practice. And from the budgetary point of view, the hospitals and Medical School cost the university serious amounts of money, since patient fees and student tuition never entirely matched costs, and research grants, when available, did not help much with hospital overhead either.

To be sure, some important medical research took place on the Midway. For example, Charles Huggins, who later won a Nobel prize for his work on cancer, chose to remain at the university from the inception of the Medical School. But for one dedicated research worker like Dr. Huggins, scores of doctors came and went without achieving distinction either as teachers or as researchers. This was a disappointing situation, but incurable inasmuch as servicing patients in the hospitals became an end in itself which the university could not forego as long as hospital finances depended on keeping beds occupied.

The Divinity School, before and after Dean Mathews' retirement, retained a special sort of intellectual eminence in Protestant circles for its thoroughgoing espousal of a historical vision of the Christian past that embraced every sect and denomination and emphasized what they had in common rather than what divided them. Many found liberation from sectarian blinkers in such ecumenicity. But there was a cost, for the Divinity School's historical perspective denied the immutability of doctrine. Indeed it was because they viewed doctrine as a human invention that professors could and did deplore all the disputes that had long divided Protestants into rival sects. But a vision of the Christian past that explored how changes in theology and changes in society marched hand in hand was anathema to true believers. This isolated the Divinity School from the most emotionally vibrant Protestant groups in the country; while the Roman Catholic hierarchy, intent on defending the decrees of the Vatican Council of 1870, proclaimed eternal, unchanging Christian truth and abhorred the historical gospel seeping from the Divinity School's new home in Swift Hall.

Although anyone suffering from a mind open to the evidence had to admit that doctrine had in fact changed across the Christian centuries, the mere fact that it was true did not endow the historical vision prevailing in the Divinity School with the sort of moral authority needed to provide a practical guide to action in a time when established social landmarks all seemed adrift. If society and theological doctrines alike were liable to constant change, what ought a puzzled human being to do when things went wrong? Where was salvation to be found? The Divinity School version of Christianity had no clear and firm answer. Irenic benevolence tied to a rather ambiguous belief in progress was not enough.

Exactly the same difficulty confronted the sociologists and other social scientists. Their efforts were descriptive and analytical, not historical: but the facts of urban behavior, as measured by sociologists, and the regularities of economic behavior, even when analyzed mathematically by economists, did not tell anyone how to answer the only question that really mattered in the early depression years, which all boiled down to Lenin's famous question: What is to be done?

In the back of everyone's mind lurked the recollection of old-fashioned life on the farm where all human needs were routinely met by family and neighborly action, and where, in time of business depression, subsistence farming could keep everyone going until the exchange economy recovered. That Eden had vanished from America with World War I or before. The professorate of the University of Chicago knew it had disappeared, yet still clung to moral attitudes and expectations inherited from that rural past. Such a posture was a recipe for indecision, confusion, distress. It meant that Chicago's social scientists—and the faculty at large who shared America's rural and small-town Protestant past with them—were unsure of themselves as never before. Resulting uncertainty, in turn, created an opening among students for wielders of radical new doctrines, Thomist and Marxist alike.

In the Humanities Division a different sort of demoralization was latent as well. The delights of philological scholarship, correcting texts and establishing chronological and other factual details about old manuscripts, verged on triviality when those skills were applied to texts and ideas that no one thought really important. Yet this is what was happening. Biblical criticism had been the lifeblood of philological scholarship in Harper's day; it continued into the 1930s, but no really big new interpretations emerged, and details worth debating became more and more recondite, of interest only to experts. Incipient triviality also haunted purely secular studies. In the first decade of the century, John Manly's philological skills, applied to the manuscripts of Chaucer, seemed a worthy match to biblical scholarship; but when he retired in 1932, with Chaucer's text established beyond all but minor cavils, what next? The same methods applied to authors of less and less importance, and to texts which had fewer variations because they originated in the age of printing, were hard to get excited about. Why spend a lifetime's effort on typographical errors in early editions of eighteenth-century writers like Oliver Goldsmith? Why indeed?

Overall, therefore, it seems fair to say that the graduate Divisions of Humanities and Social Sciences had started downhill in the early depression years, partly through the attrition of retirements, and partly from a loss of confidence in the scholarly enterprises they were embarked on. No general appraisal of how the professional schools fared seems possible; but the efflorescence of the School of Social Service Administration remained exceptional, if only because the harsh restrictions of a shrinking budget and diminishing student numbers pervaded all the other schools, as well as the graduate divisions. Hard times in these, deservedly famous, sectors of the university provoked a defensive reaction. Professors tried to hold on to what had been, defending the way things were, hoping for better times. Small wonder, then, that a straw poll in the election year of 1932 showed the faculty overwhelmingly for Hoover, who was also holding on, defending the way things were, and hoping for better times.[5]

It was different in the College, where the (largely accidental) timing of reform launched the New Plan just as the depression was heading toward its lowest depths. From October 1931 on, official regulation of student life and the curriculum of the Junior College were radically new. Soon the College as a whole became remarkably buoyant. But, as we saw, Hutchins was not satisfied with the survey courses that had emerged so hastily from the work of faculty committees and hoped for further curricular reform, not just in the Junior College, but throughout the university. At the same time, of course, he had to wrestle with the university's budgetary problems and had the mournful task of imposing cutbacks wherever possible.

In May 1933 he seized eagerly upon what looked like a constructive solution to his dilemmas. The project was in the grand tradition of American corporate management, as exemplified both by John D. Rockefeller and by William Rainey Harper, for Hutchins envisaged a merger between Northwestern and the University of Chicago (with Lewis Institute thrown in for good measure) which would allow rationalization of higher education throughout the city on a grand scale. By eliminating overlaps the new super university could save money, while simultaneously, by dint of the organizational upheaval itself, opening a way for the radical kind of curricular experimentation he thirsted after.

As finally projected, Hutchins' scheme had much to recommend it, and in a different time and climate of opinion, he might have been successful in overcoming institutional vested interests. He broached the idea to President Walter Dill Scott of Northwestern, reputedly while they were returning from Springfield after testifying before the Illinois legislature about pending legislation against communism in private universities. Scott, who confronted acute budget problems of his own, was attracted by the idea; accordingly, negotiations for a merger proceeded apace from May to December 1933. The plan was simple. As Hutchins explained to a student assembly in Mandel Hall on 12 December 1933, when the whole scheme first became public: "With emphasis in Evanston on undergraduate education, in the South Side on research and on improvements in collegiate education, and downtown on

professional education and community service we might have the strongest
centers in these three areas in the world."[6] Hutchins also envisaged the establishment of three junior colleges on the north, west, and south sides (perhaps in cooperation with the city's Board of Education, using existing high
school buildings for evening classes). He also hoped to set up three parallel
technical institutes, each associated with a junior college, and initiated negotiations with Lewis Institute (later merged into IIT) in the hope of adding
expertise in technical training to the projected merger.

What he had in view was a privately managed, citywide scheme of higher
education, beginning with the junior year of high school (when, he felt, genuinely liberal education ought to begin) and extending to the postdoctoral
level. Such a university might indeed embrace the city as a whole, providing
a model for excellence and diversity at one and the same time. It was a vision
comparable to other grandiose schemes that had characterized Chicago's
past—reversing the flow of the Chicago river, building the park system,
erecting the first skyscrapers. But the city's leaders no longer responded enthusiastically. Instead Northwestern's trustees drew back, preferring the hap-
penstance fractionation of private higher education to the grand architectonic for metropolitan Chicago that Hutchins projected.

Tax-dodging possibilities raised by the merger did much to muddy the
waters and made public authorities highly suspicious. This arose from the
fact that Northwestern's charter exempted it from taxes, even when funds
were invested in real estate, whereas the University of Chicago had to pay
local real estate taxes on any investment in income-producing property. Pru-
dence and good citizenship alike persuaded Hutchins to propose that even
after the merger "The Chicago Universities on the Foundation of Northwestern and the University of Chicago," as the hybrid was legally dubbed,
would continue to pay taxes on the university's existing real estate holdings.
But the projected merger was to operate under Northwestern's charter, so
that eventually, by selling off Chicago's less profitable investments little by
little, the new institution could attain the favored tax situation that Northwestern already enjoyed.

In public, Hutchins denied that the scheme was a grandiose tax dodge,
but the fact remains that when the plan went public, Chicago's spokesmen
remained favorable while cries of anguish arose on the Northwestern campus, where most faculty and a majority of the Board of Trustees chose to
interpret the plan as a way of decapitating Northwestern and turning it back
into an undergraduate college. From Chicago's point of view, the financial
advantages of tax exemption that might eventually be reaped from the merger

surely did enter into private calculations. This made the plan far more attractive on the Midway than it was in Evanston and assured opposition from public officials.

Legal complications were considerable. By 23 November 1933 a downtown lawyer had worked his way through the tangle, producing a draft agreement for the merger. But before the plan could come before either of the two Boards of Trustees for formal action, experts decided that the legality of the plan must be tested in Illinois courts. This required going public, which was done in mid-December. Vigorous and vocal opposition at once arose in Evanston, and soon it became clear that President Scott was almost the only person at Northwestern who thought well of the idea. Accordingly, the whole negotiation was broken off on 12 March 1934. Hutchins' grand scheme for creating a citywide multiuniversity, anticipating the statewide structure that emerged in California after World War II, thus fell to the ground. The collapse came as no surprise. As Hutchins said to Chicago's students in December when first making his scheme public: "The whole proposal may turn out to be impractical, inexpedient, and impossible. If it does, I shall shed some natural tears, for the conception is a grand one, and one that is consonant with the high traditions and glorious past of your alma mater."

Indeed it was, for Harper, too, in his day, had planned to establish junior colleges as affiliates of and feeders to his new graduate university; and the sort of bold departure from established curricular practices, which Harper had carried through at the graduate level, Hutchins had hoped to pursue afresh within a revised, streamlined, and altered institution. Merger with Northwestern might have allowed him to shape the educational establishment on the Midway more to his liking, since the ensuing general upheaval would have weakened vested interests and shaken up fixed habits all across the board. But such was not to be, and with this failure, Robert Maynard Hutchins' string of triumphs, and apparent triumphs, came to an end. He did not surrender his hope of transforming the university; but it took the dislocations of World War II to allow him to move forward again—and then only on the college level and at the cost of arousing bitter and unforgiving animosity.

The collapse of negotiations with Northwestern left Hutchins in an anomalous position vis-à-vis the College. He disapproved of the new curriculum, yet it turned out to be a great success with those who enrolled in the new survey courses and took the new general examinations. In public he dutifully praised what he privately deplored. "Every day seems to me to show its wisdom, for every day it is more successful," he wrote in a *Report to Alumni* in February 1935. But the practical success of the New Plan for the College simply strengthened resistance to further reform along the lines that Hutchins and Adler advocated. It was a frustrating situation for a president whose name was firmly associated with an innovative success for which he had slight responsibility and little sympathy.

The success of the College was twofold. On the budgetary front, student numbers in the College held up better than elsewhere in the university so that tuition (which remained unchanged at $100 per quarter) brought in almost as much as during the heydey of the booming twenties.[7]

On top of that minor miracle, the new survey courses cost less than the miscellaneous hodge podge of departmental courses they displaced. This was because big lecture classes and once-a-week discussion sections with a standard thirty students per section established a far higher student-teacher ratio than had prevailed before, when, amidst a multiplicity of courses, some enrolled only a handful of students but could not be canceled without crippling student progress toward satisfying departmental requirements for a degree. As Vice President Emery T. Filbey wrote to the comptroller on 29 February 1932: "Reduction of income is offset somewhat by economies brought about by the reorganization of our curriculum."[8]

This financial advantage was, in fact, a principal reason why other institutions became interested in imitating the Chicago reforms. A cheaper curriculum that could also be defended on intellectual grounds made an all but irresistible appeal to hard-pressed academic administrators on other campuses. Chicago's survey courses therefore became widely influential, especially the humanities course. It was, in fact, the principal prototype for introductory courses in the history of Western civilization that became an important part of core curricula for innumerable colleges and junior colleges, beginning in the mid-1930s and lasting until the mid-1960s.

But the success of the College in the early 1930s was not solely a matter of money. The new survey courses, together with the new system of exams and freedom from required class attendance, soon had the effect of attracting high-level undergraduates to the Midway in unprecedented numbers. The intellectual intensity they brought to the College made it unique in the country and soon began to shower incendiary sparks upon at least some of the graduate departments.

In an odd way, Hutchins' University spited him by becoming a theater for philosophical debate and curricular controversy just *because* of the discrepancy between what Hutchins and Adler wanted the College to be and what it actually was. Clear, logical, and necessary truth, with direct moral applications to the ills of American society, did not emerge from the debates, though this is what Hutchins yearned for. Instead he got vehement dissent from his prescriptions for liberal education from most Chicago professors, while still commanding the reverence of most undergraduates, and creating a small following among the faculty that advocated (but never agreed upon) grandiose projects for further reform of the university. Vigorous missionary efforts by partisans of reform merely intensified the opposition of those defending the old regime. Under these conditions, argument sometimes degenerated into irascibility. But on the whole, most who recall those days or recorded their impressions of the university in the early 1930s remember it as a golden age; and such it surely was—turbulent and strife-filled, as golden ages always are, but enormously exhilarating for all whose minds were being shaped in the midst of intense debate over educational and intellectual issues.

No one could stay long on the Midway without having to take a stand about fundamental questions of science and society. No doubt, undergraduate opinions were emphatic in proportion to the shallowness of the experience that lay behind them. But shallow or not, everyone's views were continually exposed to contrary winds of doctrine. Really probing young minds had to wrestle with epistemological and metaphysical questions which everywhere else remained buried under classroom rituals and routine assumptions. It was, in short, a wonderful place to be young.

The uniqueness of Chicago's College can be measured in terms of the extraordinary scholastic attainments of entering classes. In 1933, for example, when the publicity surrounding the New Plan had begun to affect recruitment, one out of fourteen entering freshmen was a high school valedictorian; one out of eight had been editor of the high school newspaper; and one out of four had been a member of a high school athletic team. A more significant figure, perhaps, was that 47.3 percent of Chicago's freshmen had grade records that put them in the top 10 percent of their high school graduating classes. Indeed, the academic quality of Chicago undergraduates rose so high that in April 1935 Hutchins complained, in a confidential report to the Trustees: "The excellence of our students and the high quality of work required for the College Certificate make it extremely doubtful whether the scheme as it is now organized can have the widest influence. . . . Our standards are so high that we are beaten from the start when we recommend our program to most other institutions." [9]

If one remembers the reproach graduate faculty members had made before 1931 when they complained that the undergraduates were intellectually unworthy of the university, the remarkable change in Chicago's pattern of College recruitment becomes apparent. It was almost entirely spontaneous. To be sure, Dean Boucher and other official spokesmen, including Hutchins, put considerable effort into advertizing the New Plan. But organized efforts at student recruitment focused almost entirely on athletes. The influx of academically ambitious, intellectually vigorous, and highly motivated students was the result of self-selection. Bright high school seniors were attracted by the prospect of not having to attend classes, of advancing toward a B.A. at their own (perhaps accelerated) pace, and of enjoying access to the vaunted intellectual resources of the university. What had seemed to many a very risky venture of treating undergraduates as grown-ups actually had the effect of selecting for Chicago a group of students who were in fact able to handle the freedom and responsibility the New Plan gave them.

There was a negative side to this happy result, for students who could not discipline themselves to prepare for exams by effective use of their time soon dropped out. Nearly half of the first class that entered as freshmen under the New Plan fell behind the normal rate of progress toward a degree, some for financial and some for academic reasons. Only 52.2 percent graduated by June 1935, but of those who did earn a bachelor's degree within that standard time span, no fewer than 29 percent had accelerated their education by a quarter or more. Moreover, of the 363 who graduated on time or before the expected four years were up, no fewer than 330 went on to study for a higher degree.[10]

A statistical study of the entering class of 1932 showed that a growing proportion of the College freshmen came from out of state, but 62.7 percent still lived at home and commuted to classes. Nearly two-thirds of the freshmen aspired to a professional career, while only 8 percent wanted to go into business or commerce. They came from relatively humble homes. A question about parental education showed that 40 percent of their parents had not graduated from high school, 28.4 percent had one parent who had gone to college, and only 8.9 percent had two parents with at least some college-level education. Blacks and Orientals totaled less than 2 percent; but 26 percent identified themselves as Jewish, 72.3 percent as gentile, leaving 1.8 percent without religious identification.[11] In the next academic year, when the entering class more fully reflected the impact of the New Plan, the percentage of Jewish students rose to 29 percent.[12] I did not find later statistics pertaining to the religious backgrounds of Chicago students, but impressionistic recollection suggests that the Jewish presence on campus remained at about that same level throughout the 1930s.

This, indeed, was the sociological fact that made the College of the University of Chicago unique in the country. Nowhere else did so large a Jewish contingent meet and mingle with a predominantly Protestant college population. The reason was simple. Other private colleges discriminated against Jews, not so much by setting definite numerical quotas, as by admitting only those whose family wealth and assimilation to upper-middle-class manners made them acceptable.[13] Like Chicago, the City College of New York kept its doors open to Jews who lacked the wealth and polish other prestigious colleges demanded; but the fact that CCNY students lived at home meant that the sort of mingling that occurred at Chicago was not really replicated in Manhattan. Moreover, as Jews whose parents had arrived in the United States early in the twentieth century came of college age, they flooded into CCNY in such numbers as to establish a nearly self-contained Jewish community on that campus. Only at Chicago could upward-bound New York Jews find easy entry into a version of American society that was more nearly mainstream. Hundreds availed themselves of the opportunity, and their presence made Chicago's undergraduate body distinctly different from any other.

Hutchins believed in a career open to talent and had no prejudices against Jews. Many faculty members and deans concurred, though not all of them. The matter was never discussed in public nor much considered in private. It seems safe to say that the influx of Jews that took place in the early 1930s was due not to policy or principle so much as to the university's financial need. In a time of declining income, student tuition mattered; and, as we saw, the College shrank less than the graduate and professional schools—a feat which would not have been achieved had Chicago's admissions policy replicated that of Columbia and other eastern colleges.[14]

But however mixed the motives that lay behind Chicago's open door, the fact remained that from the early 1930s an upwardly mobile and intellectually vigorous student body took shape on the Midway of which almost one-third came from Jewish homes. For most Jews, the whole point of coming to Chicago was to escape from the constriction of their socioreligious background. A professional career was the goal; and doing well in school was the path to success. The gentile majority had exactly the same goal, and, like the Jews, often asserted a new identity for themselves by abandoning or at least modifying the religious and sectarian beliefs of their parents. The University of Chicago became a place to rise in the social scale, where old ideas, old habits, and old prejudices were left behind and where secular truths, tested by reason and embodied in science, could be counted on both to liberate the mind and prepare a self-selected body of students for successful professional careers.

No other college replicated this sociological mix. Ivy League schools took pains to attract sons and daughters of the upper classes who set a comparatively relaxed, genteel tone for undergraduate life. Some College administrators at Chicago would have liked to do the same, but, pinched by the depression, the New Plan College instead attracted so many academically gifted students from the lower middle class that it was they who set the pace and defined the texture of College life on the Midway.

The pace was strenuous because education was taken seriously. Though money was short, ambition burned bright. Doing well in school was habitual, and the heady sense that Chicago expected students to study of their own accord and prepare for impersonal, objective examinations in any way they chose gave classroom encounters a distinctive timbre. Teacher and student alike could afford to be interested in the subject to the exclusion of other considerations. Currying favor with a teacher made no sense when grades were assigned by performance on an examination that was administered and graded anonymously. And since many of the College faculty had themselves come to professional life from humble backgrounds, they had much to share with their students, not least a faith in reason and its superiority to inherited religion as a guide to life. This, indeed, was the dominant theme of the College survey courses, implicit rather than overt, but resonant and strong all the same.

The humanities survey made this especially plain, in effect playing Socrates off against St. Paul (and Moses). The effect was telling for students nearly all of whom were veterans of Sabbath and Sunday schools. The course was brought to life by Ferdinand Schevill, a product of German *Bildung*, Cincinnati style. He was one of Chicago's original faculty members, having become an instructor in 1892 on the strength of a fresh Ph.D. in history from Freiburg. In 1917, when anti-German feeling ran riot on campus, he resigned from the university, but continued to live in the neighborhood and was recalled in 1930 when the new Humanities Division could find no one else willing and able to take charge of the new survey.

Not surprisingly, Schevill built the course historically, beginning with ancient Greece and continuing the story of Western civilization through medieval and modern times. But it was history with a difference: art, literature, and (to a very limited extent) music were folded into the course, partly by inviting experts from relevant departments to lecture from time to time on appropriate topics, but mainly by assigning a rich diet of readings (and viewings). These provided the subject matter for weekly discussion sections, which were entrusted to graduate students recruited from various departments of the division. Schevill was the anchor man. He gave most of the lectures and presided over weekly staff meetings where he and the young instructors debated how best to approach each week's assignments.

A graduate student, busy with a thesis on nineteenth-century German politics or on English Romantic poetry, had to struggle when conducting discussions based on Plato's *Apology,* Anselm's *Cur Deus Homo,* or Flaubert's *Madame Bovary.* My discussion leader most certainly was embarrassed by spending an hour on the significance of a clutch of Matisse nudes, come to class in the form of an Art Institute reproduction. But that put teacher and students on nearly the same plane. Both parties had a lot to learn from the readings and lectures and from the limited exposure to art and music that the course allowed. The fact that all concerned, teachers as well as students, were engaged in a strenuous process of discovery gave Humanities I an extraordinary liveliness, at least in its first years.

It was a coming of age for me, when I took the course in 1933–34. Week after week new perspectives opened. I learned the Christian doctrine of sin, grace, and salvation from reading Anselm—a subject that had been discreetly avoided in my Sunday School. I encountered a different sort of sin by reading Flaubert—a subject that had been carefully skirted in my high school classes. And I was shocked by Matisse—more the distortion of bodily shapes, perhaps, than bare skin: but both were puzzling, repulsive, and new. A shining panorama of the past opened, as dazzling to me as the flood-lit White City of the Columbian Exposition had been to millions of viewers forty years before. Those who took or taught the course were never quite the same again. The world took a new shape, governed by the notion that human beings had accumulated amazing knowledge and skill across the centuries by using the power of reason to overcome irrational impulses and institutionalized stupidity. A liberal, individualistic gospel was what Schevill and his colleagues had to offer, inviting us to prefer the pursuit of rational truth to the foolishness of faith in constituted authority—religious or otherwise. Education meant leaving old prejudices behind, thus qualifying for full membership in American civil society where careers were and ought to be open to talent.

The other surveys echoed the same message, without making it so explicit. In Social Science, for instance, Harry Gideonse vigorously defended the rationality of free markets and lampooned what he called "symptom thinking," whether found on the front page of the *Chicago Tribune*, which he marked up and posted daily outside his office door, or in arguments on behalf of tariffs, socialism, and other forms of government intervention in the market place. Louis Wirth presented value-free sociology in a much less flamboyant style, and Jerome Kerwin's political science was still less memorable. Some of the readings assigned in the Social Science Survey had enormous impact. I particularly remember John Dewey's *Human Nature and Conduct*, and *The Communist Manifesto;* but it is fair to say that much of the reading was textbookish and almost entirely bypassed European theorists like Weber, Mannheim, Durkheim, and Freud. This was largely a function of the departmentalized structure of the course, for the youthful instructors felt obliged to try to sum up, in textbook fashion, the subject matter of the three departments they represented: economics, sociology, and political science.

The same observation applies to the natural science surveys, although in biology, years of experience with the survey course called "The Nature of the World and of Man" allowed a well-integrated introduction to diverse departmental subject matters. By comparison, the physical science survey was an undigested jumble of astronomy, mathematics, chemistry, meteorology, and geological paleontology, with no particular effort to connect one sample of departmentalized information or theory with what went before or after.

In a sense, both courses were obsolescent even when new. The physical science survey explored a Newtonian universe and merely hinted that recent experiments and theory had called the certainties of nineteenth-century physics into question. Similarly, the biological science survey dwelt upon the orderly grandeur of Linnaean taxonomy, but skipped biochemistry because it was so complicated (and, like relativity, confusing). Yet that was the most active sector of the biological science research at the time and remained so for years to come. But in preferring clarity and simplicity to contemporary confusion, these courses were faithful to the general posture of the university faculty, which, in a time of trouble, was trying to hold fast to an inherited faith in reason and progress. The vision of the world that the humanities course made explicit was therefore implicit in each of the other survey courses. Surprisingly, the helter skelter efforts of faculty committees to create the new survey courses actually resulted in presentation of a remarkably coherent worldview. It was rational, scientific, optimistic, and put responsibility for acting with appropriate knowledge and skill squarely on each individual's shoulders.

These courses had a considerable impact beyond the university itself. Several successful textbooks were generated from the departmentalized segments of the Bi Sci and Phy Sci courses, and, as I said before, the humanities course became a model for innumerable Western civ courses on other campuses. Interesting experiments were also made with the then still very new media of motion pictures and radio. In particular, a commercial company, ERPI Films, undertook to make eighty ten-minute motion pictures in consultation with the teaching staffs of the survey courses. According to the original plan, the University Press was to sell course syllabi together with a package of twenty films for each course, and the university would collect a royalty for each film sold. But this pioneer scheme to use motion pictures in the classroom never took off, and the effort ground to a halt in the late 1930s with only a few films in Phy Sci and Bi Sci actually produced. Failure was due partly to the fact that teachers on other campuses were not accustomed to using films and lacked access to projectors and screens. In addition, the films that were actually marketed offered only isolated snippets of natural science and often relied on cheap, amateurish techniques of presentation. Basic to ERPI's ill-success, however, was the fact that other schools did not subscribe wholesale to Chicago's courses and, even when they did borrow, insisted on making adaptations of their own. As a result, the survey course syllabi, with films, never became the backbone of junior college curricula, as Dean Boucher had once imagined they might.[15]

As for radio, the humanities course lectures were broadcast at 1:30 P.M. three days a week on WJJD, beginning in 1932, and, beginning in 1931, Chicago professors were heard every Sunday on WMAQ, the Chicago NBC station, in a Roundtable discussion of some topic of current interest or importance. The Roundtable was strikingly successful and went national in 1932 on what was still innocently called NBC's Red Network. For the next twenty years this program was by far the most powerful public relations instrument at the university's command. It played a role in formulating opinion on national issues, turned its first moderator, Professor T. V. Smith, into a congressman, and projected the name and fame of the University of Chicago across the nation in prime time every Sunday.

Other radio programs originating on the Midway paled before the success of the Roundtable, but there were many additional, relatively short-lived ventures. Filling the broadcast day was still a problem for commercial stations, and a few radio programmers entertained the hope of making the new medium into an instrument of public enlightenment. As a result, in 1934 no fewer than ten programs originated each week on the campus, including regular features like the broadcast of the Sunday morning service at Rockefeller Chapel, and one-time events such as an Oxford-Chicago student debate broadcast in January 1934 simultaneously by NBC in the United States and by the BBC in Great Britain.

In 1934 Hutchins proposed cooperation with Northwestern and Loyola to create a comprehensive program of education by radio for the city of Chicago, aimed at all ages, from preschool to retirees;[16] but the institutional jealousies that had defeated his more radical plan for a merger with Northwestern also torpedoed this attenuated plan for concerted, citywide action. The University of Chicago was too far ahead and cooperation looked too much like domination from the Midway for the scheme to work.[17]

The attention the survey courses received beyond the university's own walls confirmed undergraduates in the belief that the College was at the very forefront of curricular advance. This engendered a cocksure, smart-alec attitude among many Chicago students. Having been one myself, I can attest that we felt we knew more than our parents, more than our contemporaries at other schools, and more, even, than most of the university's professors, confined, as they were, by departmental blinkers. Hutchins' criticism of the departmentalization of learning rubbed off on us readily enough, but we paid little attention to his equally emphatic reservations about the general education we were getting in the College, partly because he kept his criticism within a limited circle, lest it hurt student recruitment, and partly because we had been so won over by the liberal, rational faith embodied in the surveys that we refused to listen. We preferred to believe that President Hutchins, the man who had launched the New Plan, was really in sympathy with its actual implementation; and his public praise of the excellence of the College and of the university certainly lent themselves to this interpretation.

Yet the fact that a solid majority of the College students affirmed the intellectual posture implicit in the surveys did not mean that the liberal, rationalist worldview imparted by the College faculty went unchallenged. Quite the contrary. Adler's version of Aristotelian rationality continued to attract much attention. Indeed, his assault on the logical shortcomings of social and natural science as practiced at Chicago achieved a sort of climax in 1933–34. This took two forms. Most spectacular was a debate in Mandel Hall on 9 February 1934 that pitted Adler against Professor Anton J. Carlson, a physiologist, who was famous for asking his laboratory students: "What is the evidence?" The debate took place under the auspices of *The Daily Maroon*, the student newspaper. John Barden, editor of the *Maroon* and a graduate of the Hutchins-Adler class in great books, had launched a noisy campaign criticizing the survey courses. Barden fancied himself as a champion of Hutchins' ideas and summed up his criticism of the surveys by claiming that they taught facts, not ideas. The *Maroon's* simplistic formula, "Facts vs. Ideas," lifted (and twisted) phrases from Hutchins' speech to the faculty at the annual trustees' dinner in January 1934. The effect was to pit the practice of the College faculty against a more or less mythical, or at least misunderstood, Hutchins.

Carlson, who, with his heavy Swedish accent, was by far the most picturesque lecturer in the Bi Sci survey course, took the *Maroon* attack seriously enough to welcome a public debate with Adler, who, of course, was presumed to speak for Hutchins. But Carlson did not reckon on the general excitement that *The Daily Maroon* had managed to arouse. In fact, the debate filled Mandel Hall to the rafters, and an overflow audience listened next door in the Reynolds Club to a hastily wired loudspeaker. Carlson did not prepare very carefully, and Adler made him seem boorish and clumsy. The whole debate was shrill and superficial, largely because of the absurd antinomy of facts vs. ideas that the *Maroon* had invented. Consequently, Adler's ability to confuse his opponent left most of the audience quite as confused, though perhaps not as angry, as Carlson was himself.[18]

A more serious effort to clarify the issues dividing Adler from his elders in the graduate departments took the form of a seminar in the Division of Social Sciences, presided over by Dean Ruml. Once a week, throughout the academic year 1933–34, Adler chastised professors and graduate students of the social sciences division for their failure to understand Aristotelian philosophy. Mutual (sometimes angry) incomprehension prevailed, and the next year, after Ruml had departed for Macy's in New York, Adler gave up trying to convert his seniors from the error of their ways.

More and more, after the climactic year of 1933–34, Adler's ambitions turned away from the university, where his argumentative prowess had won him innumerable enemies and few friends. He gradually backed away from the quarrels he had provoked and allowed the crusade for reform of the College and the clarification of faculty minds to pass into other hands. His principal successor was Richard McKeon, Adler's friend from Columbia, who came to Chicago in 1934 as visiting professor of history, and then, by a remarkable sleight of hand, was swiftly transformed into professor of Greek and dean of the humanities division in 1935. But McKeon was more discreet and cautious than Adler. His impact upon others therefore took a while to develop, took a different direction, and belongs in later chapters.

Another wind of doctrine began to blow across the campus in the deep depression years of 1932–34. Small, vocal, and energetic groups of students turned to Marxism, believing that it offered the only true explanation of the depression and a recipe for curing it. Accordingly, a small Communist Club appeared on campus and arranged a well-attended public meeting in Mandel Hall in April 1932. Other Marxists formed a Socialist Club in the following year, and until 1936, when "united front" tactics were decreed by the Comintern, the two rival organizations proceeded to slang each other at least as vigorously as they attacked capitalist exploiters. A handful of members and elected officers, formally recorded, allowed these clubs to register with the Dean of Students as student organizations, thus acquiring the right to meet in university buildings, organize lectures, or arrange demonstrations on campus. But such lists were largely window dressing. The real movers and shakers of the Communist cause on and off campus preferred to remain in the background. 'Boring from within' was a sanctified tactic for members of the Communist party, and their secretive methods of sowing confusion pushed socialists, who were the primary object of communist infiltration, along a parallel, semiconspiratorial path. Intrigue and counterintrigue turned into a lively game for a dedicated few; and their rivalry perhaps had the effect of increasing the attention Marxist doctrines attracted.

More important, of course, was the reality of the depression and the inability of anyone to find an effective cure. The New Deal in Washington did head off outright starvation by organizing public relief works and extended governmental regulation across much of the economy. But the National Recovery Act did not bring recovery and was declared unconstitutional in 1935. It certainly looked as though democratic government as practiced in Chicago and in Washington could not solve the puzzle of pervasive hardship and poverty, arising from the strange juxtaposition of idle men haunting the gates of idle factories, looking vainly for work. The whole capitalist world suffered similarly, while in Russia, Stalin's first Five Year Plan had been declared "overfulfilled" in 1932, just as the depression plunged toward its lowest depths; and a second even more ambitious program of industrial construction was trumpeted to the world just before the United States government had to proclaim a bank holiday—halting all financial transactions for a few days in order to head off panic and nationwide bank failures.

Against this background, revolutionary Marxism began to seem a plausible answer to what ailed the United States. If the Russians could put millions of men to work, why couldn't we? Why not take over the factories and start them up again? Indeed why not? But communism was un-American; and most students and all faculty members resisted the simple logic of pursuing the Marxist revolutionary cure. Finding persuasive reasons for opposing the advocates of revolution took some doing however. The abstract arguments of economists like Frank Knight, who vigorously defended the efficiency of free markets, were hard for most people to understand. Accepting the virtues of a free market simply on faith was even harder when the actual market (only partly free of course) was functioning so badly. Discussion therefore raged late into the night among Chicago's students. Advocates of socialism and advocates of communism competed for converts, while the majority wondered and held back without finding very much in the way of persuasive arguments with which to rebut the Marxists.

The resulting interplay between the powerful but unformulated liberal gospel of the College courses and the extremely articulate Thomist and Marxist doctrines was intricate and pervasive. Every student encountered all three, though Marxism and Thomism were entirely extracurricular, since no professor taught Marxism, and Adler did not teach Thomism, even though his public defense of the rationality of the Saint's views did set the scene for the emergence of a band of student converts whose commitment to Thomism far outran his. Consequently, a few incandescent Thomists began to compete with Marxist sectarians for the allegience of the general body of students. As often happens in such situations, there were a few conspicuous cases of cross conversion when a leading Marxist became a Thomist or vice versa. But the great majority merely muddled along, refraining from commitment to either extreme while listening to both.

No other campus came close to such a mix. To be sure, Marxism spread to other university communities for the same reason that it took root on the Midway, encountering rather less in the way of intellectual opposition than it did at Chicago. For only at Chicago did Marxists have to compete with a rival Thomist sect, whose argumentative skill was equal or superior to anything Marx had to offer. The fact that most of the university community remained uncommitted and bemused did not diminish the vigor of the controversy. Rather, the prospect of converting the unconverted by refuting error in all its multitudinous forms fired each competing sect to new heights of public propaganda, as the pages of the *Maroon* for 1934–36 amply attested.

This extraordinary intellectual climate was supplemented by a vigorous array of extracurricular activities of a more traditional kind. Fraternities and clubs faced acute financial troubles, but most survived and continued to support a spectrum of social affairs that, at least occasionally, extended beyond the campus into downtown hotels and the like. Citizens of Chicago were still interested in the football team; and the Interfraternity Sing, with thirty-two fraternities taking part, was among the special campus events broadcast on NBC in June 1932. Dances and theatricals were almost as vigorous as in the booming twenties, while lectures, concerts, and charitable activity probably intensified.

Intercollegiate athletics also flourished. Between 1933 and 1939, Chicago was second only to Michigan in winning Big Ten championships, thanks to marked success in such sports as tennis, gymnastics, and fencing. This was not accidental. Chicago offered more athletic scholarships than any other Big Ten school. Consequently, even though Stagg's methods of recruitment for football and basketball lost most of their effectiveness in the mid-twenties (when other schools began to devote serious attention to these games), Chicago retained its old primacy in the minor sports without difficulty.[19]

Even in football, the quintessential college sport, something of a revival began in 1933, when a spectacular player named Jay Berwanger first took the field. He attracted widespread newspaper attention by his unusual skill as runner, kicker, and passer and made All-American in his junior year, followed, in his senior year, by the award of the first Heisman trophy in 1936. Berwanger's fame was greater than the success of his team, but still, the Maroons did manage to win some Big Ten games and easily downed Ivy League teams like Dartmouth and Harvard. Stagg had retired, much against his will, in 1932; but Clark Shaughnessy, his successor as Chicago's football coach, seemed entirely capable of carrying on Stagg's tradition. As a result, Chicago's students, when they got tired of debating socialism and metaphysics, could go to class with nationally famous athletes and watch them in action for the price of a $5 season ticket.

Poised in this remarkable fashion between sharply contrasting ways of pursuing excellence, the undergraduate community attained a new sort of prominence within the university as a whole. Educational debate focused primarily upon the college curriculum, and the ideological storms of the early thirties were much more intense among undergraduates than elsewhere, largely because graduate and professional school students were too busy becoming experts to spend much energy on abstract, theoretical questions. And in the eyes of the general public, undergraduate athletics, and the success of the football team in particular, continued as before to define the university's repute, rivaled only by the Roundtable.

Yet, beginning in 1934, the university acquired another reputation that became a severe embarrassment to Hutchins and the administration as a whole. The activity of communist and socialist groups on campus provoked collision with the wider community of Chicago, where public and private authorities were angered by amateurish efforts made by a few students who tried to foment revolutionary sentiment among the city's poor. The first overt sign of a mounting tension between town and gown came in May 1933 when a Chicago suburbanite and shrill defender of the American way named Elizabeth Dilling denounced the university as a seat of subversion in her book, *The Red Network*. Words turned into action in the fall of 1934 when three students were arrested for distributing revolutionary handbills in a black neighborhood, attracting newspaper attention and ACLU support before the police released them.

But these were mere premonitory rumblings of the avalanche of publicity which descended on the university after 13 April 1935 when Charles Walgreen, the founder of a very successful chain of drugstores, wrote a letter to President Hutchins announcing that he was withdrawing his niece from the College because: "I am unwilling to have her absorb the Communist influences to which she is assiduously exposed." Walgreen released his letter to the Chicago newspapers without waiting for a reply. He acted in concert with (and his decision had probably been precipitated by) the editor of the *Herald Examiner*, who was under orders from the newspaper's owner, William Randolph Hearst, to mount a campaign against campus radicals. Inflammatory articles had already appeared in the *Herald Examiner*, beginning in February 1934,[20] but with Walgreen's letter in hand, the editor suddenly had much more plausible ground for attacking the university. In Springfield, a Hearst-friendly legislator promptly introduced a bill to outlaw tax exemption for universities that taught communism and scheduled hearings in mid-May, ostensibly to collect information in support of his bill.

In the lull between the initial bombshell in April and the hearings in May, the editor of the *Herald Examiner* tried to keep the scandal going by asking an inexperienced young girl to move into International House and act as an undercover reporter. She was instructed to dig up scandal about the sex lives of students and professors, but, having found nothing worth printing, her increasingly provocative behavior led to detection and a shamefaced confession. Hence, "Little Beverley," as the *Maroon* gleefully called her, completely failed to satisfy her boss; but the sinister comedy she participated in aroused campus opinion against the Hearst press and all it stood for.

A well-attended outdoor Peace Rally on May Day 1934 showed the enormous gap that had opened between university's students and the climate of opinion prevailing in the city at large. The rally was sponsored by many campus organizations in addition to the Communist and Socialist Clubs. It climaxed in a public recitation of the so-called Oxford Oath, administered by the leading student socialist, Quentin Ogren. Participants swore never to fight on behalf of their country. Several hundred young men—nearly all of whom subsequently served in World War II—duly recited the subversive words and, of course, were castigated as traitors by the downtown newspapers.

Formal hearings, when they began two weeks later, turned out to be something of an anticlimax. Walgreen's testimony was obviously coached and not very heartfelt. He accused Frederick L. Schuman, assistant professor of political science, of preaching free love and declared that two of the college syllabi taught Marxism. But his niece, when called to the stand, scarcely supported her uncle's charges and confessed that she had never attended any of Schuman's classes. A firebrand of the right, a student from Texas, who had tried to organize patriotic demonstrations on campus by bringing American Legionnaires to the Fieldhouse and succeeded in provoking a scuffle there, came closer to reality when he accused the student community of being infiltrated by leftists; but his own psychological instability was obvious and detracted from the force of his testimony.

In fact, Walgreen's charges were absurd. Chicago's professors were nearly all conservatives. The two self-professed socialists on the payroll, economists Paul Douglas and Maynard Krueger, were not revolutionists nor even Marxists. Marxism was extracurricular. The university's sin, in the eyes of the downtown newspapers, was permitting leftist students to speak and enjoy other civil liberties guaranteed by the Constitution. Hutchins and others who testified on behalf of the university pointed this out in rebuttal and defended the inclusion of the *Communist Manifesto* in the social science survey (and another Marxist text in English I) as the only way students could discover Marxist errors.

The accusation against Schuman could not be completely discredited. He was a convinced "fellow traveler" who admired Stalin's Russia, and the charge that he advocated free love rested on a real but facetious remark he had made at a public meeting. Similarly, an accusation brought against Robert Lovett, professor of English, to the effect that he frequently voiced his distrust of the United States government and of all constituted authority, was entirely true; but he did so as a citizen, not in his class lectures, and, as befitted his New England patrician descent, adhered to Thoreau, not to Marx.

When the hearings ended on 28 May 1934, all but one of the committee of Illinois legislators voted against carrying the proceedings any further. The university was formally cleared of the charge of teaching communism; but the committee recommended that Professor Lovett be dismissed. Hutchins flatly refused to penalize Lovett for his eccentric opinions; but since he was about to reach retirement age anyway, both the committee's recommendation and Hutchins' defiance were a sort of shadow boxing. (Lovett retired in 1936, and Schuman took a job at Williams College in the same year, so the two faculty radicals who had attracted so much unwelcome attention in 1935 left the university within the ensuing fifteen months.)

Yet a nasty aftertaste remained. Day after day, Chicago newspapers had trumpeted charges against the university in front-page stories, and the rebuttals never quite caught up with the accusations. Moreover, though the faculty could in fact be cleared of the charge Walgreen had made against them, the university community as a whole continued to harbor a lively sect of Marxists who did in fact advocate revolution, often in extreme and childishly irresponsible fashion. Professional patriots and red hunters felt cheated by the way the hearings had turned out, while the general public, and some of the university's trustees, concluded that so much smoke was indeed evidence of fire.

Hutchins' eloquent defense of intellectual freedom, broadcast nationwide by NBC in the wake of Walgreen's accusation on 18 April 1935, reflected the tensions of the time, for he said: "Americans must decide whether they will longer tolerate the search for truth. . . . If they will not, then as a great political scientist has put it, we can blow out the light and fight it out in the dark, for when the voice of reason is silenced, the rattle of machine guns begins." But the assertion, in this same speech: "I have never been able to find a Red professor," even if true, merely infuriated the university's foes, for it treated them as children, not as equals.[21]

To be sure, Hutchins' boldness in defending freedom of speech did win support. On campus he was very much the hero for faculty and students alike. He carried the Board of Trustees with him too, in spite of some doubters. And an upsurge in gifts to the university in 1935–36, though undoubtedly affected by a partial recovery from the depression, may also have reflected the readiness of some donors to support an institution where the defence of intellectual freedom was so emphatic. Charles Walgreen himself was converted. He soon realized that he had been shamelessly manipulated by the Hearst press. Accordingly, when spokesmen for the university reproached him for the harm he had done, he proved surprisingly contrite and eventually agreed to establish a Walgreen Foundation for the Study of American Institutions with a gift of $550,000. He and Hutchins, in fact, became real if distant friends, and when he died, soon after setting up The Walgreen Foundation in 1938, the family asked Hutchins to speak at his funeral. It was a famous victory, but the university's reputation for radicalism persisted, exacerbating long-standing problems of student recruitment, fund-raising, and public relations generally.

In face of this difficulty, Hutchins turned to an old Yale friend, William Benton, for help. Benton, who had been on the debate team with Hutchins as an undergraduate, went into advertising and soon teamed up with another youthful Yale graduate, Chester Bowles, to found a firm of their own. Specializing in radio advertising, which was then a new, expanding field, the two young men grew rich, in spite of the depression. But getting rich by selling soap and other such things on the radio did not satisfy Benton. Accordingly, as soon as he had accumulated a million dollars, he withdrew from the firm. In 1936 he was therefore at loose ends, casting about for a new career. Hutchins seized the opportunity, inviting him to come to the university and make a study of its public relations. Benton set vigorously to work. He soon came to admire the university and what it stood for and eventually agreed to become vice president with special responsibility for public relations—a post he assumed in October 1937. His arrival on campus helped to shape the years after 1936 into a distinct era for university affairs, to be dealt with in the next chapter.[22]

Another landmark that made 1936 a turning point was the publication of Hutchins' first book, *The Higher Learning in America* (New Haven, 1936). Its pages publicized the radical views about higher education that Hutchins had matured over the first years of his presidency at Chicago. His convictions had taken shape largely through conversations with Adler, reinforced and sometimes sharpened by collisions with members of the faculty who opposed experiments Hutchins wished to make, both with the curriculum and with the organization of the university.

Hutchins devoted his primary effort toward reshaping the College more to his taste. This meant bringing the last years of high school and the first two years of college together to allow coherent training in the liberal arts of grammar, logic, and rhetoric. Reading and discussion of authentic texts of great books seemed the best way to achieve this goal. Accordingly, in 1934–35 Hutchins and Adler tested what could be done with younger students by recruiting juniors and seniors from the University High School into a special honors section to study such books under their own personal supervision. This doubled Hutchins' teaching, for his course for college students was not interrupted. The high school experiment met with somewhat ambiguous success, whereupon Hutchins handed the high school honors course over to a pair of high school teachers of English, devoting himself to trying to persuade faculty committees of the feasibility and desirability of remaking the curriculum along the lines he and Adler had tested out in their classes.

But faculty committees talked and talked and did not agree on much of anything. Resistance to Hutchins' and Adler's prescription for the improvement of liberal education was vigorous, and the palpable success of the New Plan strengthened the vested interests of those teaching the existing survey courses. Dean Boucher defended his handiwork vigorously, which, of course, put him in opposition to Hutchins. The resulting impasse was not resolved even when Boucher left Chicago to become president of the University of West Virginia in 1935. His departure merely deprived the College of strong leadership. Aaron J. Brumbaugh, a professor of education, became acting dean, but he never won Hutchins' confidence and therefore remained only an acting dean despite holding that office until the early 1940s. In this ambiguous position, Brumbaugh chose the role of honest broker. Taking no distinct initiative of his own, he played along with Hutchins' plans by chairing committees that toyed with proposals for radical reform and never actually agreed on anything of importance. For a man of Hutchins' impatient temperament, open defiance might have been less exasperating.

Blocked in the College in this fashion, Hutchins was not much more successful in the divisions. It is true that in 1935 in three of the four divisions he was able to appoint youthful deans who were keen on reforming the departments entrusted to their jurisdiction. But Robert Redfield in the social sciences, Richard McKeon in humanities, and William H. Taliaferro in the biological sciences were unable or unwilling to attack the prevailing departmentalization of research and teaching precipitately, even though they all were in sympathy with at least some of Hutchins' animadversions against the fragmentation of learning that resulted.

The three young deans were men of intellectual distinction and nobody's pawns. In particular, Redfield and McKeon soon developed open disagreement with Adler on theoretical and practical issues. Hutchins therefore found himself presiding over an unruly and more than three-ring circus—much more if one thinks of the professional schools and the separate departments, each of which had a life and autonomy of its own. But projects for reform of the Ph.D. degree, touched on in his inaugural address, and the development of a coherent Master's program, which in his optimistic moments Hutchins also envisaged, had to wait until he made better sense of the College—or so it seemed to him.

Meanwhile public events and Hutchins' increasingly strained relationship with his wife combined to increase his impatience. Democratic government and liberal society were fumblingly on the defensive in Europe, threatened by the apparent successes of Stalin's communism and of Hitler's fascism. In the United States, the New Deal's principal effort to reorganize the national economy had been declared unconstitutional in 1935, and President Roosevelt's subsequent scheme for enlarging the Supreme Court stirred bitter controversy before it ultimately failed.

For Hutchins, who cared deeply about justice and the law, and who probably cherished the ambition of becoming a member of the Supreme Court some day, the whole course of events, at home and abroad, within the university and within his own home was acutely unsatisfactory. Where brutal violence did not reign, confusion and deadlock prevailed. Clearly, the world needed rational principles and resolute action. But where were the necessary principles to be found, and how could people be persuaded to agree on them? Obviously, proper education was needed; yet he was unable to persuade the professors of the university he headed to agree on first (or any) principles and teach accordingly!

Hutchins' speeches reflected his gloom. "The world seems to be rushing towards the destruction of liberty of conscience, of worship, of speech and of thought," he told entering freshmen in September 1936; and in a speech he later judged to be the best he ever made, he told the graduating class in June 1935: "I am not worried about your economic future . . . I am worried about your morals. Time will corrupt you. Your friends, your wives and husbands, your business and professional associates will corrupt you; your social, political and financial ambitions will corrupt you." He went on to deplore the prevalent "resistance to uncomfortable truths" and the "decay of the national reason," concluding with a really despairful injunction to his hearers to hold fast to virtue as best they might, for: "Believe me, you are closer to the truth now than you will ever be again." [23]

Hutchins vented his frustration in four lectures on "The Higher Learning in America" delivered at Yale and subsequently published by the Yale University Press in 1936. He sketched his four-year College ideal, uniting senior high school and junior college; explained that great books ought to be the staple of a sound liberal education; and concluded by declaring that advanced work and research ought to be conducted, not by fractionated departments, but by synthetic and interrelated faculties of metaphysics, social sciences, and natural science.

This was radical enough, but what really set critics' teeth on edge was Hutchins' assertion that metaphysics alone could provide a basis for ordering higher education aright because theology, on which older generations had relied, was gone. "We are a faithless generation," he remarked, yet "consciously or unconsciously" we are trying to get back to first principles."[24] Other assertions were almost equally provocative. For example: "Knowledge is truth. The truth is everywhere the same. Hence education should be everywhere the same." Or: "Real unity can only be achieved by a hierarchy of truths."[25]

Hutchins failed to explain what he meant by metaphysics, and indeed he may have had no firm and definite propositions in mind when he used the word. Yet he concurred with Adler's impassioned argument that some sort of metaphysical first principles were a logically necessary basis for practical action, which is what he always aimed at. As he wrote in an effort to explain what he meant: "Morals degenerate into mores unless they have a higher meaning imparted to them by theology or metaphysics."[26]

Hutchins was obviously yearning for firm and clear principles like his father's in proposing that metaphysics take over from theology. The trouble was that metaphysics proved just as slippery as theology, reason just as deficient as faith, in guaranteeing what he always craved: a definite set of rules about right and wrong that could guide everyday behavior. His father had derived such rules by reasoning from scripture, and, for him, the truth of scripture was, of course, guaranteed by God. Hutchins, the son, sought the same result by reasoning from great books, whose truth could be guaranteed only by the same sort of reason required for their explication. But whose reason? And what if reasonable men disagreed? Hutchins had no answer, yet felt there had to be one. Otherwise morals became mores; and "Anything goes"—the refrain of the song that had haunted his youth at Yale—became a naked, abhorrent truth.

Most Americans felt the strain of uncertainty far less strongly than Hutchins did, shaped as he was by his father's example, and rubbed raw by his wife's tantrums and by the vigor of Mortimer Adler's arguments. Most Chicago faculty members were simply puzzled, but some were appalled at ideas "conceived and born in authoritarianism and absolutism, twin enemies of a free and democratic society," to quote Harry Gideonse, in his polemical rebuttal, entitled "The Higher Learning in a Democracy."[27] Gideonse claimed that "unfettered competition of truths," confusing and disorderly though they might be, was a necessary support for democratic society and accused Hutchins of seizing upon "a certain stage of human thinking as final," to wit, the long since discredited Middle Ages.[28] Yet Gideonse dodged the issue that was central for Hutchins, for the "unfettered competition of divergent truths" he recommended provided no practical guide for action. Private persons, acting on a personal version of truth and justice could, in logic at least, only lead to a war of all against all.

This is what Hutchins wanted to forestall by discovering a proper, rational education for all citizens. Yet he never spelled out what the metaphysical and moral principles or the detailed content of such an education would be. He was too busy with administration to be a philosopher in his own right. He hoped instead to provoke faculty members to undertake the task he set before them. But, as we saw, and as Gideonse's polemic reaffirmed, the faculty at Chicago refused to try. Disagreement prevailed, and the suspicion that Hutchins meant what he said and would use his authority as president to impose his (or Adler's) outlandish ideas on the university gained considerable ground among indignant and often uncomprehending faculty members.

That suspicion reached a farcical climax in the academic year 1936–37 when Hutchins used a gift to the university, earmarked for the purpose, to set up a Committee on the Liberal Arts and then invited a number of Adler's former friends to come to Chicago to take part in this new venture. Arthur Rubin was the impressario behind this venture, for after his failures of 1933–34, Mortimer Adler had abandoned his personal effort to reform the university. In this situation, Rubin, a man of private means and no professional occupation, stepped forward. An associate of Adler and McKeon at Columbia, Rubin was a man whose thrust after a single, saving truth made Adler seem almost like a middle-of-the-road moderate. Nonetheless, he contrived to find enough money to allow Hutchins to offer suitable salaries to a number of discontented and reflective men, of whom the most prominent were Scott Buchanan and his colleague, Stringfellow Barr, a professor of history at Virginia with whom Buchanan had become closely associated. The committee was initially projected to become part of the humanities division; but the new dean, Richard McKeon, quickly decided that it ought not to come under his jurisdiction lest it irreparably damage his relations with the rest of the division.

Thus orphaned, the Committee on Liberal Arts quickly turned into a disaster. The problem was that the coterie from Columbia, once reassembled at Chicago, no longer agreed on key issues. This hamstrung the committee on the few occasions when it met. A single truth turned out to be just as elusive among Adler's (and Rubin's) former friends as it was in the university at large. This upshot was all the more embarrassing because many faculty members regarded the appearance of Scott Buchanan, Stringfellow Barr, and other members of the Committee on Liberal Arts at Chicago as a covert method for bypassing the legal procedures of appointment that had been formally agreed to in 1931 when Adler had been forced out of the Department of Philosophy. The newcomers belonged to no department, yet enjoyed the status and perquisites usually reserved for members of the faculty—and all by virtue of Hutchins' personal invitation.

In fact Hutchins did seek to overcome the prevailing departmentalization of learning; and if the Committee on Liberal Arts had succeeded, he might well have tried to pursue the path of creating new, cross-departmental committees on a permanent basis. As we shall see, several such committees did take root subsequently, but in the short run, this particular experiment failed dismally. Anger and suspicion blew very hot against the newcomers, who began by quarreling and ended by sulking. Accordingly, when the prospect of taking over the management of St. John's College in Annapolis, Maryland, came to their attention, Buchanan and Barr decided to seize the opportunity. They swiftly removed themselves to St. John's and proceeded to institute a four-year program of study based mainly on great books.[29]

Hutchins and Adler stayed behind, thereby forfeiting an easy chance to act on their principles as far as undergraduate education was concerned. Hutchins rejected the presidency of St. John's, although Barr and Buchanan offered it to him; and Adler preferred retaining his association with Hutchins to remaking undergraduate education in collaboration with friends with whom he no longer fully agreed. Altogether, the Committee on the Liberal Arts turned out to be as farcical a failure for Hutchins and Adler as Little Beverley had been for the Hearst press. Afterwards, Hutchins lay low for a while, bruised by the distrust he had created and disappointed at the way his words were construed by those among the faculty who defied him so vehemently.

For the university as a whole, it marked the end of an era. The depth of the depression lay behind; the years ahead were to be dominated instead by approaching war. A more diffused push toward university reform persisted on the campus itself; and an influx of European refugees began to impinge on some of the more parochial dimensions of the university's intellectual traditions, especially in the humanities and social sciences. These changes require a new chapter.

4

THE DRIFT TOWARD WAR
1937–1941

Events in Europe echoed so loudly across the Atlantic in the late 1930s that life at the University of Chicago, as in the rest of the United States, was gradually transformed by the shadow of approaching war. The ugly side of fascism became apparent as Hitler organized assaults on Jews at home and then, beginning in 1936, began to expand the borders of the Reich by a combination of propaganda, subversion, military threat and coup d'état. The Nazis had few friends in the United States, and none to notice on Chicago's campus; but what, if anything, to do about their threat to the balance of power became the most urgent question of the day, displacing (but not yet curing) the domestic depression with its continuing unemployment.

Peace rallies and the like seemed silly in the face of Hitler's overt glorification of force. War was coming, all too clearly. Many expected the United States to recapitulate its role in World War I, but dreaded and loathed the prospect. What to do? Avoiding another war seemed as much beyond human capability as was finding any real cure for the depression. Confidence in rationality was hard to maintain with an incurable depression at home and international politics locked into a fated, foreseeable pattern from which there seemed to be no escape. Hitler's successes provoked pessimists to say that liberalism had failed—forever.

Communists posed for a while as stalwart enemies of fascism, yet their cause, too, lost much of its former appeal. Earlier in the decade, when Russian feats of industrial construction were trumpeted to a world sunk in the toils of economic depression, revolutionary Marxism had attracted the allegiance of a small but energetic group of rebels. But their confidence waned and the glamour of Stalin's achievement began to fade between 1936 and 1938 when a series of public trials in Moscow purported to show how Trotsky and other prominent Bolsheviks had betrayed the Party by conspiring with agents of foreign powers. The accused confessed their treason in open court, and some even asked for (and got) capital punishment. This was strange enough, but when some details of their confessions proved to be patently false—for example, a rendezvous in Denmark at a hotel that had been destroyed a few years before the supposed meeting took place—it became impossible to believe that the trials were not rigged. The sinister image of a Communist police state began to emerge—paralleled only by events in Germany, where organized attacks against Jews and a brief, bloody purge of the Nazi party in 1934 rivaled the long-drawn-out, and far bloodier purges that Stalin perpetrated during and after the Moscow treason trials.

As far as American opinion was concerned, both Nazis and Communists were deeply discredited by these events. The Nazis never had any significant following, but student Communists, who had become a small but noisy sect on campus in the early 1930s, were much embarrassed by the news from Moscow. In the wake of the treason trials, a new Trotskyite group formed. The ferocity of the resulting debate over the pieties of Marxism, Leninism, and Stalinism dimmed only after 1940, when Trotsky was assassinated in Mexico by a Russian agent.

Shortly before that quietus, the Molotov-Ribbentrop pact of August 1939, which made Russia an ally of Germany and paved the way for the outbreak of World War II, had dealt American Communists an all but lethal blow. Ever since 1936 they had led a crusade for a united front against fascism, trying to patch up old quarrels with socialists, liberals and, indeed, with anyone whom they could attract to the cause. A new organization, the American Student Union, carried the united front banner into student politics and flourished vigorously at Chicago during the next three years. Liberals occupied all the conspicuous leadership positions of the ASU, but a handful of dedicated Communists usually managed to run things from behind the scenes.

This pattern of student politics suddenly fell apart in the autumn of 1939 when party directives required Communists to defend Russia's cooperation with Hitler. Their new targets were French and British imperialists, whom they held responsible for the continuation of war in Europe after the brief Polish campaign had ended in the partition of that unfortunate country between Hitler and Stalin. (Stalin also annexed the Baltic republics of Esthonia, Latvia, and Lithuania in 1939; and when Finland refused to admit Russian troops, he launched the so-called Winter War, which ended with Finnish capitulation in March 1940.)

Such a sudden kink in the party line made it perfectly clear that the Communists slavishly served the interests of the Russian government, as Stalin chose to interpret those interests. This was more than many true believers and their former allies and sympathizers could swallow. As a result, in 1940, Communists and Trotskyites both disappeared from campus as organized entities, the ASU broke up, and Marxist recipes for revolution lost nearly all of their appeal. A few ingenious apologists succeeded in following every twist and turn of the party line, to be sure; but they spoke without conviction and commanded less and less attention on the campus, where Marxism had once rivaled Thomism in extracurricular debates.

The decay of Marxism after 1936 was gradual, and its effective disappearance from campus life was brief, because political volatility on the international front did not cease with the shocks of 1939–40. Instead, Hitler's attack on Russia in June 1941, followed by Japan's attack on Pearl Harbor in December of the same year, transformed Russia into an ally whose desperate struggles against the common enemy soon began to command considerable admiration and sympathy in the United States. As a vehicle for youthful rebellion against constituted authority, Marxism therefore reappeared on campus during the war. But the naive hope and missionary faith of the first years of the depression, when Soviet successes in building new factories contrasted so starkly with the inability of American capitalists to keep the population employed, did not return. Memories of Stalin's brutal methods of repression could never be entirely erased. Moreover, it was obvious that Russian policy reflected state interests, which were not necessarily (or even plausibly) identical with the international solidarity and proletarian brotherhood prescribed by Marxist teaching. Consequently, Marxism on campus (and in the country at large) tended to degenerate into a convenient vocabulary of reproach against constituted authority and ceased to be taken seriously as a recipe for social betterment.

Simultaneously, the course of public events made the reach after simple, total systems of belief—a frame of mind that had characterized both Thomists and their Marxist rivals in the early 1930s—a good deal less urgent. First of all, as the depression decade of the 1930s approached its close, unemployment began finally to dissipate. Stimulated by rearmament, the American economy started to revive. Simultaneously, an increasingly emphatic enmity toward Germany and Japan invited everyone to rally around the government in Washington, which, from its side, made serious efforts to seek support from Republicans and businessmen who had been targets of opprobrium in the early New Deal era. With the national economy and polity gearing up for war in this fashion, Chicago's students, like the nation at large, were more and more inclined to subscribe to the existing American way of life. They no longer found it really necessary to try to base a personal system of belief on first principles, and as that occurred, the bloom departed from Marxism and Thomism alike. To be sure, Hutchins' pronouncements lost none of their eloquence, but he, too, fuzzed the commitment to metaphysical first principles that he had declared to be necessary in 1936 by explaining at a trustees' dinner in January 1937 that "the answers to these questions are not so important as asking them." [1]

A second and more enduring consequence of the course of public events in the late 1930s was the arrival on campus of a handful of European intellectuals who were fleeing from official persecution in Germany and Italy. Refugee students were few and played inconspicuous roles; but the handful of Europeans who secured faculty appointments did exercise considerable influence within some departments and affected the political tone of the campus at large.

University finances remained under strain, and the first refugees were only appointed thanks to gifts specially earmarked for the purpose. This was the case, for example, with Ulrich Middeldorf and Ludwig Bachhofer, who brought instruction in art history at Chicago to a new level of sophistication after joining the Department of Art in 1935. They were the first refugees from Nazi Germany to secure faculty appointments at Chicago and did so on the strength of a gift from a wealthy Chicago businessman and art collector, Max Epstein. Three years later, the appointment of Nobel Laureate James Franck in chemistry also depended on a special gift earmarked for the purpose. But once the possibility of hiring men of high capability for comparatively low salaries became obvious, the university opened its doors to other refugee scholars, even without special outside funding.

Such appointments, of course, squeezed out American-trained individuals, which hurt a good deal in a time when academic employment was far from buoyant. Moreover, transplanted professors did not always turn out to be effective teachers of students whose general background and prior training were far different from the best German patterns of education. But the prestige of German scholarship carried the day, and Chicago, like other leading American universities, proved remarkably hospitable to refugees.

The overall effect of the influx of foreigners varied from case to case. The art department was the most thoroughly transformed. Soon after his initial appointment, Middeldorf became chairman and proceeded to attract a cluster of other German scholars like Otto von Simson, Peter von Blanckenhagen, and others. In their hands, art history transcended prior American academic efforts at art appreciation and became a remarkably erudite, sophisticated, and incisive branch of intellectual and cultural history.

On the other hand, the renowned classicist, Werner Jaeger, who came to the Department of Greek in 1936, kept pretty much to himself, pursuing his own line of thought and scholarship in a detached and private way. He presupposed a higher level of familiarity with classical languages and scholarship than American schooling provided and therefore attracted few students, while the brevity of his stay at Chicago and his toploftical reclusiveness meant that he had little impact on his colleagues. When he left Chicago for Harvard in 1939, he therefore left little trace behind. American-trained professors remained what they had been, and their students continued to lag behind European levels of linguistic and philological mastery. Thereafter, the best work in classics at Chicago, as elsewhere in the United States, tended to concentrate on archaeology and related investigations, where American training was abreast of the best practice in Europe.

In natural science, the major influx of refugees came only after 1941. Perhaps Chicago's physicists, chemists, and other scientists shared a common discourse so fully and were already so closely in touch with the latest research results from Germany that they had less to gain from closer association with top-notch Europeans than did humanists and social scientists. At any rate, I am unable to assess the impact of Chicago's principal prewar appointment in science—that of James Franck in chemistry.

A different sort of strengthening came to the Department of Astronomy in 1936, when its chairman, Otto Struve (himself Russian by birth), attracted Bengt Stromgren from Sweden, Gerard P. Kuiper from Holland, and S. Chandrasekhar from India, by way of Cambridge, England. These were not distinguished refugees, but young men of special promise picked by Struve to work on the stream of new data that the McDonald telescope in Texas was about to provide. His choices turned out to be excellent and assured the continued distinction of the Department of Astronomy throughout the Hutchins era and beyond.[2]

Appointment of able young men, preferably younger than himself, was Hutchins' way of reconciling budgetary pressures with the necessity of finding worthy successors to famous faculty members who had retired. He continually kept looking for youthful talent and made every effort to persuade the relevant department to appoint those who somehow caught his fancy. Thus, for example, when visiting England in 1936, Hutchins met David Daiches at Oxford and invited him to come to Chicago on the spot, presumably because he was confident of being able to persuade the Department of English to accept Daiches as a junior colleague. The young Scotsman, a Jew from Edinburgh, duly arrived in the autumn of 1937 to find the Department of English in a particularly vivacious state of intellectual turmoil, to which I shall presently turn.[3] Daiches stayed at Chicago only until 1942, but another young man who caught Hutchins' eye, the Irish classicist, David Grene, spent his entire career on the Midway, though he did not remain in the Department of Greek because of clashes of personality and of viewpoint that became acute in the mid-1940s. Another brilliant protégé was Edward Shils. Hutchins did not bring him to Chicago, but did contrive to keep Shils there despite an invitation to London.[4]

Hutchins was clearly capable of recognizing young scholars with a gift for words, and in the fields of learning where words prevailed, he thought it his right and duty to act on his personal impression and judgments. But some humanities and social science departments were so suspicious of Hutchins' intentions and so jealous of their prerogatives that any candidate he might propose was almost sure to be voted down, especially if the person in question represented a departure from existing departmental outlook and practices. After the fiasco of Adler's appointment and withdrawal from their department in 1930–31, Chicago's philosophers were particularly hostile to Hutchins, and it is perhaps not surprising therefore that they refused to appoint the French Catholic philosopher, Jacques Maritain, as Hutchins proposed after Maritain first visited Chicago in 1938.

Yet, unlike some of the professors whom he offended, Hutchins was not vindictive. Part of the deal contrived in 1931, when Adler left the Department of Philosophy for the Law School, was the appointment of Charles Morris, a graduate of the Chicago department and a representative of everything in philosophy that Adler most detested. Five years later, perhaps as a gesture of defiance, the Department of Philosophy proposed the appointment of Rudolf Carnap, a logical positivist from Prague. Carnap was a leading figure in European philosophical circles, and Hutchins therefore concurred with the department's nomination, despite Adler's privately expressed disdain for "that sap Carnap."[5]

When he got to Chicago, Carnap launched a vast collaborative work, intended to demonstrate the unity of science as defined in positivist terms. Morris served as coeditor. Two initial volumes of the resulting *International*

Encyclopedia of Unified Science were published by the University of Chicago Press, but when war broke out in 1939 the enterprise had to be suspended owing to interruption of communication with European philosophers who constituted a majority of the contributors. Oddly, therefore, after 1936 the university became the base for an ambitious synthesis of positivist thought at a time when Adler and Hutchins were busy denouncing positivism as a pernicious intellectual error.

Yet, despite his great reputation, Carnap had little effect on campus life at close range. His ideas (and those of Charles Morris) contributed to the recent rise of semiotics, but had little impact at the time. Though exiled from Prague and living in Chicago, Carnap much preferred to cultivate his connections within a circle of like-minded philosophers in Europe and paid almost no attention to local controversies. These turned, more and more, upon what Richard McKeon had to say.

McKeon, after becoming dean of the humanities division in 1935, induced the Department of Philosophy to admit him to its ranks in 1937. Thereafter, Carnap's positivism—and the pragmatism that had dominated the department before Hutchins' arrival, represented by men like T. V. Smith and Charner Perry—coexisted awkwardly with the new broom of McKeon's idiosyncratic method for dissecting and classifying philosophical writings. Yet just because their disagreements were so fundamental, the philosophers refused to confront one another openly, being both too busy and too polite to argue fruitlessly in public.

Tolerating, and in practice neglecting, such differences over truth was anathema to a man of Adler's temperament. He vehemently wished to silence every opponent with a stream of rapid-fire argument; and by choosing his own terms for debate, he could in fact prevail, yet without being able to convince those whom he so volubly overpowered. His frequent verbal victories confirmed Adler in the conviction that he was right, while the obduracy of his opponents who, even when defeated in debate, stubbornly refused to accept his demonstrations of philosophical truth, disgusted him with the whole academic world. He therefore withdrew more and more from campus affairs, intervening only sporadically and from afar by unburdening himself in characteristically extreme and provocative fashion.

After this withdrawal, Adler's principal epiphany on campus occurred in November 1940 when the *Maroon* published a special issue on "The New Medievalism." The occasion for such an unusual event was an address, entitled "God and the Professors," that Adler had delivered two months earlier at a conference in New York. The *Maroon* republished Adler's speech in full along with vigorous rebuttals by professors Ronald Crane, Frank Knight, Quincy Wright, and Malcolm Sharp (Adler's colleague in teaching a course for students of the Law School), together with a burlesque of the whole debate written by the university's public relations expert, Milton Mayer.

Adler's exasperation was evident. "Since professors come to a conference of this sort with the intention of speaking their minds but not of changing them, with a willingness to listen but not to learn, with the kind of tolerance that delights in a variety of opinions and abominates the unanimity of agreement, it is preposterous to suppose that this conference can even begin to realize the ends which justify the enterprise," he declared, and then laid down a series of propositions about philosophy and religion which, he asserted, simple logic required all men to affirm. Instead of recognizing various "systems of philosophy," as the professors were wont to do, Adler affirmed that there was "only philosophical knowledge, more or less adequately possessed by different men" and "there is only one true religion, less or more adequately embodied in the existing diversity of creeds." But what offended his audience in New York most sharply and echoed just as strongly in Chicago was his conclusion: "Until the professors and their culture are liquidated, the resolution of modern problems will not begin" because "democracy has more to fear from the mentality of its teachers than from the nihilism of Hitler." [6] Chicago professors were outraged, and Hutchins, who, as always, refused to dissociate himself from Adler's pronouncements, suffered guilt by association because Adler went out of his way in this speech to praise Hutchins' abortive curricular proposals and left the impression that his great and good friend agreed with everything he had to say.

Short-lived recurrence of such extremism in logical dress did not signify any real restoration of Adler's influence on campus however. Instead, intellectual controversy focused more and more on McKeon's way of addressing philosophical and curricular questions. He differed completely from Adler both in the substance of his doctrine and in the manner of his discourse. Adler, having failed to establish any influential academic base at Chicago, was in danger of becoming no more than Hutchins' court jester. He was a perpetual outsider—a voice crying in the wilderness—by temperament and by choice. McKeon, by contrast, preferred to operate from within the academic hierarchy. Having become dean of humanities, he occupied a strategic position from which to influence others through a combination of intellectual persuasion and administrative action. This allowed him to exercise independent, personal authority within the university. Consequently, during the next decade McKeon's influence far outweighed anything either Adler or Hutchins did to reshape the curriculum in the Division of Humanities and, after 1942, in the College as well.

McKeon's impact upon the university arose in large part from the fact that he refrained from the sort of headlong assault on all who differed from him that Adler always preferred. Instead of arguing for any particular doctrine or set of philosophical conclusions, he developed a method for analyzing texts that purported to be able to discern the inmost structure of any philosopher's thought. Whether a particular doctrine was true or false did not really matter; the task was to analyze and understand what thinkers, caught in their respective modes of discourse, had, as it were, been compelled to conclude. The superior insight McKeon's method seemed to confer on those who practiced it caused his disciples to assume a posture of intellectual condescension both toward the philosophers whose arguments they dissected and toward anyone who failed to embrace their method or agree with their conclusions.

In this backhanded way, a new dogmatism, far more recondite than Adler's straightforward affirmation of Aristotelian doctrine, gradually gathered force. Consequently, among the diverse schools of thought represented in the Department of Philosophy after 1937, only McKeon's method of argument and analysis mattered as far as the rest of the university was concerned. This was mainly due to the enthusiastic way a few scholars of literature, particularly Ronald Crane, chairman of the Department of English, embraced McKeon's ideas. Carnap, by comparison, only mattered to a small circle of professional philosophers, nearly all of whom lived in Europe.

Other departments where refugees found lodgement usually behaved like Greek and philosophy, admitting the newcomers and respecting them without reacting very strongly to whatever novelties of learning and outlook they brought with them from the other side of the Atlantic. This was clearly the case in economics, for instance, where a Polish socialist, Oscar Lange, accepted appointment in 1938. His efforts to set forth criteria by which socialist administrators could expect to allocate resources efficiently without recourse to free market prices commanded some professional curiosity among the dedicated market economists who dominated the Chicago department, but neither side was able to convince the other. In Romance Languages, a fiery Italian, Giuseppe Borgese, who arrived on campus in 1936, likewise added a new strand to university life without affecting the established style of literary scholarship that prevailed in the department that gave him refuge. Borgese's interests were public and political rather than philological or narrowly literary and, as such, had almost no impact on his departmental colleagues, though his book, *Goliath: The March of Fascism,* published in 1937, met considerable public success. Borgese hated Mussolini in a thoroughly personal way and, in attacking him, invited his American readers to lump Italian fascism and German Nazism together as equally oppressive and repugnant regimes.

In the field of history, Hans Rothfels, like Borgese, came to Chicago with firm political commitments, for he was a deep-dyed German (actually Prussian) conservative; and, like many other exiled German professors, he never got used to the slender background American students brought to the study of his subject, which was German and central European history. His best students were themselves exiles, and his intense German patriotism—anti-Nazi though it was—tended to isolate him from colleagues in the history department, especially after the United States went to war against Germany once more in 1941.

Yet for all the obstacles that limited the establishment of effective intellectual intercourse between European scholars and their new American colleagues and students, there is no doubt that the overall effect of the influx of refugees in the late 1930s was a wholesome tonic that eventually propelled the university toward a far greater cosmopolitanism of learning than it had known before. In the 1920s and 1930s, much American scholarship in the humanities and social sciences was provincial in the sense that most professors paid little attention to anything that was not published in English. Before 1914, the prestige of German scholarship had enticed many Americans to study at German universities and assimilate what they could of German learning; but World War I broke this connection and it languished thereafter. Chicago actually took the lead in turning away from speculative social theory of the sort that continued to flourish in Germany, preferring direct observation and measurement of human behavior as exhibited close at hand in the city of Chicago, or, for the anthropologists, in Indian villages of North and Central America.

The rather naive faith of Chicago's social scientists in their own objectivity as observers had already come under attack from Adler and other philosophers, and this perhaps helped to prepare the way for a fruitful renewal of contact with German and European speculative social science. But it took a while to establish effective communication across the linguistic and conceptual barriers that separated German and European thought from American and English traditions of learning; and, except when wholesale transplantation occurred, as happened to the Department of Art, the first years of encounter between European refugees and their hosts in Chicago were not particularly productive.

The hard sciences were already cosmopolitan, with a common language of mathematics and chemical notation. For that reason, there were fewer obstacles to fitting refugees into the natural sciences, and, for the same reason, they had less to offer in the way of redirecting research into new channels. Or so it seems to an outsider like myself, who cannot claim to know where the impetus for new investigation in physics, chemistry, and biology actually came from, whether at Chicago or in the country at large.

In effect, the impact of newcomers from across the ocean could not be fully felt in social science and the humanities until younger people, who encountered German learning as graduate students while their minds were still flexible, began to succeed the old guard of professors whose intellectual postures had been defined in the 1920s or earlier. Slowly but surely, retirements produced this result, changing the posture of Chicago's departments little by little, and eventually allowing them to combine German with English and American intellectual traditions more firmly and fully than ever before. The drastic disruption of German learning that Hitler brought about meant that after the war German academics were impelled to apprentice themselves to the English-speaking world. Only the French retained a distinct intellectual autonomy (at least in some fields, such as history) that could command respectful attention from bearers of the enriched cosmopolitan tradition that took root in the United States as a result of the influx of refugees from Europe. This constitutes a notable shift in the world's cultural and intellectual landscape, and the University of Chicago played a worthy part in what happened, as we shall see in later chapters.

No doubt it was the course of public events, and the obvious approach of war, that gave the years 1937 to 1941 their special character for the life of the university; but internal currents played a role as well. First and foremost was the continued friction between Hutchins and a considerable proportion of the senior faculty. After the flare-up over Hutchins' endorsement of metaphysics in his lectures at Yale in 1936, ideological debate softened, not because the parties managed to agree or even to understand one another, but because Hutchins, like Adler, had begun to despair of making the sort of changes he wished.

As he explained in a document entitled "Annual Confidential Statement to the Board of Trustees," dated 30 September 1938: "One member of the Board asked me this winter why I had not put into the College the program for general education advocated in my books. The College faculty and its committees have three times rejected my recommendations on this subject." He went on: "Actually the President's power is the privilege of trying to persuade the faculty to accept his views of persons and policies." Although, as he admitted, some university presidents had accomplished a good deal even with such limitations, "I think it will be found that these accomplishments are limited either to the first years of an administration before the president had time to alienate the faculty through adverse decisions, or to periods of financial and educational expansion." But Hutchins was in neither of these happy situations. Instead he found himself locked into the "unenviable position of having to persuade persons against whom he is making decisions every day of his life." Only with new money coming in would the "normal rule against shooting Santa Claus" be likely to prevail. Instead, "the problem of the University of Chicago is one of integration. This involves trying to improve what we have, trying to make some sense out of it, trying to get out of entangling alliances, dropping courses, men, departments, even schools, and putting everything we are doing on a defensible basis. This program . . . threatens vested interests." [7] No wonder, then, that faculty opposition made it impossible for him to act on his educational principles.

What provoked this *cri du cœur* was a falling out over academic tenure. When the depression hit, Hutchins had tried to guard the budget against future constriction and improve his power of maneuver by withholding tenure whenever possible. Promotion to associate professor therefore no longer carried tenure with it; and by 1938, there were even a few full professors without that accustomed prerogative. The Chicago chapter of the American Association of University Professors took note of this decay of status in 1937–38 and complained so vigorously that the University Senate decided to appoint an official committee to study the matter of tenure and make formal recommendations about future policy.

Hutchins regarded this as a personal attack on his prerogatives and good judgment. The administrative issue was in fact colored by a diffuse but intense ideological hostility, largely because Harry Gideonse had become a leading spirit within the local AAUP chapter. Gideonse fancied himself as Hutchins' principal opponent, having taken a leading part in defending the College curriculum against Hutchins' reproaches, and hurrying into print with his criticism of *The Higher Learning in America* as well. Hutchins perhaps suspected that Gideonse and his friends were deliberately trying to increase support for their ideological position among the faculty by shifting debate from educational principles to the question of tenure, whereas Gideonse and others who distrusted Hutchins' intentions feared that without the safeguard of academic tenure the faculty might find itself at the mercy of an irresponsible president's personal whims.

Hutchins, in fact, felt that academic tenure was unwise and unnecessary. From his point of view, it protected the weak and, above all, inhibited change. "The problem of eliminating mediocrity and getting something done seems to me much more pressing than that of protecting the faculty," he told the trustees.[8] And for the first but not the last time, he complained of the Senate's ineffective governance of the university, which allowed small cliques of specially interested individuals to veto any departure from existing routines simply because most professors were indifferent to anything that did not affect their personal careers and only attended Senate meetings when their own special interests were somehow at stake.[9]

Hutchins' frustration was therefore acute, but his distaste for academic tenure was no match for the faculty's addiction to it. After appropriate deliberation, the Senate Committee recommended a regular pattern of promotion whereby after four years as an instructor, reappointed annually, junior members of the faculty would have to become assistant professors or be dismissed, and then, after two three-year terms as assistant professor, the process would be repeated, with the choice becoming either promotion to indefinite tenure as associate professor or dismissal. No fixed term for promotion to full professor was suggested, however; and the higher dignity of a named professorship, together with adjustments of salary within each rank, were left entirely to the discretion of the administration. In due course, the Senate endorsed this policy and the Board of Trustees made it official in June 1940.

Hutchins' power over appointments was not really reduced by this action, for ever since 1931 he had been compelled to persuade departments and schools to approve anyone he wished to invite to the university; but it did mean that a larger proportion of the faculty had the right to stay exactly where they were until retirement, and this obviously reinforced all the vested interests that Hutchins found so galling. It was, therefore, a defeat for the president and one which steeled him to extraordinary action in 1942, as we shall see in the next chapter.

As for Gideonse, he did not stay at Chicago to savor victory. The up or out rule had a cutting edge, after all; and Gideonse's colleagues in economics declined to support his promotion to a full professorship, simply because he had no research to publish, being far too busy with his teaching and leadership role in the College. It was an ironical upshot, intensified by the fact that

Gideonse, after becoming president of Brooklyn College, New York, shortly after leaving Chicago, began a long series of clashes with rebellious faculty members there who resented his administrative highhandedness.

The professional schools underwent two significant changes in the period we are concerned with, one positive, one negative. On the positive side, the Law School developed a new four-year curriculum that came into effect in 1937. Departing from exclusive attention to legal case studies such as that which had dominated Hutchins' own training in law, the new curriculum featured courses in psychology, constitutional history, ethics, business organization, and economic theory to provide a proper setting for mastery of details of the law as actually applied in the courts. To make time for the new courses, aspiring lawyers were expected to start the Law School curriculum while still seniors in the College, but an abbreviated three-year curriculum was maintained for those entering from other colleges.

The Law School also attracted a cluster of bright young teachers, including Edward Levi, the future president of the university; and when Dean Bigelow retired in 1940, Hutchins found a vigorous, youthful successor in Wilber G. Katz. Katz took over just in time to see student numbers plummet when compulsory military training made it difficult or impossible for a physically fit young man to stay out of the armed forces after reaching draft age. Nevertheless, in the long run the new curriculum was a solid success, even though in the short run the Law School suffered through troubled times during the war, when most of the faculty dispersed for government service and students almost disappeared.

The Medical School suffered no parallel difficulty when war came, since medical students were exempted from the draft and their training was actually subsidized by the armed forces in return for compulsory military service afterwards. But there were difficulties of a different kind. First of all, the long-standing problem of relations with Rush Medical School led to a not very amicable parting of the ways in 1941. This resulted from a decision to prohibit undergraduate pre-meds from enrolling at Rush, while accepting only as many medical students as could be accommodated on the Midway. Rush had a proud tradition of its own that antedated affiliation with the University of Chicago. As a result, faculty and alumni rebelled against accepting such a sharply diminished role, especially since it was being dictated from the South Side. Rush accordingly resumed full independence and became a rival rather than an ally of the Medical School on the Midway.

Another affiliation agreement turned sour when Provident Hospital, serving the black ghetto on Chicago's South Side, was cast adrift, largely because the university found it difficult to induce white medical students and doctors to serve there and was unwilling to admit black doctors and patients into the university's hospitals for fear that their presence would drive away the white patients upon whom the finances of the Medical School had come to depend. On the other hand, Lying-In Hospital, which had once been a proprietary and separate institution, was successfully folded into the university hospital system in 1938.

Finances remained difficult, even after the Rockefeller Foundation was persuaded to make a final grant to help out with the Medical School's persistent deficits. No solution could be found for the gap between academic salaries and the level of income a doctor could attain in private practice. As a result, the Department of Medicine remained a revolving door, bringing newcomers to campus every year who stayed for only brief periods of time before setting out on their own. The ideal of making teaching and research into a full-time occupation for the faculty of the Medical School remained firmly in place, but doctors who were so devoted to their research and teaching as to forego enlarged incomes remained a small, though honored, minority.

No very conspicuous changes came to the other professional schools in the years just before the war, although an episode in 1941 raises an interesting question of what might have been, at least in retrospect. In April of that year, a wealthy man named Walter P. Murphy proposed the establishment of a School of Engineering at Chicago and offered to endow it, at least partially. But Hutchins felt that the university needed to consolidate and concentrate upon what it did best and should not expand into new fields. The problems besetting the Medical School showed how distracting a new venture could turn out to be, even when launched with clear principles and lofty goals. Moreover, Hutchins had a certain disdain of material things and perhaps felt that engineering was a trade more than a profession, with no legitimate place in a university. At any rate, he turned the offer down flat, and any possibility of linkages between engineering and physics, of the kind that were to flourish so luxuriantly in Boston and California after the war, was thereby forfeited. In view of the role computers have begun to play in our society, Hutchins' decision may have been a serious mistake. Of course, he can hardly be blamed for not foreseeing the way computer technology now intertwines with information of every kind so as to affect all fields of knowledge. Yet his rejection of engineering, like his far more famous abolition of football, may have been more important for the university in the long run than were the curricular and organizational reforms he struggled so hard to achieve.

Conquering Hero

Or Failed Shakespearian Actor?

President and Mrs. Hutchins on their arrival in Chicago, November 1929

Hutchins sent this to a friend with the following inscription: "I am having sent to you one of these pictures of me looking like a retired second-rate Shakespearian actor gazing into his past. I do not believe that I ever looked this way."

The Man Who Hired Him

The College dean who greeted him with a radical and successful New Plan

(above) Harold Swift, Chairman of the Board of Trustees, 1922–1949

(right) Chauncey S. Boucher, Dean of the College, 1926–1935

And the friend he brought to Chicago

Mortimer J. Adler, associate professor of the philosophy of law

Work

Comprehensive Exam in the Fieldhouse, ca. 1938

Play

Formal dance in a downtown hotel, ca. 1940

Protest, May Day 1938

"Peace Strike 1938 brought out 520 paraders, almost as many signs, not ignoring the Alpha Delt swastika. While few took the Oxford Oath, one lone fascist heckled." So reads the caption for this montage from the student annual *Cap and Gown*, 1938.

Blackfriars

Male Chorus Line

Football, 1931

By 1931 Big Time football had spread from Chicago to many other schools, and Coach Stagg's team no longer towered over rivals.

Bill Haarlow   Jay Berwanger

Haarlow scored, almost at will, by setting up, back to the basket, on the foul line, then stepping forward, whirling, and shooting from the top of his jump. This tactic was later outlawed as others learned to do it, but in 1938 it made him an All American like Berwanger.

Berwanger ran, passed, and punted for the team 1935, 1936 and 1937, and like everybody else played defense as well. He won the first Heisman trophy in his senior year.

Beardsley Ruml, Dean of the Social Sciences Division

Richard McKeon, Dean of the Humanities Division

William H. Taliaferro, Dean of the Biological Sciences Division

Robert Redfield, Dean of the Social Sciences Division after Ruml left

Planning a Roundtable Radio Program

Professors Jerome Kerwin, Harry Gideonse, and T. V. Smith were frequent participants in the Roundtable in the 1930s.

Amos Alonzo Stagg

The University's reputation in the world at large depended very much on Stagg's football teams. Even when they ceased to win regularly, his reputation remained very high until his reluctant retirement in 1935.

Nobel Laureates in Physics

Albert A. Michelson and Arthur H. Compton in front of Kent Laboratory, ca. 1928. Michelson was the first American to win a Nobel prize.

Three Isolationists

Robert M. Hutchins, ca. 1939

William B. Benton, vice president

Each for his own reasons resisted
the drift toward war, 1939–1941

Anton J. Carlson, professor of physiology

Undergraduates on the walk in front of Cobb Hall, ca. 1940

The Soviet-Nazi Pact of 1939 abruptly changed the tone of student politics as everyone reluctantly faced up to war's approach.

Ceremonial march on the Midway. Thousands of soldiers and sailors took special training courses at the university during the war.

Temporary housing on the south side of the Midway. Married veterans lived here after the war and brought the Baby Boom to campus. Chicago Historical Society: photo by Mildred Mead.

Dawn of the Atomic Age

Artist's drawing of the Pile where the first self-sustaining nuclear reaction occurred under the west stands of Stagg Field on 2 December 1942. No photograph of the original pile was allowed for security reasons.

The Physicists Who Built It, Ten Years Afterwards

On the tenth anniversary, veterans of the original experiment reassembled at the original site to commemorate their achievement and reflect on it. This shows Lawrence A. Kimpton speaking, while Enrico Fermi and Arthur H. Compton sit behind him awaiting their turns at the microphone.

Professor James Franck

Dean Clarence Faust

Professor Joseph Schwab

(above) Franck was one of the first German refugees to enrich Chicago's learning. He came with a Nobel prize in chemistry.

(above right) Faust presided over the reorganization of the College, 1942–1946.

(right) Chairman of the controversial Natural Sciences staff in the Four-Year College

55th Street about 1950

Restrictive covenants were outlawed after World War II, and the resulting advance of blacks into the university neighborhood created new problems for race relations and the maintenance of middle-class standards. This photo shows shop fronts on 55th Street about the time when the challenge was setting in. Chicago Historical Society: photo by Mildred Mead.

The College remained the main focus of Hutchins' reform efforts, but immediately before the war excitement and action concentrated instead in the humanities division, where a cluster of enthusiasts formed around Ronald Crane and Richard McKeon. Crane, chairman of the Department of English, was an unusually clearheaded man, which, no doubt, was what attracted him to the literature of the eighteenth century. He had established himself as a meticulous scholar by investigating the usual sort of historical, biographical, and textual questions; but, more than most of his colleagues, he felt the triviality of such scholarship when devoted to second-rate authors.

Crane's resulting dissatisfaction with his own accomplishment and with that of his fellows took a new turn after hearing McKeon explain how to analyze a text and discern its intrinsic structure and meaning. Applied to literature, McKeon's approach promised to show why some texts were great works of literature and why others fell short. This seemed a far more important goal than discovering still more historical details about all the authors of rather trivial books that scholars of English literature had hitherto, and quite properly, overlooked. Or so Crane came to believe, whereupon he rapidly communicated his new conviction to others around him, within and beyond the Department of English.

The enthusiasm of a convert carried Crane's rejection of history and social context as the main path toward a proper understanding of a text very far indeed; and since all the humanities and most of the social science departments were built around the study of texts of one kind or another, this principle was potentially of the very widest significance. As early as 1933, before he had ever heard of McKeon, Crane had scathingly rejected one sort of historical study—the loosely articulated synthesis of art, literature, and history that Schevill had made the basis of the College humanities course. "If what is meant by synthesis," he wrote, "is the putting together by one man of the results of specialized research in order to write a unified account of a given phase of civilization, then that is something with which scholars as scholars can have nothing to do. It is a task that should be left to journalists." And again: "The only histories of thought that can be taken seriously will be those written by philosophers, the only good economic histories will be written by economists, etc." [10]

When he wrote this memorandum in 1933, Crane was actually objecting to the encroachment by historians on his own and other scholars' special preserves—a style of historical writing and teaching that had been translated from Germany to Columbia before World War I and dubbed "The New History" by James Harvey Robinson. When Schevill, who drew directly on German inspiration as well as profiting from Columbia's example, set out to do the same at Chicago, he did not carry the history department with him; and, in fact, Crane was arguing against a straw man because there was no organized support within the divisions for the sort of historically framed synthesis of intellectual and cultural history that the College humanities course offered. The College staff was therefore isolated; and after Schevill's retirement in 1934, his successor as anchor man for the College humanities course, an undistinguished and unreflective historian named Arthur Scott, was completely unable to defend what he had inherited. He simply persevered, without even trying to reply to Crane's memorandum.

Nevertheless, Crane carried the logic of his attack on history as a mode for understanding anything other than past politics a step further after discovering McKeon's method. He, in effect, decided to discard the minutiae of historical context so lovingly supplied by the scholarly labors of literary experts along with the looser sort of historical synthesis that Schevill had exemplified. Neither form of historical scholarship, he came to believe, had anything important to say about works of art, which ought to be studied as objects in themselves. Only so could the real literary merit, or demerit, of a given text be discovered. Only so could authentic literary scholarship emerge from the miasma of miscellaneous historical information that professors of English had laboriously piled up, obfuscating real understanding of the literature they purported to study by attending not to the texts but to their trivial and often accidental contexts.

This, approximately, became the mission of what came to be called the "Chicago School of Criticism." The English department divided between followers of Crane and McKeon, who committed themselves to the ambitious task of reforming literary scholarship, and those who clung fast to older forms of contextual, historical study. By and large, it was younger men, like Elder Olson and Norman Maclean, who followed Crane most enthusiastically, while most of his older colleagues remained indifferent or even opposed to the effort to bring precision to literary criticism by using McKeon's analytical method.

In practice, Crane and his followers had difficulty acting on their new principles. David Daiches, when he arrived at Chicago in the fall of 1937, found himself immediately enveloped in the resulting controversy. "In Oxford," he wrote, "it would have been bad taste to ask such fundamental questions . . . In Chicago nothing was assumed, all questions were asked point blank, and you were not allowed to get away with a perfunctory answer." [11] Daiches' account of those times is both vivid and sympathetic. He describes how Crane took him aside and read aloud one of his essays, inviting Daiches' opinion about how well he had in fact been able to discern the intrinsic structure and value of a particular literary text. Crane's eagerness to invite an outsider's very youthful judgment (Daiches was not yet 30), and Crane's uncertainty about his own success in getting to the heart of literary excellence becomes very clear from what Daiches has to say; and so does the intensity of the intellectual effort Crane generated among his younger colleagues and the leading graduate students of the English department.

Daiches, having been shaped by a genteel, historicizing tradition at Edinburgh and Oxford, "remained suspicious of a purely specialist technical vocabulary for criticism"; but "in a sense I grew up," being "forced in controversy to define my own position much more carefully than I had ever done before." [12] It was, in short, a marvelous place for a young scholar to refine and define literary taste; just as the College continued to be a marvelous place for those interested in the broad spectrum of intellectual traditions embodied in the survey courses. In the early 1930s, graduate students had been too deeply committed to their professional advancement in a particular, specialized branch of learning to pay much attention to the doctrinal debates that had run so strongly among undergraduates; but after 1936 this ceased to be true in English, and in somewhat less intense degree in all the associated departments of the humanities division, wherever the study of literary texts prevailed. Everyone had to take account of the new winds of doctrine Crane and McKeon had generated, though only in English and philosophy did a substantial body of graduate students or professors do more than dabble and then dismiss the new style of textual analysis.

McKeon as well as his fellow dean, Robert Redfield in the social sciences division, entertained ambitions for altering the departmental structure they had inherited. McKeon's tactic was to create new interdepartmental committees with degree-granting power. A Committee on the History of Culture, and another entitled Analysis of Ideas and Study of Methods were the principal monuments to McKeon's effort along these lines; but he entertained, without ever acting on, far more radical notions of restructuring the humanities division so that criticism might be systematically disentangled from historical scholarship by segregating the two approaches to knowledge in different academic units.

Redfield advocated equally radical notions about how the social sciences might be more rationally organized, but prolonged discussion of what a divisional curriculum leading to an M.A. ought to be like only produced deadlock. Instead, the divisional M.A. program limped along in the form it had assumed when the divisional organization was invented in 1931, with each department offering whatever it chose as an introductory course without regard for what the other departments were doing. No satisfactory introduction to the social sciences resulted; but Redfield was unable to persuade his colleagues to think more systematically or to cross established departmental lines. Like McKeon, he had to content himself with setting up a few interdepartmental committees, like the Committee on International Relations, the Committee on Human Development (jointly with biological sciences), and the Committee on Statistics (jointly with physical sciences).

Such committees, because their members all held departmental appointments, did not do much to alter the traditional pattern of Chicago's graduate training. As long as all graduate teachers had to win departmental approval—and this was a jealously guarded prerogative after the quarrel over appointments in philosophy in 1930–31—no administrative initiative could prevail against the habits of mind that existing departmental boundaries created among the faculty. Professors found it impractical—for most, indeed, inconceivable—to abandon a disciplinary identity painfully acquired in graduate school and firmly enshrined in professional associations, journals, career patterns, and specialized vocabularies.

In face of this elemental fact of American academic life, despite Hutchins' rhetoric and the reformist ambitions nourished by the two young deans he had chosen for the humanities and social sciences divisions, interdepartmental curricular reform at the graduate level met with very limited success. Interdepartmental committees certainly did allow a few students to pursue unusual paths toward a Ph.D., but no real synthesis across departmental lines emerged from such enterprises. The Chicago School of Criticism, involving, as it did, both philosophy and literature, was about as far as genuinely interdisciplinary graduate study ever got; and, intense though it was, the enterprise never won over everyone within the relevant departments. Yet the furor of debate that Crane and McKeon generated enlivened the minds even of those who rejected their approach to truth and beauty. As Daiches said: fundamental questions were asked point blank, and no one could get away with a perfunctory answer. That made the humanities division an unusually lively place in the years just before the war.

The College, where intellectual effervescence had concentrated in the early 1930s, became comparatively quiet. The deadlock between Hutchins' hope for a drastic restructuring of liberal education and the satisfaction of those actually teaching the survey courses with what they were doing meant that no important change came to the undergraduate curriculum until 1942.

To be sure, a formal act of the Board of Trustees set up a four-year college in 1937, embracing the junior and senior years of the University High School and the first two years of the College. High school teachers caught up in the new administrative structure were much more willing to experiment than were those who taught the survey courses in the College. Thus, for example, Russell Thomas and other high school teachers of English carried on with the experimental course in Great Books that Hutchins and Adler had introduced into the high school. Social studies teachers also reorganized the study of American history around important debates on public policy, using original documents. But these reforms affected only a few students in University High School, and Hutchins' advocacy of great books did not persuade those teaching the humanities and social science survey courses in the traditional College to change their ways very significantly. Authors like Hobbes and Locke did displace some textbook reading of political science, and a more sustained effort to connect the separate segments of the physical science survey sought to discover a common pattern of inquiry among the separate sciences. But the humanities and Bi Sci courses held firmly to the patterns of the early 1930s, even after the men who had been principally responsible for their initial formulation retired. In humanities, Schevill's successor, Arthur Scott, simply soldiered on, in anticipation of his own imminent retirement. The retirement of Anton Carlson, along with Frank Lillie and H. H. Newman in 1940, likewise signaled the departure of a group of biologists who had nursed the archetypical survey "The Nature of the World and of Man" into being in the early 1920s, and whose collective imprint on the Bi Sci course was as strong as Schevill's individual imprint was upon the humanities course. Their designated heir, the botanist Merle Coulter, was as faithful to their outlook as Arthur Scott was to Schevill's. Both were epigones, all the firmer in holding fast to what they had inherited because they (quite rightly) recognized themselves as intellectually inferior to their predecessors.

The quality and numbers of Chicago's undergraduates held up very well under the adverse publicity that had been generated by the Walgreen investigation. This was at least partly due to skillful and energetic efforts to increase the university's reach, not only through radio, where the Roundtable went from strength to strength under Vice President Benton's careful nursing; but in magazine and newspaper publicity as well.

Radio remained central to the university's public relations. The Roundtable became a good deal more professional after Benton persuaded the Sloan Foundation to subsidize it to the tune of several thousand dollars a year. This paid the salary of a full-time manager, who made it his business to recruit suitably prominent outsiders to supplement Chicago professors. The standard format balanced two spokesmen from the university against a single visiting expert. Printed transcripts of each program circulated to many thousands of subscribers; and as interest in public affairs intensified with the approach of war, the role of the Roundtable in Washington and across the nation tended to grow.[13] Benton made some tentative efforts to jazz things up a bit, experimenting with replying to questions sent in by letter and even trying to get the professors to sharpen their thoughts ahead of time so as to be able to get them down in writing and speak from a script. But faculty members resisted Benton's tinkering with their free and easy format; the major impact Benton had was on the choice of topics to be discussed and whom to ask. Hutchins, too, took a very active interest in each week's program and was in the habit of sending notes to the program's manager, urging him to get rid of some and praising others for their performance.

Topics discussed week after week ranged very widely, and the manager tried always to select a panel that would disagree in some important fashion, so that discussion could be lively, real, and spontaneous. This, indeed, was the secret of the program's success. To assure that result, a few well-spoken mavericks on campus got more than their share of exposure on the Roundtable, sometimes to the distress of Benton and Hutchins. T. V. Smith, the politician-philosopher, was one such figure; so was Maynard Krueger, an economist and candidate for vice president on the Socialist ticket in 1940.

A tendency to concentrate on economic policy as against other possible topics for public debate became clear as war approached. This made economists into the university's best-known spokesmen. The transmutation of economists into public soothsayers was, of course, a general phenomenon of the time, reflecting the real accomplishments of theoretical macroeconomics and the new forms of national management that came into effect during World War II. The Roundtable played a real, if modest, part in elevating the economics profession to its new dignity.

Behind the scenes, Benton's influence may have mattered too. As a business man, he was much interested in economic questions and habitually ate lunch with the university's economists in the Quadrangle Club. Moreover, since most of them were conservative defenders of free markets, by appearing on the Roundtable they could counteract the university's reputation for radicalism. This was always one of Benton's chief concerns; and, as he was acutely aware, the Roundtable was and long remained the university's principal way of addressing the American public. Very potent it was, far outdistancing all other university-based programs throughout Hutchins' twenty years at the university.

Benton supplemented the Roundtable with a second syndicated radio series, entitled "The Human Adventure." This was scripted and undertook a far wider range of themes than the Roundtable. Particular programs dealt with such varied subjects as Darwin, vivisection, Lucian of Samosata, Pepys, Melville, tourists in America. In all, over three hundred half-hour programs were broadcast between 1939 and 1945. But "The Human Adventure" never attracted anything like as large an audience as the Roundtable routinely did; and its production, entrusted to professional scriptwriters and actors, never became as much a university enterprise as the Roundtable was. To be sure, writers consulted professors in preparing their scripts; but it was the taste and judgment of radio experts that dictated exactly how the program took the air. Faculty members were often dissatisfied by the way their expertise was transmogrified and popularized for radio broadcast; and no satisfactory compromise between the professionalism of radio scriptwriters and the qualms of the university's professors was ever achieved.

Benton's best effort to make the mysteries of university scholarship accessible to the American public therefore fell short. He was trying to mix oil and water, for as radio writers and program managers developed a sharper ear for popular tastes, the incompatibility between academic and radio professionalism became total. Yet Benton kept a foot in both camps and was always eager to mediate between radio professionals and academics. He believed in both and never gave up his populist faith in the educability of the American public—if only the proper skills were brought to bear to make learning palatable. "The Human Adventure" was his first ambitious effort in this direction, but not his last, as we shall see in subsequent chapters. Its very limited success illustrated the difficulty even William Benton had in creating popular understanding of such a peculiar and specialized a place as the University of Chicago had become. The Roundtable, being less ambitious and more spontaneous, fared much better, but it presented only one, very limited, aspect of the university—a few professors' concern with current issues of public affairs.[14]

Benton did not confine his efforts on behalf of the university to radio. Connections in the advertising world allowed him to gain access to such stalwart upholders of popular American values as the *Saturday Evening Post* and *Readers Digest*. As a result, in 1937–38 Hutchins published three (largely ghostwritten) articles on education in the *Saturday Evening Post;* and *Reader's Digest* also found room for a very complimentary article about the university.

But the main ally Benton could rely on in his effort to improve the university's public image in print was Henry Luce, publisher of *Time, Life*, and *Fortune*. Luce had known Hutchins when they were both undergraduates at Yale. His missionary background in China resonated with Hutchins' post-Presbyterian earnestness and prepared him to sympathize with Hutchins' yearning for a firm basis of moral action. Accordingly, it is not surprising that *Fortune* sent a correspondent to Chicago in 1937 who wrote a very sympathetic account of what was going on at the university and praised Hutchins' efforts at further reform of the College.

More important was the fact that *Time* regularly published bits of information from the Midway, insinuated into its pages partly by means of telephone calls Benton made to another Yale man named Ralph Ingersoll, who was a vice president of Time, Inc.; and partly by contacts with the magazine's humbler staff writers, several of whom were graduates of Chicago and kept in touch with friends on the Midway even after moving to New York. The result was an almost steady flow of notices about Hutchins and the University of Chicago, together with frequent quotes from Chicago professors in the pages of *Time* magazine.

Readers certainly came away with the impression that important and interesting things took place on the Midway. Indeed, the university was a place where even trivial happenings somehow became noteworthy. Thus, for example, in its gossip column "People," *Time* once chose to take note of the fact that the author Thornton Wilder (another Yale man) had appeared on the Mandel Hall stage in an amateur performance of *Xerxes*, one of Handel's little known operas, with the responsibility of singing a single word! Wilder was a visiting professor in English at the time, a personal friend and warm admirer of Hutchins, and, of course, an acquaintance of Luce as well. An old boy network obviously influenced the way the University of Chicago was treated in Luce's publications, and as a result Benton was able to win wider and far more favorable public notice for the university than ever before.

His efforts undoubtedly helped student recruitment and fund-raising. In addition, the frequency with which national publications referred to persons and events on campus, and the enormous public reputation President Hutchins continued to enjoy, gave everyone a sense of being at a very special place, where big ideas, big projects, big problems, and promising solutions all came dazzlingly together. Undergraduates are always inclined to be self-centered, facing, as they do, the challenge of growing up intellectually as well as emotionally; but in retrospect it seems scarcely an exaggeration to suggest that many of us (I graduated in 1938) felt and acted as though the universe revolved around the flagpole in the center of the campus. Or if not the material universe, at least the universe of intellect, where ideas and their implementation were what mattered.

Hutchins' habit of slanging other universities and asserting Chicago's superiority was translated by most of us into a warm appreciation of our own peculiar wisdom and virtue simply for being where we were. To outsiders we must often have seemed exceptionally callow and conceited, even for undergraduates. But in fact we *did* know more than our contemporaries attending other colleges, and, of course, we thought we knew far more than we did. All of which means that the College of the University of Chicago was a fine place for a youngster to find himself growing up, despite the war clouds overhanging the campus, the country, and the world in the late 1930s.

Life in the College did not center wholly on intellect. Fraternities and women's clubs continued to concern themselves with parties and everyday living; and all the usual extracurricular activities helped to absorb undergraduates' excess energy. Blackfriars and the *Daily Maroon* were the two biggest student activities, measured by their respective cash flows. But dances, lectures, the Chapel Union, YWCA, and other religiously sponsored groups abounded; and sports continued to matter. The tennis team won Big Ten Championships in 1938 and 1939; and All-American Bill Haarlow was succeeded in basketball by an equally spectacular player, Joe Stampf, who in 1941 scored more points than anyone else in the Big Ten, even though the team had a losing season.

But in sports the central fact was that Chicago's football team fell on evil days after Berwanger graduated in 1936. Other Big Ten schools were professionalizing their football teams, building big stadiums, and filling them with loyal alumni and other fans on Saturday afternoons, thanks to the new mobility automobiles allowed. Physical education departments[15] trained coaches for high schools by giving academic credit for athletic skills and knowledge. This permitted football players to retain academic eligibility while concentrating almost their whole effort on sports.

But Chicago's compulsory curriculum left no room for professionalized athletes. Football players had to pass the same examinations as other students. To be sure, a few old-fashioned College teachers, like Teddy Linn in English, were notorious for giving passing grades to football players, whom they rewarded more for their feats on Saturday afternoons than for anything done in class. But no athlete could get through the College by taking courses from Teddy Linn. The survey courses and their formidable comprehensives constituted an unsurmountable obstacle in the path of anyone seeking a cheap B.A. As a result, athletes who scamped schoolwork learned to stay away from Chicago, despite the athletic scholarships which the Admissions Office had at its disposal. Tennis players, swimmers, and gymnasts could still be successfully recruited to Chicago, because other Big Ten schools paid little or no attention to sports that commanded only very modest spectator interest and therefore brought in no money. But football and basketball had gone big time, and Chicago could not keep up without systematically compromising academic standards for athletes.

What to do about the situation became an acute issue in 1939, when the football team, beaten by Beloit in its opening game, ended the season with successive losses to Harvard (61–0), Michigan (85–0), Virginia (47–0), and Ohio State (47–0). It was small comfort that *Look* magazine designated Chicago's football team "Amateur All-American." [16] A group of downtown alumni, in conjunction with members of the "Order of the C," decided that Chicago's reputation could only be redeemed by gathering a war chest with which to buy players. They talked more than they acted, but Hutchins and the athletic director, T. Nelson Metcalf, were well aware of their mood and intentions.

Metcalf had come from Oberlin, whose team Chicago managed to defeat even in the disastrous football season of 1939. He was committed to intramurals and to moderation. "There is no necessity for athletics to be overemphasized to the extent of interference with academic work," he had announced on taking office in 1933. "I believe in light schedules, playing natural rivals only, with a minimum of absence from class and with short practice periods." [17] Such a program left no place for Chicago in the Big Ten, once the other schools professionalized their football and basketball teams. But, as Beloit's victory over the Maroons showed, there were no "natural rivals" within easy reach of the Midway with whom Chicago could comfortably compete. To be beaten by Beloit hurt as much as being lopsidedly defeated by Big Ten rivals that Stagg once had humbled as a matter of course when the University of Chicago, thanks to its urban location, had been the principal center for college-based spectator sport in the entire country.

Those days were gone forever, and Hutchins decided that he ought to head off the effort to professionalize Chicago's football by withdrawing from intercollegiate competition entirely. Metcalf agreed; and the demoralized coaching staff did not actively resist. Accordingly, Hutchins submitted a powerful lawyer's brief to the Board of Trustees that recommended the abolition of intercollegiate competition in football. The trustees were of two minds. Harold Swift, in particular, loved his "California boys" and other athletes whom he had helped to bring to the campus almost as much as he admired Hutchins. He voted against the recommendation—one of the very few times he openly opposed Hutchins, though he did so only within the privacy of a closed meeting. But a majority of the trustees concurred with Hutchins' logic, whereupon Swift loyally fell in line and publicly supported the move while privately regretting it.

Of all the actions Robert Maynard Hutchins took in his twenty years as president of the University of Chicago, the abolition of intercollegiate football, announced in December 1939, provoked the loudest reaction, both among alumni and across the country. The rapid professionalization of college athletics had already attracted a good deal of unfavorable attention, but Chicago's decision seemed particularly drastic, coming, as it did, from an institution that had done more than any other to introduce big-time spectator sport to American higher education. Newspaper and magazine reactions were surprisingly supportive; something like 98 percent of the newspaper editorials that discussed Chicago's move applauded it.[18] On the other hand, sports writers deplored and ridiculed the decision. Hutchins' famous wisecrack, to the effect that when he felt the need for exercise his policy was to lie down and wait until he felt better, did nothing to assuage their anger. A side effect of the Chicago sports writers' displeasure was that the university's intercollegiate teams received little or no coverage in the downtown press in those sports in which they continued to compete. Football overshadowed everything else, and the university's popular reputation as a place where radical intellect had snuffed out red-blooded, all-American games became an unhappy, half-underground counterpoint to Benton's celebration of the university's cultural and public roles.

In retrospect, it is clear that withdrawal from big-time football involved significant loss for the university. The link with downtown Chicago forged by Stagg's victorious teams had been important in Harper's day and afterwards. Citizens of Chicago, including many wealthy civic leaders, were prone to identify the university with the football team. Simplistic logic equated a successful team with a great university. This link between town and gown had already frayed, thanks to the rise of Notre Dame and the decline of the Maroons after 1924. It was severed in 1939 and has not been restored since.

The loss for the university was and remains real. It might have been avoided if Hutchins had been willing to consider affiliation with the Chicago Bears—a team which in 1939 was still on the margins of social respectability, since it played on Sundays and paid its players openly instead of covertly. George Halas, owner and manager of the Bears, might well have welcomed some form of association with the university. He was still struggling to make his team a financial success and needed the respectability a university connection would have provided. A graduate football team for a graduate university might have turned into a very profitable marriage for both parties. In its absence, Halas hurried to appropriate the "C" logo that Stagg had used and in other ways deliberately assimilated his team to the football tradition of the Midway. He even hired some of Chicago's football staff, including Clark Shaughnessy and the doctor who attended to players' sprains and bruises.

In 1938, the *Maroon* casually suggested that the university rent Stagg Field to the Bears for a percent of the gate,[19] but no one took the suggestion seriously, not even Benton, who might have been expected to sense the importance of football for the university's popular reputation. In view of what happened after the war, when television made professional football into a religion for Chicago and for the nation as a whole, the university's failure to link up with Halas and the Bears in 1938–39, when both parties stood to gain from closer association, was a missed opportunity of monumental proportions.

The university's prominence in the public mind, though temporarily sustained by Benton's artifice and his personal connections with radio executives and with Henry Luce, needed a more enduring, dependable basis. Given the fact that football prowess was rapidly becoming the popular measure of a university's merit throughout the United States, the University of Chicago could only have reconciled high academic standards with high public repute by becoming honestly and overtly professional. The advantages to the university, and to the Bears at a time when the team was still struggling to escape the marginality of professional football's working-class, part-time origin, would have been very great indeed.

This represents the greatest lost opportunity of Hutchins' regime. Hutchins muffed a chance to continue Harper's tradition of pioneering in sports and cashing in on the public attention football commanded; and the student body lost the chance of supplementing their superior intellectual prowess with a more visceral but very valuable sort of collective identity, based on association with famous athletes and cheering them on—thus associating themselves and the whole university with another, quite genuine kind of excellence.

At the time, Hutchins half expected other leading colleges to follow Chicago's example of abandoning big-time football; but nothing of the kind occurred. Instead, a different foreshadowing of things to come began to alter campus life when a government-financed program for training airplane pilots appeared on campus in 1939, followed by the establishment of a military institute in the next year. In September, war finally broke out in Europe. In anticipation of war, the United States began to rearm. Simultaneously, France and Great Britain came shopping for military supplies in comparatively vast quantities. All of a sudden, the depression faded into the past; shortages of goods and of skilled manpower began to show up in a few strategic industries, and the crying question of the hour became how to stop German and Japanese expansion short of all-out war.

Hutchins found the course of public events as depressing as the deadlock he faced anent curricular reform. His collisions with the faculty and his dissatisfaction with the governance of the university, rendered acute by the controversy over tenure, turned his thoughts toward an alternate career in government. He very much wished to become a member of the Supreme Court, and his literary and legal talents would indeed have made him a distinguished Justice. But he was unwilling to curry favor with President Roosevelt, who alone had the power to make such an appointment. Roosevelt had in fact offered him the job of administering the National Recovery Administration shortly before it was declared unconstitutional in 1935, but later reneged; and when a vacancy came on the Supreme Court in 1939, he appointed William O. Douglas to a position that Roosevelt had, perhaps, dangled before Hutchins, as well as others.

In any event, Roosevelt was well aware of Hutchins' frustrated candidacy for the Supreme Court and offered him instead the post Douglas had just vacated as chairman of the Securities and Exchange Commission. But to Roosevelt's surprise, Hutchins refused, perhaps because he was unwilling to follow in the wake of a man whom he had once brought to Yale Law School and then tried, vainly, to attract to Chicago. Hutchins and Douglas were friends, but also rivals. By winning appointment to the Supreme Court when he did, Douglas in effect reversed his youthful dependency on Dean Hutchins of the Yale Law School. Hutchins, for once, had been outstripped. He flirted with the idea of recovering from this setback by running for vice president in 1940, but his efforts to mobilize support in high circles of the Democratic party got nowhere. Roosevelt was not sure that Hutchins was really "his man," and that was decisive.[20]

The election campaign in 1940 turned very much on Roosevelt's promise to keep the country out of the war, while still making sure that Hitler would not win by extending all aid "short of war" to Britain and Britain's by then rather bedraggled allies. (The Nazis had conquered France and most of western Europe between April and June 1940.) Hutchins, listening to FDR's words, decided that he was, in fact, leading the country into war. His own personal memories of World War I led Hutchins to deplore the course Roosevelt was taking, and his irritation at having demeaned himself to seek political favor only to be rebuffed lent a cutting edge to his dissent. In addition, Benton, for reasons of his own, had become an emphatic isolationist, as those who resisted involvement in European struggles were then called. Benton soon persuaded Hutchins that it was his duty to try to influence American opinion by going public with his criticism of the way Roosevelt was conducting the nation's affairs.

The result was two radio speeches broadcast nationally. On 23 January 1941, Hutchins spoke on "America and the War" on the NBC Red Network, beginning: "I speak tonight because I believe the American people are about to commit suicide" because "the President now requires us to underwrite a British victory." In May he was more specific in his warning. War, he said, "will produce bankruptcy and revolution in this country. We know that instead of helping us to make democracy work, this war will end our chance of achieving democracy in our time." He went on: "I believe that we shall have a totalitarian government after the war . . . When we start out to impose our conceptions of the four freedoms on the rest of the world, we shall end up by establishing an empire. . . . I have no more desire to see the world enslaved by the United States than I have to see it enslaved by Germany." [21]

Sentiment on campus was much divided. Some of Hutchins' close associates sympathized with Roosevelt's policy of supporting Britain against the Nazis, even at the risk of war. Adler and McKeon were among them, while Anton Carlson, from retirement, sounded forth in favor of "America First" and isolationism. Hutchins himself never joined the organized "America First" movement, preferring, as he said, "to join a Committee for Humanity First" on the ground that "national selfishness should not determine national policy." [22] He was a somewhat reluctant warrior in the whole affair, pushed from the rear both by Benton and by his wife Maude, who had become a rabid foe of FDR, demanding the president's impeachment at every opportunity.[23]

Aside from personal distaste for some of the bedfellows that his public attack on Roosevelt condemned him to, Hutchins had a second reason for his reluctance about taking on an active political role. The university celebrated its fiftieth anniversary in 1941, and the trustees decided to exploit the occasion by launching a mammoth fund drive. Hutchins took the lead in fund-raising as always; but many felt that his political posture would alienate donors, as perhaps it did in some cases. At any rate, the fund drive was declared a success when gifts of over $8.75 million were totted up—a sum that fell short of the initial goal of $12 million, but far outstripped receipts in any previous year. Hutchins may not have been satisfied by his success as a fundraiser. It nonetheless was substantial and allowed the university to maintain itself in something close to a steady state through 1941.

Everything changed after Pearl Harbor. Government-financed research and training, unimportant before the war, grew enormously; student numbers plummeted; faculty dispersed for war work. Hutchins stayed where he was, having foreclosed all chance of government service by his attack on FDR. He used the opportunity presented by the disruption of normal university life to ram through radical changes in the College, thus inaugurating a new era in the history of the university, and a new chapter of this memoir.

5

THE WAR YEARS
1941–1946

The Japanese attack on Pearl Harbor on 7 December 1941, followed by Germany's declaration of war on the United States three days afterwards, compelled Hutchins to reverse course abruptly and publicly promote what he had previously decried. Within a month of the commencement of hostilities, he declared that the university had to be turned into "an instrumentality of total war." This required the faculty to invent or foster "vocational training courses that will help win the war." On top of that, "the manufacture of gadgets that will help win the war is a necessary and laudable part of the university's work." Intellectual tasks, "the symbols of everything we had to defend," remained as ever, an unchanged responsibility. But for the time being, the duty of contributing directly to the war effort "will make it hard, perhaps very hard, perhaps impossible to carry on our basic function." [1]

In the event, the university actually did both, with extraordinary and strangely bittersweet success. The university accommodated thousands of sailors and soldiers assigned to special training courses. That was completely commonplace; but as a maker of gadgets, Chicago exceeded all expectation by becoming, for a brief period, the principal center for research and experimentation with the controlled release of nuclear energy—the most awesome of all the gadgets ever invented for winning (and losing) wars. And while a galaxy of supremely talented physicists and chemists were bringing the atom bomb finally into being, a newly assembled college faculty devised a four-year College curriculum that more nearly conformed to Hutchins' prescription for liberal education than anything previously available at the university.

Yet both successes carried heavy long-range costs, to Hutchins and to the university, because the physicists' hope of developing peacetime uses of atomic energy fell far short of their expectations, and the curricular innovations emerging from the war years at Chicago failed to catch on at other institutions. In effect, Hutchins' second decade at the university raised the educational stakes by making the university more obviously different from other places. Yet, at the same time, his personal role in what occurred on campus became more and more marginal. He left curricular pioneering within the new four-year college entirely to others, devoting himself to various extracurricular enterprises which were, at least partly, surrogates for his heightened frustrations within the university itself.

The most obvious impact of the onset of war was the proliferation of military uniforms on campus. In effect, the university went shopping for contracts with the armed forces, offering to accommodate various special training courses on university premises. Sometimes faculty members served as instructors, sometimes the university only supplied classrooms and dormitory spaces. Some programs had rapid turnover, bringing sailors and soldiers to campus for only a few weeks. Others involved lengthy courses and quite traditional sorts of academic study. The three most substantial military programs at the university dealt with meteorology and weather forecasting, civil affairs training, and area and language training for future administrators of conquered and liberated territories. These, and many other training courses, brought thousands of uniformed students to Chicago, with the result that as the number of civilian students dwindled, available space was taken up, and more than taken up, by military programs and personnel.

By the end of 1942, the university had entered into 103 separate contracts with the federal government, and, as Hutchins remarked in his annual "State of the University" report to alumni and other interested parties, "The university is rapidly becoming a technological institute." By 1944 the annual budget had swollen to $31 million, three times the prewar level; and of this total, $22 million came from government contracts.[2] By far the largest flow of government funds resulted from the hectic effort to produce an atomic bomb before the Germans succeeded in doing so—an effort in which Chicago's physicists and chemists played a prominent role, beginning in 1940. Altogether, the university received $3 million as overhead from the Manhattan Project (the code name for the atomic bomb project).[3] In effect, cost plus contracts, standard for war work, solved the university's budget difficulties for the duration, but at the price of making the university dependent on government programs and grants as never before.

The campus was full to overflowing. Sailors drilled on the Midway in such numbers as to make the university look like an annex to the Great Lakes

Naval Training Center. Wooden emergency buildings grew like mushrooms on vacant lots south of the Midway and elsewhere. The metallurgical project (Chicago's code name for atomic research) overflowed from Eckhardt, Kent, and Ryerson to take over the Oriental Institute completely and invaded other parts of the campus as well—not least the west stands of Stagg Field, where the first controlled and self-sustaining nuclear reaction occurred on 2 December 1942. Secrecy and security checks proliferated. Everyone knew that something important was afoot. Insiders hinted; outsiders wondered. Everyone—insiders and outsiders alike—hurried, and hoped and feared what war might bring.

Half a century's subsequent experience with atomic energy makes it difficult to reconstruct the spirit of those times; and exactly why and how Chicago supplanted Columbia and was in turn supplanted by California as the principal vehicle for government-financed experiments with nuclear energy is even harder to tell. Columbia was the place where Enrico Fermi, after abandoning his native Italy in 1938, first tried to create a controlled and self-sustaining atomic reaction; and his combination of practical and theoretical insight made him the key figure for that breakthrough when it was achieved on 2 December 1942 under the west stands of Stagg Field.

Chicago's part was marginal at first. The university's first contract for atomic research, totaling $9,500, ran from January to August 1941. It paid for Professor Samuel Allison's investigation of the uses of beryllium for enhancing the pace of atomic reactions. Allison had begun to investigate the fission of uranium before government funds and secrecy enveloped such researches. Other Chicago physicists—Robert Mulliken, Arthur Dempster, and William Zachariasen—were at the "very top of their respective fields" of research, according to a memorandum Arthur Holly Compton wrote to Hutchins soon after becoming dean of the Division of Physical Sciences in 1940;[4] and this made it possible for him to attract government money and contracts on an ever increasing scale once authorities in Washington decided to make a bomb as quickly as possible.[5]

But there were other centers of atomic research: Columbia, Princeton, and California chief among them, and the decision to concentrate the principal effort to achieve a chain reaction at Chicago, which was made in January 1942, depended very much on Compton and his personal standing within the community of research physicists in the United States. He had the prestige of a Nobel Prize, conferred upon him in 1927 for youthful experiments with X rays and electrons. At a time when most of the leading figures in atomic research were foreign-born, Compton had the additional advantage of being indubitably American, having been born in Wooster, Ohio, in 1892 and holding a Ph.D. from Princeton, followed by professorships at the University of Washington, St. Louis, and then, beginning in 1923, at Chicago. His work with cosmic rays in the 1930s had been inconclusive and disappointing; but after shifting to administration, he launched himself on a second and very successful career as bridge-builder between three diverse and separate sorts of people, each inclined to be rather suspicious of the others: to wit, government and the military, business and engineering, and a hastily assembled array of academic physicists and chemists. Since he was able to command the confidence of all three groups, Compton turned out to be the right man in the right place to hurry the atom bomb into being.

He also had President Hutchins' confidence, or at least compliance. Exactly how much Hutchins knew about the atomic enterprise before 1945 is unclear. He raised no objection when Compton decided, in January 1942, to concentrate all work on atomic chain reactions at Chicago. (Compton had been put in charge of the national effort to create such a reaction on the day before Pearl Harbor.)[6] This involved bringing Fermi and his collaborators from Columbia and transferring other physicists from Princeton. And when health concerns came to the fore, Compton put a radiologist from California in charge. Within a few months, a truly dazzling array of talent assembled at Chicago to build the first self-sustaining atomic pile in a spooky, echoing slate-walled squash racquets court under the west stands of Stagg Field. The guarded door, and an array of exhaust pipes peeking out of pseudo-gothic apertures in the stuccoed and (absurdly) crenellated stands, advertised the unusual character of what was going on inside. But whether Hutchins or any other high administrative officer of the university actually knew what was being done or understood anything about nuclear energy and the physics of fission is entirely unclear to me.

Constructing the pile, controlling the flow of neutrons, regulating a,d measuring the reaction, and guarding against excessive exposure to radioactivity—all at the same time—was an extraordinary feat, performed in haste and confirming theoretical calculations with admirable and satisfying precision. Thereafter, far larger and equally venturesome construction aimed at producing fissionable material on an industrial scale dwarfed the original pile. New sites, where suitable quantities of electrical energy were available, had to be found for the purpose. Oak Ridge in Tennessee, where the TVA could provide the necessary power, was the first such site; and, as backup, another plant using a different method for producing plutonium was built at

Hanford on the Columbia River in Washington state. The team of physicists, chemists, and medical radiologists that Compton had assembled at Chicago continued to play important roles as advisors and consultants to the Du Pont Company, which undertook the task of constructing these new atomic facilities.

But Du Pont had been a target of public outcry against "merchants of death" after World War I and was unwilling to operate the new plants for fear of future backlash. Accordingly, on 10 March 1943, General Leslie Groves, the army officer in command of the Manhattan Project, invited the university to undertake what the Du Pont company shied away from. "The War department," he wrote, "requests the University of Chicago to enter into contract for the full management and operations of a semi-works plant for the production of experimental quantities of a new product. The plant is to be located in the State of Tennessee. . . . The War Department has given careful consideration to the question and is of the opinion that the University of Chicago is the best fitted organization for the work and that it would be most unfortunate if the University should feel itself unable to undertake it."[7] In a memorandum to Hutchins, dated the next day, Compton explained that Du Pont had refused the role now proferred to the university and that his team of scientists would have special responsibility for health hazards and for the soundness of the physics and chemistry of the design.[8]

Management and operation of a large industrial plant in Tennessee (and later of the even larger installation at Hanford) was an unusual role for any university to play; but Hutchins and the Board of Trustees did not blanch. Chicago therefore became the vehicle through which vast sums of federal money flowed to Oak Ridge and Hanford for the production of plutonium. This arrangement endured until the end of active hostilities in July 1945. These contracts inflated the university's budget enormously; and paperwork on campus multiplied proportionately. But in practice, Chicago's role as legal contractor for the two big atomic plants made little difference. Administrators administered—mostly on the spot where work was going ahead; and a few of them darted in and out of Chicago from time to time to check up on the accountancy. That was about all that General Groves' invitation and President Hutchins' acquiescence amounted to as far as life on campus was concerned.

A more significant change for the university was the establishment nearby of what became Argonne National Laboratory. After the initial success of 2 December 1942, nervousness about what might happen if some accident allowed radioactive gases or other materials to escape from the pile under the west stand persuaded the scientists in charge of the Metallurgical Project to transfer further activity and experimentation to a safer site. They chose a location on public land about twenty miles west of the city, and when suitable buildings had been erected there, the original pile was taken apart and reassembled at the new site so that various measurements and further experiments with nuclear fission might continue safely.

The university managed this establishment also and continued to serve as prime contractor for Argonne after the war, when the new Atomic Energy Commission assigned it the task of developing peacetime uses of atomic energy. At a time when optimism about what cheap atomic power could do for the country was still widespread, it seemed entirely appropriate to continue a mutually advantageous relationship. The university's atomic scientists required federal funds to sustain the enormously expanded scale of operation they had become accustomed to, and federal administrators were eager to supplement their continued production of warheads in secret with something of use to the general public. The arrangement therefore lasted until long after Hutchins left the university.

Yet in spite of Argonne and the university's continuing involvement in nuclear research, Chicago's primacy waned long before the end of the war. Experiments with dangerously large quantities of poisonous and explosive materials called for emptier landscapes than any available in the Middle West. Consequently, after March 1943, when another new laboratory started operations at Los Alamos, atop a remote mesa in New Mexico, Chicago ceased to be the main center of research and testing connected with the manufacture of atomic bombs. Robert Oppenheimer from Berkeley became the chief administrator at Los Alamos, and the University of California served as prime contractor for the laboratory there. Experts from Chicago as well as from many other universities and research institutions assembled at Los Alamos, as they had previously done at Chicago, and in a remarkably short time inaugurated the atomic age by exploding a test bomb at Alamagordo, New Mexico, on 16 July 1945. Both Allison and Fermi were present for the occasion; and Allison actually conducted the final countdown.

The subsequent explosions over Hiroshima and Nagasaki were anticlimactic as far as the atomic scientists were concerned; and many of them felt that the destruction of these Japanese cities was unnecessary. They readily believed that a demonstration explosion over an uninhabited offshore island, such as the test they had witnessed at Alamagordo, would have sufficed to bring Japanese resistance to an end. The resulting rift between government and the military on the one hand and leading spirits among the atomic scientists on the other never healed completely.

For that matter, the wartime marriage between big government and big science had not been completely amicable; and the spectacular upshot of the Manhattan Project—far surpassing ordinary expectation and straining the imagination even of experts—did not ease the ambivalence with which scientists served the military. Many of them bridled at having to conform to security rules and obeying orders from men whom they often regarded as ignorant or incompetent. Yet they were captivated by the soldiers' access to hitherto unimagined resources—the Manhattan Project disbursed about $2 billion dollars by the end of 1945—which allowed them to carry out experiments they could not have financed on any other basis.

Before Hitler's defeat in May 1945, scientists in general and refugees from Europe in particular justified their subordination to General Groves and his minions on the ground that they were competing in a fateful race against the Nazis. Germany had been the world leader in atomic research and theory in the 1930s, and after Fermi won the 1938 Nobel Prize for splitting uranium by bombarding it with slow-moving neutrons in a makeshift laboratory in Rome, research physicists everywhere became well aware of the theoretical possibility of creating a nuclear explosion. Hence, even as late as the early months of 1945, when the war in Europe was drawing to a close, many U.S. scientists believed that Hitler's public references to secret weapons that would yet wring triumph from defeat could only refer to atomic warheads. But in the event it turned out that rockets and jet-engined aircraft were what Hitler had counted on, and after Germany's surrender in May 1945, it became clear that the Nazis had made no sustained effort to create atomic weapons. This provoked a crisis of conscience among the scientists who were then on the verge of success in the United States, for they suddenly realized that they, and they alone, were the world's potential destroyers.

Yet at the time, with war against Japan still to be won, most Americans and many atomic scientists felt that the American government could be trusted to use the new weapon wisely and for good purposes. The official War Department news release describing the Alamagordo test may not have distorted the truth very much in claiming that "the explosion had far exceeded the most optimistic expectations and wildest hopes of the scientists. All seemed to feel that they had been present at the birth of a new age—The Age of Atomic Energy—and felt their profound responsibility to help in

guiding into the right channels the tremendous forces which had been un-
locked for the first time in history.

"As for the present war, there was a feeling that . . . we now had the means
to insure its speedy conclusion and save thousands of American lives. As to
the future, there had been brought into being something . . . that would prove
immeasurably more important than the discovery of electricity or any of the
other great discoveries which have so affected our existence." [9]

It is still too soon to appraise the full consequences of the atomic scientists' spectacular feats between 1942 and 1946, but it is easy to see some of
the consequences for the university. Departures from previous routines
seemed only temporary during the war itself. Only a few insiders knew what
was going on, and they were too busy to do much thinking ahead. After the
end of active hostilities in the Pacific in mid-August 1945, when the university was allowed to announce to the public what the Metallurgical Project
had been doing during the war, news of Hiroshima and Nagasaki was still
fresh. Accordingly, from the start of public deliberation about future policies
and relationship with government, pride in the university's very considerable
part in making the bomb mingled with fear, guilt, and regret at what the
atomic scientists had achieved.

Even before the explosion at Alamagordo, maintaining top-level research
in nuclear physics at Chicago became a major goal for the university. Efforts
to attract funds from private industry never got very far, with the result that
Chicago's continued participation in atomic research came to mean continued dependence on government funding. Physicists led in establishing this
new relationship, but other disciplines hurried to imitate them when government grant programs proliferated after the war. The resulting linkage between official agencies of the federal government and the academic world
was, indeed, the major change brought to campus by the war.

Compton's success in getting contracts for the university between 1940
and 1945 pioneered this transformation as far as Chicago was concerned;
and like the force of atomic explosion itself, the result was ambivalent. It
made expensive research enterprises possible and channeled activity into
paths approved by bureaucrats whose aversion to risk put a new kind of obstacle in the way of innovative individual inquiry. Government funding also
compelled the university to construct a proliferating bureaucracy of its own
to cope with paper generated by the granting agencies. Privateering as a basis
for fund-raising in support of a single professor's research, which had prevailed before World War II, became marginal in the most prosperous disci-

plines, since bureaucratic procedures also enveloped the big philanthropic foundations that competed with the federal government in directing academic research.

To be sure, the humanities division and some of the professional schools lagged conspicuously behind. But an enterprising clique of humanists compensated for their exclusion from the bureaucratized business of research by undertaking a sweeping reform of the College, thus provoking the major intellectual upheaval that beset the university during and immediately after the war.

A critical factor in allowing humanists to assume the leading role in reforming the College, beginning in 1942, was the fact that much of the rest of the university went off to war. As we have just seen, the Metallurgical Project engaged the university's physicists and chemists so totally that in effect they withdrew from ordinary campus activities between 1941 and 1945. Other faculty members found other ways of abandoning familiar routines. Paul Douglas, the economist, surprised his friends and forwarded his political career by volunteering as a private in the Marine Corps; but most faculty members who entered the armed forces did so as commissioned officers and were assigned tasks that had some connection with their professional expertise. Leon Smith, a teacher of French and Dean of Students in the College, for example, became an army intelligence officer and then recruited a clutch of bright Chicago undergraduates to decipher enemy codes. Similarly, the historian James Cate joined the Air Force and ended up as one of the editors of its official history, while the anthropologist Captain Fred Eggan stayed on campus as head of the university's training program for future civil affairs officers in the Far East.

Others went on leave to take government posts in Washington and elsewhere. Economists and lawyers were in special demand, so much so that the Law School almost closed down completely. Anyone who really wanted to leave the university could find some sort of war work to perform, since jobs abounded and skilled manpower was desperately short. Sudden interruption of academic routine became commonplace as students, staff, and faculty drifted off into wartime jobs or were drafted into the armed services. For example, as early as 1940, Harold Gosnell of the political science department dropped his classes part way through the spring quarter to take a job in Washington, suddenly handing them over to two graduate students, one of whom waited until the end of the quarter to leave the university, while the other was drafted into the army a few months afterwards.[10]

This sort of volatility altered the nature of the university community.

Commitment to accustomed routines faltered when so many individuals were changing careers, often on very short notice. War's impact was sharpest among the young, of course, but even full professors changed careers in sufficient numbers to undermine the conservative character of the Senate, the university's ruling academic body. This allowed President Hutchins to have his way on 22 January 1942, when the Senate, by a vote of 63 to 48, approved a motion "that the Bachelor's degree be awarded in recognition of the completion of general education, as redefined by the College faculty." [11]

Hutchins had advocated such a reorganization of higher education for more than a decade; and ever since 1937, when the trustees formally placed the last two years of the University High School under the administration of the College, faculty committees had labored to define a coherent curriculum of general education, starting at the junior year of high school and concluding with the sophomore year of conventional college. This enterprise languished as long as Aaron J. Brumbaugh served as acting dean of the College and as long as teachers of the existing survey courses dominated the College faculty. But in 1941, Hutchins found a new broom in the person of Clarence Faust to take over from Brumbaugh. Simultaneously the wartime dispersal of College faculty weakened resistance to radical change.

In the tumult that ensued, Faust played a central role. Born in Iowa in 1901, he prepared for the ministry by getting a B.A. from Naperville and a Bachelor of Divinity from its associated Evangelical Theological Seminary in 1924. But after four years of preaching, he changed course and enrolled at Chicago as a graduate student of English, where he specialized on the writings of Jonathan Edwards and other Puritans. With the exception of a year of teaching at Arkansas, he remained on campus thereafter, slowly climbing the academic ladder by starting as instructor in 1929, becoming assistant professor six years later in 1935 when he received his Ph.D., and associate professor in 1939. In the late 1930s he was among those who followed Ronald Crane in his effort to learn from Richard McKeon how to escape the trivialities of history by analyzing literary works in their own terms. As dean and professor of English, and in accord with his newly acquired convictions, he therefore led a Crane-McKeon party within the College until, exhausted by the resulting controversy, he resigned in 1946.

How much he personally did to assure the dominance of this group, and how much he was the tool of others in forcing through controversial decisions, is unclear to me. McKeon's ideas and influence, sometimes exerted in extreme forms by his more enthusiastic disciples, were the driving force, and Faust may have merely tagged along, habitually deferring to their views.

Then in 1944, when Crane led a faculty attack on Hutchins for trying to undermine departmental autonomy, Faust found himself awkwardly caught between quarreling, strong-minded men whom he had been accustomed to revere. Resulting tensions, which became acute throughout the university, made Faust miserable and persuaded him to resign the deanship at a time when success for the College he had striven to create still hung in the balance.

In 1941, when active planning for a new four-year liberal arts curriculum got into high gear, Crane, McKeon, and Hutchins were still allies. Yet from the start, conflicts were acute. Reformers envisioned a four-year curriculum of liberal studies, emphasizing the capacity to read, write, and speak accurately and fluently. Mastery of the medieval trivium—grammar, logic, and rhetoric—was the provocative way some of them chose to describe their aim. Mingled with this was a further notion that textbooks and other merely contemporary material should be eschewed in favor of sharpening students' skills on time-tested texts. (Only great books of the Western tradition mattered; the reform party knew no others.) What to do about mathematics, natural science, and foreign language study was something of an embarrassment for them. Their concerns were philosophical and, to a lesser degree, moral. Because they wished to stimulate the young to become intelligent, competent adults, rather than preparing them for professional careers, they tended to regard "tool courses" in language and mathematics as unfortunate nuisances. As for natural science, most of the Crane-McKeon party knew little and cared less about what biologists and physical scientists had to teach; yet the prestige of modern science was such that everyone conceded that scientific texts and concepts had to find a place in the curriculum—somehow.

In the biological and physical sciences divisions, the great majority of the faculty had no patience with what these reformers were after. The scientists were, in general, well satisfied with the existing introductory survey courses, taught, as they were, by instructors whose central identity was securely lodged in one or another graduate department. In addition, a somewhat tattered old guard of historians and social scientists—consigned long since to the College (and more or less dismissed as being "unproductive scholars") by their respective departments—believed in and wished to maintain the survey courses they had been teaching ever since 1931.

Reflecting these opposed outlooks, the College committee charged with the task of defining what the new four-year B.A. program would look like came before the Senate on 10 March 1942 with a majority and minority report. The vote was 6–5; and exactly half of the majority came from the English department where the winds of new doctrine were already blowing strong.[12] The majority's proposal became basic for subsequent planning. It prescribed three-year sequences in humanities, social science, and English; three years of natural science, but with variants to allow emphasis either on biology or on physical sciences. In addition to this core, the majority report prescribed a single year of mathematics and of a foreign language and allowed room for two year-long elective sequences in more specialized subjects. This last provision was intended to satisfy specific requirements for undergraduate training dictated by various professional bodies. Chemistry courses needed for entrance to medical school were the most imperious; but advanced work in foreign language and mathematics was just as important for other professions and careers.

What is striking about this curriculum is the total absence of history. In the *Poetics,* Aristotle had remarked that history, being concerned only with particulars, was the lest philosophical of the sciences, and the whole point of Crane's conversion to McKeon's analytical method was to escape the tyranny of history over literary studies. The elimination of such a trifling study was therefore deliberate, although the doctrine could not be applied in its full rigor because state law required the study of American history in the final years of high school. This was accommodated by devoting the first year of social science to a study of selected public policy debates, thus salvaging the history of the United States from mindless particularity by focusing upon the more philosophical aspects of politics.

It is true that the industrial revolution attracted some attention in subsequent social science courses, and as a form of literature, books of history also figured in the humanities sequence, where they were analyzed like any other work of art in terms of their internal coherence and structure. But the grand historical architectonic of the survey of Western civilization worked out by Schevill in 1931 was deliberately banished from the curriculum, on the ground that historical accounts of changing tastes, styles, and ideas lacked all rigor, summoning imaginary entities like "the spirit of the times" or economic determinism to explain differences that were in fact intellectual and reflected the accomplishment of individuals who used deliberately chosen terms to correct predecessors' errors and capture the beauty of truth and the truth of beauty.

Historians, who might have been expected to defend the way their discipline approached truth, were totally unprepared to meet the Crane-McKeon party on their preferred, abstract level of argument. The professors of the graduate department of history had, as a matter of fact, never embraced Schevill's sort of *Kulturgeschichte*, each being far too deeply committed to a particular speciality (eighteenth-century France, the United States since 1865, and the like) to think about the history of Western civilization as a whole, or how it ought to be taught to undergraduates. Finding themselves tongue-tied by commitment to a completely different style of discourse, Chicago's historians, and the vast company of historically minded scholars in other departments and schools, therefore made no concerted effort to defend the place of their discipline in the College until 1946.

Scientists also tuned out the Crane-McKeon style of thinking, but, for the most part, were too busy with war work to take much notice. When the reformers' schemes came to their attention, almost all scientists objected, but a final showdown over undergraduate education was postponed, in effect, by a provision of the Senate action of 22 January 1942 that gave the two natural science divisions the right to continue to confer old-fashioned B.S. degrees in the accustomed way "for the duration of the war." The new four-year curriculum was designed for those who entered the College after only two years of high school; and various compromises and half measures made it possible for students arriving on campus with a high school diploma in hand to be excused from part of the new requirements for a B.A. degree. In practice, therefore, as long as the war lasted, nearly all of those who actually took the new College courses were students from University High School. A smattering of "early entrants" from other high schools, attracted by scholarship grants and the prospect of getting a B.A. before reaching draft age, swelled their numbers only slightly.

Nevertheless, the handwriting was on the wall. If the reformers were to have their way, a single required curriculum would eventually prevail and would leave no room either for the history of Western civilization or for the sort of advanced training in chemistry, mathematics, and foreign language that graduate study and some professional careers required. Many of the university's professors felt that this was absurd and unreasonable; and, on reflection, they began to deplore the whole idea of awarding a B.A. for general studies two years earlier than was conventional. Departmental self-interest was at stake, since a B.A. for general studies meant that the departments had no direct access to undergraduates and no chance to attract them to "major" in their particular speciality. Moreover, appointments to the College no longer required departmental approval, and since the new College proposed to retain and promote instructors on the basis of teaching rather than scholarly accomplishment, faculty standards would surely be lowered. Or so a great many departmental stalwarts believed.

Another factor in the situation was that the announcement of Chicago's new B.A. provoked widespread criticism. This came as a surprise to Hutchins, who had sounded out other university presidents ahead of time and came away with the impression that they favored the change, especially since earlier award of the B.A. would allow students to complete their undergraduate training before being drafted. "I have the impression," he wrote, "that if the University will take the lead in this matter it will not be without followers." [13] But when Chicago did take the lead, the North Central Association, whose main function was the accreditation of academic programs in colleges and universities in the Midwest, condemned the move emphatically, and it became clear that Chicago's new B.A. would stand no chance of winning accreditation. Phi Beta Kappa also threatened to withdraw its chapter from Chicago.

The sharpness of the reaction was due to the fact that nearly all liberal arts colleges felt threatened by what Chicago had done. They were in difficulty already, due to wartime withdrawals. If Chicago's redefinition of the B.A. were to prevail, they would have to become junior colleges and student numbers would decay still further. That looked like a recipe for suicide. The response was to denounce the debasement of educational standards that Chicago was seeking to perpetrate. Angry and fearful, spokesmen for the threatened colleges were entirely deaf to Hutchins' rationale for giving clear and distinct meanings to both the B.A. and M.A. degrees. The president of Stanford did remark that Chicago's move made sense, but refrained from imitating what Chicago had done. Unlike what had happened in 1931, it very soon became clear that this Chicago New Plan would be opposed by the whole educational establishment, since high schools, too, were loathe to see their most promising juniors and seniors enroll elsewhere. [14]

All these considerations came to a head in April 1942 when George Bogert of the Law School and eight other prominent professors announced that they would move to rescind the Senate action of 22 January, when redefinition of the B.A. had been approved. Only full professors were members of the Senate; and when that august body met in special session on 9 April, the vote came out an exact tie, 58 yea and 58 nay. Hutchins, who presided, ruled that the previous action therefore stood, allowing implementation of the four-year College curriculum to go ahead.

Yet this narrow victory was a larger defeat, for Hutchins achieved the tie only by two very dubious moves. First of all, he promoted several persons whom he knew would support the new College plan to the rank of full professor just before the crucial meeting. Only three or four persons were so favored, including Dean Faust, and it is possible that the promotions in question might have been made anyway and were not deliberately timed to affect the vote.[15] But the defeated party thought otherwise and believed henceforth that Hutchins would stop at nothing in order to get what he wanted. Their suspicion was reinforced by the way the tie was achieved, for Hutchins cast a vote himself, despite the fact that it was highly unusual, though not, it seems, illegal, for a presiding officer to do so.[16]

The slenderness of this victory is worth thinking about, for if the Senate had reversed its earlier decision and nullified the effort to create a new four-year College curriculum, the subsequent history of the university and the course of Hutchins' presidency would have been utterly different. Accident played a role. Despite the intensity of feeling that surrounded the issue, attendance at the special meeting of the Senate was far from complete. Only five more votes were tallied in April than had been counted at the meeting of January, and something like one-third of those eligible to vote failed to show up at all. Some were away on leave; a good many others deliberately distanced themselves from the controversy and wished to take no part in it. My father, a professor in the Divinity School at the time, was one such. He was walking home when he remembered that the Senate had been called into special session and reluctantly decided that it was his duty to retrace his steps, arriving just as debate concluded. Rather hesitantly, he cast his vote in favor of Hutchins and College reform, not because he understood or sympathized with what was being attempted, but out of a sense of deference to Hutchins' constituted authority as president and his presumed expertise in questions of university organization and management.

Hutchins somehow became aware of my father's role on this occasion. A year later when he resigned from the university, Hutchins went out of his way to be gracious. My father responded: "In accordance with your request, I write this memorandum on the University of which I have been a member for seventeen years. . . . It is regrettable that Chicago professors once, even recently, loyal to the administration should now be alienated and agitating against policies advocated or instituted by the President. . . . To bring the University out of this crisis will require invincible patience on your part. You are a very talented man and I believe you can do it. . . . I think the new college plan will have a good chance of success. I voted for it somewhat doubtfully but I am glad that I did not deny you the majority you needed and so narrowly obtained." [17]

But Hutchins was not a patient man. In retrospect, he confessed: "My lack of patience was one of my principal disqualifications as an administrator. . . . It is one thing to get things done. It is another to make them last. I should have known that a large and embittered minority, which felt that fundamental alterations of the University had been pushed through without consideration of its point of view, destined such alterations to endure only until the minority could muster the strength to become a majority." With patience, he mused, "I would have accomplished fewer things but they might have survived longer." [18]

At the time, however, he felt very differently. The narrow squeak of April 1942 impelled him to protect the College and its fledgling curriculum from the hostility of the university's senior professors by changing the university's constitutional structure. Accordingly, on 16 November 1942, he submitted a proposal to the Board of Trustees whereby the president, appointed for a seven-year term, would be subject to dismissal at any time that the faculty refused him a vote of confidence. But the meat of his proposal was that the president should have the power to act in matters of educational policy and organization and risk the consequences—with the proviso that if he chose to override faculty advice coming from a particular department, school or committee, implementation would wait until a vote of confidence had either sustained or, alternatively, overthrown him, together with the policy he wished to promote. [19]

The trustees responded by suggesting consultation with the faculty. Hutchins then wrote a rather petulant memorandum to the Senate, on 31 December 1942, suggesting that it address the question of whether the president should be turned into a mere chairman of the faculty or accorded effective power. In response, on 8 January 1943, the Senate elected a special committee, chaired by Leonard White, professor of political science, to meet with a committee of trustees, chaired by Laird Bell, to consider Hutchins' proposals for changing the governance of the university.

Deliberations were long-drawn-out and for the next two years tended rather to exacerbate than to calm Hutchins' relations with the faculty. Almost a year later, on 13 December 1943, he felt compelled to spell out the argument for constitutional change anew. "The question," he declared, "is whether there is to be an agency in the University responsible for educational policy and for educational and scientific standards. The Senate Committee insists that the faculty is and must be responsible on these issues. But this is a meaningless use of the term. . . . No man is responsible unless others can hold him accountable for what he does. Who can hold the faculty accountable for its decisions? It is absurd to talk about responsibility of a group which cannot be removed, or even rebuked, without violation of the most sacred canons of academic life."

He went on: "Important decisions must be made and made quickly. Some agency must make them. But the agency which is making them during the current emergency, the President, is making them illegally, and there is no effective way of holding him accountable. If this continues, the President will become an irresponsible dictator . . .

"The question is whether it is possible to have both democracy and efficiency. . . . Everybody knows that an organization based on distrust of the executive does not prevent the executive from exercising great powers; it merely impedes and harasses him and drives him to extra-constitutional, if not illegal, methods of getting things done. . . . The remedy is to encourage, even to require, the executive to act and hold him strictly accountable for what he does." He then repeated his recommendation for giving the president executive authority and suggested "annual review of the administration by a joint trustee-faculty committee, which, if unfavorable, must produce the President's resignation."

Hutchins concluded his case for constitutional reform by suggesting overthrow of the professorial oligarchy that had caused him so much trouble. "The Senate" he suggested, "should consist of 50 members elected by all assistant, associate and full professors. The Senate Committee should consist of seven members elected by the Senate as a whole. The Senate should be required to express itself affirmatively on all matters coming before it.

"Such an organization would encourage initiative, discourage political chicanery, and fix responsibility. It therefore looks like a significant attempt to solve one of the most baffling problems of democracy . . . I do not believe that if the members of the Senate Committee understood the issues and the proposed remedy they would want more."[20] But no decision was made, despite Hutchins' skillful pleading. Too many professors distrusted everything he had to say after the way he had achieved the tie vote in April 1942.

These lengthy controversies generated intense emotion. Cliques formed and broke apart. Rumor distorted reality. Suspicion ran rampant. In August 1944 Hutchins boiled over in a private letter to Laird Bell, saying: "If your object was to depress me, you have succeeded . . . Everything said by the members of the Faculty is irrelevant. . . . If the Committee of the Senate represents the firm and abiding conviction of the Faculty as a whole, then I think that a change in the administration is clearly indicated."[21] Altogether, it was a very difficult time. Civilian students were few, professors had scattered, the whole future of the university was uncertain. Apocalyptic anxiety, fed by the war, pervaded the university community. Hutchins set the tone by telling the faculty at the very beginning of active hostilities that the fate of civilization rested on their shoulders. "To formulate, to clarify, to vitalize the ideals which should animate mankind, this task is the incredibly heavy burden that rests, even in total war, upon the universities," Hutchins had said in January 1942. "If they cannot carry it, nobody else will, for nobody else can. If it cannot be carried, civilization cannot be saved."[22] Hutchins was no compromiser. He reacted to prolonged deadlock and mounting personal frustration by acting, with or without consent of the faculty. His opponents among the faculty behaved in the opposite fashion, resisting almost every kind of change more and more stubbornly.

The whole question of university governance was soon distorted and exacerbated by a clash of doctrines in the College, where the burning issue was whether the second year of the humanities sequence should be based on McKeon's style of textual analysis. Edgar Wind, a specialist in Renaissance art and philosophy and a newcomer to the university, became a member of the fledgling Humanities 2 staff in autumn 1942. Almost at once, he quarreled with McKeon's followers, who dominated the staff, and asked to be relieved from teaching a course which required him to subscribe to a doctrine he deplored. Wind accordingly retreated to the Department of Art, but he had become a marked man in McKeon's book, and when John Nef invited him to lecture under the auspices of his newly established Committee on Social Thought, McKeon tried to veto the enterprise, arguing that as dean of humanities he had jurisdiction over what faculty members could rightfully do outside the division. Nef exploded, asking "What are you trying to do, bully me?"

Although Wind did deliver his lectures, shortly afterwards he left the university. Before he departed, however, in May 1944, Wind, Nef, and Ralph Tyler, soon to succeed Redfield by becoming acting dean of the social sciences division, signed a memorial asking for a Senate inquiry into McKeon's conduct. "There is interference with the self government of departments, with the freedom of teaching, and with the development of inter-departmental studies," they wrote. "A particular philosophical doctrine is being imposed," which they ascribed to an "abuse of power by the Dean of the Humanities. He officially combines in his person the functions of Professor of

Greek, Professor of Philosophy, Acting Chairman of the Latin Department and Dean of the Division, not to speak of his presence in about a dozen committees in and through which he exercises influence." [23]

A more judicious assessment of the situation on the Humanities 2 staff came from David Grene, who after teaching the course in its second year, 1943–44, wrote to Hutchins: "It is at least more than questionable whether the examination of a work of art 'in itself' without any external reference means anything at all. And yet one is expected to teach this method (of 'scientific criticism') to students, not as a personal point of view but as an accepted method of literary procedure about which qua method there is no ground for dispute." In practice, Grene felt, it turned into "a tissue of absurdities" relying upon "the isolation of certain words, usually called 'terms,' in the book studied, and the creation of a quite arbitrary interplay among them." [24]

But opposition to McKeon and his followers was a risky business in the mid-1940s, when their influence was at its peak. Just as Wind found it best to leave the Department of Art, Grene's dissent from the reigning orthodoxy was duly followed by his dismissal from the Department of Greek and from the College. Nef, however, came to his rescue by inviting him to join the Committee on Social Thought in 1946. Hutchins may have had his own reservations against the way McKeon's disciples were imposing their doctrine in the College. At any rate, he concurred in Grene's new assignment and made Ralph Tyler acting dean of the Division of Social Science just a month after he had signed the accusation against McKeon.

A new alignment seemed about to emerge. Hutchins had talked about escaping the departmentalization of graduate study ever since his inauguration; and in 1942 John Nef decided to do something about it. After a slow start, Nef had become one of the few members of the faculty who enjoyed social relations with President Hutchins and his wife. He was a distinguished economic historian, yet, as an aesthete and collector of French art, met Maude Hutchins' exacting standards—more or less. He was also wealthy (through his wife) but childless and disdained the narrowness and philistinism of his colleagues in economics and history. Like Hutchins, his interests shifted toward morals and religion during the war, and he came to feel that what the world needed was a new vision of society, of beauty, and of truth. [25]

The Committee on Social Thought, established within the social sciences division in 1942, was the result. Chaired by John Nef, and funded in large part by his wife's money, the Committee on Social Thought became an elite group. Nef simply gathered persons he liked and admired, picking them from quite diverse professional backgrounds, and asked them to supervise the studies of a select handful of graduate students. Presently he began to entertain grander visions of what the committee might become. In a memorandum to Hutchins he sketched an Institute of Graduate Studies at the University of Chicago that would "encourage men and women to discover, rediscover and maintain the principles that will help humanity to form its ultimate community." The Committee on Social Thought would dissolve into the Institute in order better to pursue a "synthesis of the accumulated knowledge, thought, art and wisdom of the race." [26]

Hutchins' reactions to this proposal are not recorded in the files I saw, but it seems clear that Nef believed that he was Hutchins' true champion against the departmental myopia of the faculty. Yet, as we saw, he also clashed sharply with McKeon. Obviously, if both Nef and McKeon were cats' paws for Hutchins' nefarious schemes to revolutionize the university, as Hutchins' foes believed, the president's partisans were in remarkable disarray. In fact, Hutchins never endorsed any detailed scheme for reconstructing the College curriculum or for remodeling graduate study. He preached, but never came to grips with exactly how to implement his ideals. Instead he let the deans attend to academic and curricular infighting and devoted most of his personal attention to affairs beyond the walls of the university.

His friend, Mortimer Adler, pulled vigorously in this direction. He had given up on the university long since and believed that the grand reform of thought he aimed at, and the reform of society that Hutchins craved, could best be pursued through Great Books classes for adults, together with the development of an index to the Great Books that would give everyone easy access to the knowledge needed for living a good life.

Adler's new faith fed on the success he met when, with Hutchins' rather sporadic assistance,[27] he began to offer a class in the Great Books to members of the Board of Trustees, beginning in 1943. This replaced the analogous course for undergraduates they had conducted from 1930 to 1940. The fact that many of the trustees rose to the challenge of reading and discussing serious books on a weekly basis convinced Adler that such classes, aimed at the business and professional elites of the country, were more promising than anything he had been able to achieve among undergraduates.

His hopes were further encouraged by association with another significant educational institution, the *Encyclopaedia Britannica*. After migrating to America, this famous reference work had fallen on hard times. The giant mail order and department store, Sears Roebuck, bought it in the 1920s, but did little to keep articles up to date, so that the encyclopedia was in danger of losing its intellectual respectability. The *Britannica* was rescued from this fate when, after two years of negotiations, William Benton concluded a deal whereby Sears Roebuck transferred ownership to him; or rather to a new company he organized and headed. Benton agreed to advance $100,000 from his own pocket to start the new company off, but as part of the deal also agreed that royalties from sales would accrue to the University of Chicago. In return, the university faculty was expected to give advice and counsel about revising out-of-date articles.[28]

Hutchins became president of an editorial board that Benton established to advise him about the content of the encyclopedia. Benton also bought ERPI films, the company with which the College had been allied in the early 1930s, and launched a scheme for producing additional educational films. Then in October 1943 the new company announced that it would branch out still further by publishing a uniform edition of the Great Books. As a result, Hutchins was soon presiding over a committee charged with the task of defining the canon. Adler was the driving force behind the Great Books project and resigned from the faculty in 1946 so as to work full time on preparing a master index, or Syntopticon, that would make what he decided were the "101 Great Ideas" of the Great Books readily available to every reader.

Obviously, the project of expanding Great Books classes for adults depended on ready availability of texts, and the new set did not become fully available until 1952. But Adler did not wait. New Great Books classes for adults were started throughout the Chicago area in 1945–46, meeting both in university classrooms and in libraries, schools and at business locations like the Marshall Field's store in downtown Chicago. The number of students skyrocketed, from 164 in 1944 to almost 2,000 in 1946. In that year, sixteen classes led by university faculty members were supplemented by no fewer than thirty-four community groups, whose leaders were sketchily trained by Adler and other experienced mentors and then turned loose to discuss the books assigned each week as best they could. Adler, the "Great Bookie" as Hutchins jestingly now called him, projected a nationwide enrollment of up to two million.

Enthusiasm was indeed real and proved surprisingly contagious among business and professional men and their suburban wives. TV was just beginning; reading was still a normal way to occupy leisure time; and the widespread decay of religious faith in suburbia made pursuit of the good life by public discussion of serious books attractive to innumerable well-to-do middle-aged men and women who found themselves somehow dissatisfied with their lives. By assembling together once a week and discussing the Great Books, they could vent and even relieve some of their distresses. The Great Books movement, in short, offered an intellectual surrogate for, or supplement to, attendance at church. As a result, for a few years Great Book classes multiplied very rapidly across the country, and what had seemed to many an absurd and reckless publishing venture turned out to be a financial success, though Benton and his new company had first to survive a cash flow crisis in 1947 which for a while threatened the successful continuation of Adler's venture.[29]

Although Hutchins' dual responsibilities toward Benton's new company took considerable time, he also busied himself with presiding over an ineffectual Commission on Freedom of the Press, funded by Henry Luce in 1944. After much huffing and puffing, the commission had little to recommend in the way of legal or other changes, though it did displease Luce by decrying the irresponsibility of owners and managers in appealing to the lowest common denominator of public taste.[30] Hutchins also acceded to Professor Borgese's importunities by chairing a Committee to Frame a World Constitution. This enterprise, initiated in September 1945, was largely a response to the dropping of the first atom bombs. Modeling themselves on the precedent of the Constitutional Convention in Philadelphia of 1787, Hutchins, Borgese, and a few of their friends presented what they called a "proposal to history" on 17 September 1947 in the form of a preliminary draft of a world constitution. By saying firmly that national sovereignty would have to go, the committee offended prevailing public opinion, and, after a few initial expression of horror, the document pretty well dropped from sight.[31]

While Hutchins was thus spending much of his time on extramural projects, others within the university were busy dreaming up a plethora of other projects for the postwar era. As early as 1941, Arthur Compton proposed the establishment of an Institute of Metals as a means of attracting major support for research in physics from "a metal-minded industrial community, such as that near Chicago."[32] And in 1946 Hutchins acted on the proposal, subsequently modified and enlarged, in hope of attracting Enrico Fermi and other key figures in the wartime Metallurgical Project back to campus. Despite problematical funding, three new bodies were set up in August 1945: an Institute for the Study of Metals, an Institute for Nuclear Studies, and an Institute of Radiobiology and Biophysics.

Compton's relationship with academic atomic scientists had worn thin during the war. He was no longer a practicing experimentalist, and his administrative, intermediary role made him seem an apologist for the military in the eyes of many. Partly for that reason, he left Chicago to become president of the University of Washington, St. Louis, just when Fermi and key figures among his colleagues (Edward Teller, Leo Szilard, and others) were returning from Los Alamos to animate the new institutes and begin peacetime work at the place where they had created the first self-sustaining atomic reaction a hectic three years before.

These new institutes were matched by several other, similarly ambitious visions of the future, though Hutchins held back from acting on most of them without better prospect of funding. A scheme for establishing an Industrial Relations Center was launched in 1945 with the participation of several big corporations as well as some labor unions. In due course, the new center even achieved a brand new building of its own south of the Midway; but support faded as expenses mounted, and the initial hopes withered soon after Hutchins left Chicago in 1950. Similarly, Rex Tugwell, after a controversial official career in the federal government, accepted appointment as professor of political science in order to establish a Program of Education and Research in Planning; but funding fell short of initial expectation for this enterprise also, and since Tugwell failed to establish effective collegial relations with other political scientists at Chicago, his Planning Program became pretty much of an orphan.

Other expansive postwar plans remained mere pipe dreams. Nef's idea of turning the Committee on Social Thought into an Institute for Graduate Study, mentioned above, fell into this category, and so did a proposal from Adler for a Philosophical Institute whose mission would be to construct a "Summa Dialectica" to give "the twentieth century the only sort of wisdom it can have."[33] Hutchins was sympathetic, but for lack of funding, Adler's institute never found a place within the university, though he did eventually create such an organization as an autonomous entity. Robert Redfield, too, hoped to expand the domain of anthropology beyond the study of hunters, farmers, and nomads to take on literate civilizations and complex societies; but his initial proposal for a special institute also failed to gain the necessary financial support. He, too, therefore went ahead on a more personal, limited basis, concentrating initially on China. Benton, an inveterate dreamer and doer, toyed with the notion of establishing a Broadcast Center on campus that would run a radio station, perhaps in collaboration with such institutions as Harvard, Wisconsin, California, and the *Encyclopaedia Britannica.* Part of the scheme was to begin to create professional standards for radio by arranging seminars for radio program directors. But the young man he had put in charge of the university's radio office, George Probst, was no fund-raiser; Benton was busy with other things, and this idea, like the others, therefore died aborning.[34]

A more important new enterprise on campus reflected the intense concern felt by atomic scientists and other members of the university over the management and control of the new force that the Manhattan Project had unleashed on the world. Hutchins took a lead by convening a high-level conference on atomic energy on 19 September 1945 where, for the first time, economists, political scientists, government officials, journalists, and other laymen, together with atomic experts, confronted the question of how the new technology ought to be managed in future. One burning issue was secrecy: another was whether the existing pattern of military control should continue into peacetime. Chicago's scientists became "the principal nerve center of the postwar movement"[35] for civilian control within the United States, and most of them backed an effort to give the United Nations authority over the new weapons. Intense lobbying in Washington, orchestrated in considerable part from Chicago, resulted in the transfer of responsibility from the army to a new Atomic Energy Commission in 1946. Edward Levi of the Law School played a key role in mediating between atomic scientists and the political process of lawmaking in Washington, while Robert Redfield and Edward Shils were the principal links between Chicago's hard scientists and the real but limited wisdom of the social sciences. Since congressmen and government officials had everything to learn about atomic energy, and since the company of concerned atomic scientists had almost everything to learn about national and international politics, the lead Hutchins took in bringing the resources of the university to bear on the hectic negotiations and briefings, back and forth, between atomic experts, politicians, and social scientists had a good deal to do with the upshot, even though hopes of international control, to which most at Chicago subscribed, were soon blasted by the growing friction between the Soviet Union and the United States.[36] Never before had the University of Chicago played so prominent a part in defining important national policy, but once the Atomic Energy Commission took over Hanford and Oak Ridge in 1946, the university's special role in the national management and control of atomic energy faded rapidly away. Argonne remained, but it was only of local and regional importance.

While these various projects, together with the wartime conversion of campus facilities to military uses, were testing the established structure of the university, a new four-year program of general education in the College was taking shape, year by year. The full array of new courses was in place for the first time in 1944–45, and rising numbers of students presaged the rush of veterans guaranteed by the provisions of the so-called G.I. Bill, passed by Congress in 1944. Then, like a clap of thunder, came the bombing of Hiroshima and Nagasaki. War's end loomed abruptly ahead; and with it an end to all the wartime programs, government contracts, and emergency arrangements that had dominated the campus since 1942.

It was against this background that the climactic constitutional struggle over the management of the university took place between February 1944 and June 1946. It was triggered by Hutchins' annual speech at the trustees' dinner for the faculty on 12 January 1944. He took this occasion to reaffirm the need for a radical restructuring of graduate study along the lines he had first set forth at the time of his inauguration in 1929. He proposed that just as the College was at last giving the B.A. a new, coherent meaning, an Institute of Liberal Studies should be set up at the graduate level to do the same for the Ph.D. In practice, Hutchins argued, the doctoral degree had become a license for college teachers. But preparation to teach the sort of general courses needed for genuinely liberal college education required appropriately general, philosophical graduate training. Only by instituting such a program of graduate studies could the university's responsibility for the reform of American higher education be properly realized.

Hutchins' scheme, of course, would have deprived departments of jurisdiction over the mainstream of graduate study, reserving specialization for an elite actually destined for careers in active research. He knew that most faculty members would oppose such a change, but was in a reckless mood. Only by taking advantage of the break in routine involved in shifting back to a peacetime basis did he see any chance of overcoming the faculty's vested interests in existing arrangements. He therefore took the occasion of this trustees' dinner speech to raise the constitutional issue anew, declaring that the university could not lead the required reforms of higher education in America unless he, as president, were empowered to override faculty opposition.

In hope of making the university into a true community of scholars, he challenged the faculty with two other shocking proposals: abolition of academic rank, and generalization of the Medical School regulation whereby all outside earnings accrued to the university. In return, he offered the prospect of better salaries, keyed not to seniority but to need, so that a "young man with three children would have a larger living allowance than a department chairman with none." Instead of allowing the university to remain "a gigantic conspiracy to preserve the status quo," he summoned his hearers to envision that "the purpose of the university is nothing less than to procure a moral, intellectual and spiritual revolution throughout the world. The whole scale of values by which our society lives must be reversed if any society is to endure." [37]

This speech alarmed a great many faculty members. Having spoken, Hutchins declined to elaborate or negotiate. Perhaps he was hoping to carry the trustees with him and force his opponents to yield. For a while it looked as though he might be able to do so, for in February 1944 the trustees accepted his proposal to authorize a new type of contract for faculty salaries, known as 4E. In return for somewhat higher annual salaries, the 4E contract required faculty members to assign to the university all additional earned income—book royalties, lecture fees, summer salaries from other institutions, and the like. The argument was that if professors had no monetary incentive to engage in outside work, they would limit themselves to tasks of intrinsic intellectual and professional worth, and by organizing their efforts accordingly would become better citizens of the intellectual community that Hutchins hoped to create on the Midway. Existing faculty members could choose the new contract and assure themselves of a raise—or refuse; but all new appointments to the university were to conform to the terms of 4E.

Introducing this change, as he did, with the trustees' backing and without faculty assent, led many faculty members to conclude that Hutchins was indeed about to ram through the other changes that he had proposed in January. Widespread anxiety and anger resulted. After months of preliminary skirmishing, a "Memorial on the State of the University" passed the Senate with a vote of 94–42 and was forwarded to the Board of Trustees on 22 May 1944. Ronald Crane was the principal author of this memorial, which expressed "deep concern for the well being of the university" because Hutchins was trying to "reverse the whole scale of values by which our society lives." After denouncing his proposal for an Institute of Liberal Studies and denying that the president had the right to override the faculty, the memorial ended up by declaring that "continued control by its members, organized according to subject matter departments" was essential because the university could not prosper intellectually "if it is committed to any particular social, moral, philosophical or spiritual ideology or other specific formulation of unity." [38]

Nef decided he should come to Hutchins' support and by 7 June had collected eighty faculty signatures for a countermemorial praising him for protecting the faculty from outside pressure, such as those that had boiled up in the Walgreen case, and affirming that he "never interfered with any individual's research or teaching." [39] Hutchins sought to calm the situation by issuing a statement on the next day, 8 June 1944, which read: "It is the duty of the president of a university to formulate and state his conceptions of the purposes of the institution. Nobody has to agree with the president's statements. The imposition of a particular doctrine would be a violation of the perfect academic freedom which the administration of the University of Chicago has always guaranteed." [40]

Controversy carried over into the summer. Extravagant rumor about Hutchins' intentions distracted the campus as the war in Europe came to a climax in the weeks after D-Day on 6 June 1944. Hutchins therefore tried to define the issue anew, explaining exactly what he wanted at a crowded meeting in Rockefeller Chapel on 20 July 1944. His address, entitled "The Organization and Purpose of the University," was published in pamphlet form and circulated widely thereafter. After a masterly summary of all his ideas and aspirations for the university, he reaffirmed his hopes. "This is a great university," he declared, "the greatest, I think, in the world. . . . The secret of the University's distinction has been its daring and its unity. The original source of both was its youth. . . . Now the University has reached maturity. . . . The question is whether, as it has lost its youth, it will lose its daring and its unity.

"We are going to have a new world whether we like it or not. The signs of the character of that world which we can see now are not encouraging. To me it seems that nothing less than a moral, intellectual, and spiritual revo- lution can save mankind, for the scale of values by which we live has given us at last the means which can be used to exterminate the human race without giving us the will, the reason or the vision to see the human ends for which these means should be used. . . .

"In the moral, intellectual and spiritual conflict which I foresee the Uni- versity may take whichever side it pleases. It may endorse the scale of values by which our society lives; or it may join the effort to reverse them. The only thing it cannot do, as it seems to me, is to stand apart from the conflict on the theory that its function places it above it. This is to doom the University to sterility. It is to renounce the task of intellectual leadership. It is to deny the great crisis in history and our responsibility to mankind." [41]

Hutchins' moral earnestness and rhetorical skill had never been more im- pressively demonstrated. His eschatological tone was soon to be reinforced by the atomic explosion over Hiroshima on 6 August 1945, and it may be that he already was aware in July 1944 of what the atomic scientists had wrought under the west stands and subsequently. As far as Hutchins was concerned, the war and its approaching end, the bomb and its implications for the future of humanity, moral reformation of modern society, reform of education in the United States, and what to do about the governance of the university all came to be wrapped up together in the debate.[42]

His apocalyptic mood was contagious and the resulting intensity of conflict on campus made it obvious that the constitutional issue, hanging fire ever since 1942, would have to be resolved. Since the Board of Trustees was legally responsible for management of the university, Laird Bell took charge and after careful consultation with everyone concerned succeeded finally in producing a document that all were prepared to accept. The new statutes were approved by the trustees on 28 December 1944. Though Hutchins liked his own, unadulterated proposals better, he nonetheless expressed the hope that the faculty would now be satisfied. In fact they were satisfied, and the statutes remain in force to this day. Despite Hutchins' grumbling, the final compromise conformed fairly closely to the pattern Hutchins had suggested in December 1943. A new ruling academic body, the Council, consisting of fifty-one members, elected by assistant, associate, and full professors, replaced the Senate. The members of the Council, in turn, elected a Policy Committee. Meeting biweekly with the administration, it was charged with preparing the agenda for monthly meetings of the Council.

Steady communication and consultation between administration and faculty was thereby assured. This had not occurred before, since the Senate represented only full professors and had met only when there was some sort of emergency to discuss. Though everyone hoped that the new arrangements would head off collisions like that of May 1944, the new statutes provided that in case the president disagreed with a resolution passed by the Council, he had the power of veto; in which case the matter would come back to the Council for reconsideration. If the Council reaffirmed its stand, the issue would then pass to the Board of Trustees for ultimate resolution.

Hutchins supplemented this new pattern for sharing authority over academic matters with the faculty by reorganizing the central administration. Benton had all but disappeared from the campus scene, owing to his multifarious other activities. He therefore shed his title of vice president and became "assistant" to Hutchins instead. His vacated office was filled by three new vice presidents: one for business affairs, one for fund-raising, and one for faculty affairs. Hutchins became chancellor of the university, with overall responsibility as before; but everyday administration was entrusted to Ernest C. Colwell, dignified with the title of president.

Colwell was an even-tempered New Testament scholar. He had come to the fore in 1943, when, as dean of the Divinity School, he negotiated a federation with a number of theological seminaries located near the campus. The participating institutions expected to benefit by allowing students to take courses freely, back and forth among the separate schools. In addition, vital budgetary relief could be expected from the elimination of overlapping courses. Colwell's irenic disposition and his ability to reach across touchy sectarian lines stood in welcome contrast to the rancor that became so widespread on campus in 1944. Hutchins therefore hurried to bring him into the central administration, putting him in charge of faculty affairs before making him president in 1945. Stung by the hostility he had aroused, thenceforth Hutchins let his subordinates manage the university as best they could and intervened himself only in unusual situations.

Unusual situations, however, refused to fade away. On 6 February 1946 by a vote of 65–43, the College faculty decided "to award only the degree of Bachelor of Arts as at present defined to students entering after the Summer Quarter 1946." [43] This language announced the coming of age of the new four-year curriculum, laboriously worked out, year by year, ever since 1942. Henceforth, the halfway houses, invented during the war to accommodate high school graduates and students wishing to prepare for scientific careers, were to be shut down. Every student seeking a B.A. would have to satisfy every requirement, either by passing a placement test on entry, or by passing a comprehensive examination after appropriate study.

Natural scientists were outraged. The three-year sequence in natural science, they felt, did not give students the grounding in contemporary science they needed to start graduate school and wasted far too much time on outmoded scientific texts. The College requirements for the B.A. would not prepare students adequately for medical school either. Scientists found allies within the humanities division, for the requirement of one year of work in a foreign language seemed grossly inadequate to prepare students for graduate work in fields in which mastery of more than one language was essential. In addition, diffuse and general opposition to McKeon's domination of the humanities courses in the College crystallized around the absence of history from the curriculum, which accordingly became a key demand of the opposition.

Emphasis on the importance of history had the further virtue of blunting the counterargument to the effect that the College aimed at producing citizens, not scientists and scholars. This was, in fact, somewhat specious. The actual makeup of Chicago's undergraduates belied the claim, since the great majority of them, as in the 1930s, were in fact headed for professional schools and graduate study. Hutchins from time to time complained that the intellectual elitism of the College defeated its purpose of pioneering a general educational reform; but, ironically, his warmest supporters in the College—faculty and students alike—embodied the high intellectuality that he deplored and, in other contexts, praised. This contradiction eventually doomed the Hutchins-Faust-McKeon College to failure; but in 1946 its efflorescence was just beginning, and its partisans were ready and eager for battle against what they saw as the pettifogging vested interests of the divisional faculties.

But in the university as a whole, divisional and professional school faculty members far outnumbered undergraduate teachers; and the elected Council inevitably reflected this balance. As a result, when the Council reviewed the action of the College faculty, on 5 March 1946, a substantial majority, 30–10, voted to "request the College to reconsider its action of February 6, 1946, by designating a committee to confer with the committee of the Council ... to conserve, through greater flexibility in the requirements for the Bachelor of Arts degree, both the objectives of general education and the interests of students intending to enter the Divisions or Schools."

Two days later, Hutchins vetoed the action of the Council; but when, in accordance with the new statutes, the matter came before the Council for reconsideration, the vote was almost unchanged: 33 to 12. Yet no one wanted the Board of Trustees to decide. Consequently, hasty behind-the-scenes negotiation led to withdrawal both of the Council's actions and of Hutchins' veto so that everyone could start anew. After long and difficult negotiations a committee came up with a compromise. A key item in the settlement that thus emerged was postponement of the effective date for abolition of alternate paths to a bachelor's degree by one year, so that the new curriculum came fully on stream only in autumn 1947 and with three critical modifications. These were: (1) the humanities sequence would introduce foreign language variants in the third year, thus opening a door for more adequate training in foreign language; (2) the scientists were authorized to maintain a course in physics tailored for the needs of students planning to enter the Divisions of Physical Science and Biological Science; and, last but not least, (3) the banishment of history from the College curriculum was to be modified by merging English 3 with Humanities 3 to make room for a course in the history of Western civilization.

Both parties felt bruised by the negotiations that led to this compromise; but when the College faculty and the Council both approved it, in June 1946 the storms of controversy that had distracted the campus for so long could begin to subside, inaugurating a new, postwar era in the university's history. The transition was marked by a widespread changing of the guard. Redfield and Compton had both resigned from their divisional deanships, and Mc-Keon kept his only until 1947. Faust resigned from the College, exhausted and distressed by the long, angry struggle.[44] Within Hutchins' circle of intimates, Benton severed all connection with the university on becoming Assistant Secretary of State in June 1946 and, simultaneously, Adler resigned to work on his Syntopticon. Hutchins, like Faust, was near the end of his tether. Having fled from Maude, he hoped to induce her to divorce him for desertion. Expecting never to return, he asked for, and the trustees granted him, a leave of absence from the university of nine months, beginning 1 October 1946. Yet his intense love-hate relationship with the faculty and with the university was destined to resume. His final years in office, replete with intermingled success and failure, require another chapter.

6

BLOOM AND DECAY:
THE END OF AN ERA
1946–1950

The immediate postwar years were a time of wrenching change in Hyde Park, the United States, and the world. For the world, the dominating fact was the emergence by 1949 of a new alignment of power, pitting the United States with its allies and dependents in a Cold War against the Soviet Union and its allies and dependents. It was nothing new for victorious alliances to split apart in response to the imperatives of balance of power politics; but this time the potential destructiveness of atomic warheads gave the process an enhanced chiaroscuro from its inception. For many Americans, the initial euphoria of 1945, when victory over Germany and Japan was expected to inaugurate an era of peace (and, perhaps, of prosperity), dissolved into haunting fear of another, perhaps irretrievably disastrous war waged with atomic warheads. This apocalyptic mood was especially strong on the University of Chicago campus, where a small but vocal group of atomic scientists felt personally responsible for the terrible weapon they had helped to create.

In the country as a whole, and on campus as well, official American actions designed to assist postwar recovery and check the spread of communism (Truman Doctrine 1947, Marshall Plan 1948, NATO 1949) commanded sometimes reluctant but nonetheless general support. The trouble was that each American action provoked a Russian reaction, and vice versa. Their emerging rivalry locked the two great powers into a struggle from which there seemed no escape. Public anxiety in the United States escalated when the Russians exploded an atomic device in August 1949, swiftly followed by a Communist victory in China (October 1949) and then, a mere nine months later, by war in Korea (June 1950). When, in the name of the United Nations, the United States decided to send American troops into action against the Communists of North Korea, who had invaded the South, no one could tell whether this localized struggle would turn out to be the prelude to another world war, with destructive potential sure to dwarf anything experienced in World Wars I and II; or whether, as President Truman proclaimed, the international police action required to restrain Communist aggression in Korea would give the Security Council of the United Nations the prestige and authority it needed to maintain international peace. We now know that neither of these scenarios for the future was correct; but at the time, extravagant hopes and equally extravagant fears ran rampant, giving these years a fevered quality that matched, and perhaps even exceeded, the uncertainties of depression and war that had preceded them.

Locally, on Chicago's South Side, another problem thrust itself upon the reluctant attention of the university community. Restrictive covenants had been devised after World War I to exclude certain groups of people from access to housing in Hyde Park and many other Chicago neighborhoods. Blacks and Jews were the usual targets of such agreements, whereby the existing owners bound themselves and their successors not to sell real estate to anyone who fell into these categories. The effect of restrictive covenants had been to draw sharp geographic boundaries around the black ghetto that formed on the south side of the city during and after World War I. Cottage Grove Avenue on the west, 47th Street on the north, and 67th Street on the south defined the area of white occupancy around the university. Within that area, no comparably definite boundaries between gentile and Jewish habitation existed; but Jews were nevertheless systematically excluded from many blocks and buildings and therefore tended to cluster together in those parts of the neighborhood where no such barriers existed.

In the 1920s and 1930s university people paid little attention to the way restrictive covenants affected their immediate surroundings. Students, faculty, and administration all accepted the way things were without thinking much about it, and many professors and students did not even know that restrictive covenants existed. Investment in local real estate was not judged the best use of endowment funds, so the university owned only a few apartments and houses in the immediate vicinity of the campus; but insofar as the university did engage in local real estate transactions, its agents sustained and may even have extended restrictive covenants as a way of protecting the university against the encroachment of the black ghetto.

Another form of discrimination prevailed in the hospitals, where black patients were refused admission on the ground that if they were allowed to come, white patients would depart. Everyday attitudes made that prediction thoroughly plausible, for blacks and whites lived very separately in Chicago. The city was largely composed of immigrant communities from different parts of Europe, whose cohesion depended on proximity of like with like. Blacks, migrating from the south, had to compete for housing and jobs with whites who were trying hard to maintain village solidarities under American urban conditions. As a result, black newcomers were unwelcome. Mutual fear and repugnance between the races prevailed throughout the city.

The university's sociologists, to be sure, studied the black community more fully than they did any other group in the city; and Robert Park, who was the leading spirit of the Department of Sociology until his retirement in 1934, had much sympathy for and some rapport with blacks. But Park and his colleagues did not make much difference in practice. Chicago's sociologists observed and measured sustained by the faith that accurate information would provide self-evident cures for social ills. Instead, their studies merely showed that the social distance between whites and blacks in Chicago was greater than in southern cities where long-standing patterns of symbiosis had been distorted but not destroyed by the Jim Crow laws of the post–Civil War decades.

The fact that the black population continued to grow and pressed hard against the boundaries set by restrictive covenants meant that Chicago's race relations (which had boiled into violent riot in 1919) remained uneasy during the boom of the twenties and the subsequent decade of depression. Friction intensified during World War II when black immigration from the rural South speeded up. Peace did not check the flow of blacks into the city, thanks, largely, to the increasing use of cotton-picking machines, which had been invented in the 1930s. As jobs in the cotton fields disappeared, more and more field hands headed north to Chicago, despite the fact that urban employment did not readily keep up with their swelling numbers. Job scarcity and insecurity therefore made adjustment to an already hostile city especially difficult for black newcomers.

One important element in the situation changed when, immediately after the war, restrictive covenants were declared illegal, so that blacks were suddenly able to buy from any owner who was willing to sell. Since long-standing shortages within the ghetto had compelled blacks to pay more for housing than whites did, they were ready to bid higher than whites, with the result that blacks began to infiltrate rundown neighborhoods across the ghetto's erstwhile boundaries. Panic flight to some safely segregated suburb was a widespread white reaction to the appearance of blacks on the block. Unscrupulous real estate agents practiced the art of "turning" a block, scaring white owners with anonymous telephone calls, offering to buy, and, when that failed to produce results, sometimes arranging drunken curbside parties in front of stubborn holdouts' houses. In this fashion, the boundaries of the ghetto began to expand, block by block, making room for the growing black population of the city by seeping across both Cottage Grove Avenue and 47th Street and by rushing east along 63d all the way to Jackson Park.

By 1949, the market, as shaped by prevailing real estate practices in the city, made it clear that the neighborhoods surrounding the university were headed toward engulfment in the black ghetto. What, if anything, to do about it became a serious question for all the members of the university community. Only a few fled to the suburbs, because the advantages of walking to work were so great and the boundaries of the expanding black ghetto had not yet reached the area closest to campus where most of the faculty and other university employees lived.

Nevertheless, the advancing tide made itself felt on campus and in the university's immediate vicinity where students and faculty congregated. By far the most troublesome symptom was the rise in crime that made campus life more nerve-wracking than before. During the depression, street holdups had been uncommon, so that Hyde Parkers felt safe walking home at night, even when alone; and burglary was so rare that professors simply locked the front door when going away for the summer quarter, or at any other time, and could count on finding everything in order on their return. This ceased to be true during the war, with the result that during the 1940s an increasing fear began to pervade everyday life in the university community, especially after dark. The rising tide of violence in Hyde Park achieved particularly nasty advertisement in 1946, when William Heirens, a student in the College, was convicted of three squalid rape-murders, all perpetrated in the immediate neighborhood. His trial generated a blizzard of newspaper stories, leaving almost though not quite as great a residue of horror as the Loeb-Leopold case had aroused in the 1920s.

All the same, professors, students, and other middle-class whites continued to live in and around the university as they had done ever since its foundation. Indeed, Chicago was unique among urban universities in the United States inasmuch as most of the faculty and much of the staff walked to work and, in fact, constituted a sort of village in the city. A good many members of the university stayed in the neighborhood for weeks on end—working, sleeping, shopping, and socializing in the immediate vicinity. On some blocks, faculty and other university employees constituted a clear majority, and they often knew one another, at least slightly, both as neighbors and in their professional capacity at the university. This created a network of acquaintanceship that undergirded and enlarged the more strictly professional contacts that occurred on campus and made the university community far more coherent than it could otherwise have been. In particular, university wives could and did know one another through neighborly contacts, as well as through various volunteer organizations, on and off campus.

When, after 1950, the university community organized effective action to preserve middle-class occupancy of Hyde Park, these women played a leading role in the effort, which could not have succeeded without them. But that is another story, for as long as Hutchins remained in office, no one tried to organize the local community to enforce legal standards for housing and to combat crime. Instead, the market forces that impelled the black ghetto to expand across all its borders continued to operate in Woodlawn, Kenwood, and Hyde Park, and whatever real estate managers, acting on behalf of the university, may have done to try to keep the immediate neighborhood lily white—and some efforts were made to that effect—they did in secret and without the moral support of the higher administration, or of the faculty and students.

The fact was that Hutchins and many other university people were of two minds about what was happening. Hutchins detested racial or any other form of discrimination and took a leading part in compelling the Quadrangle Club to open its membership to blacks when that question arose in 1946.[1] He had not made an issue of restrictive covenants, as long as they were legal; but when the law changed he declined to use university resources to put new obstacles in the path of black expansion, even though that expansion made the life of the white community around the university more difficult.

The university also opened its hospitals to blacks in 1945, but did so without fanfare so as to minimize white reaction. But blacks were inconspicuous to begin with. This provoked a few campus radicals and black activists to picket the clinics on 9 December 1946, demanding a larger role for those who had formerly been excluded. Despite such dissatisfactions, in principle and to a large degree also in practice, after 1945 the university's hospitals, like its classrooms, were open to everyone on an equal basis, regardless of skin color.

What held blacks back from full equality was no longer deliberate, blanket discrimination. Instead, economic and behavioral differences excluded a great many blacks from participation in the university community because they lacked money and/or appropriate skills. Maintaining standards therefore was, or at least looked, discriminatory. There was no escape from this form of racial inequity, short of complete erasure of behavioral differences between black and white populations. Financial costs had to be met somehow; and deliberate lowering of standards for black students and professors—a policy the university never followed—would confirm by forgiving the inadequacies of their skills and knowledge.

For someone who believed, as Hutchins did, in careers open to talent, removal of formal barriers was welcome and appropriate. But he, and many other members of the university, were dismayed at the prospect of having to defend the middle-class style of life in Hyde Park against the slums that started to advance on the university community with the breaching of restrictive covenants. Action that could really check the expansion of the ghetto was sure to strain, and might radically worsen, black-white relations, which were already embarrassingly tense. What to do was hard to decide; and as long as Hutchins remained at the helm, trustees and the administration dithered. Nearly everyone tried not to notice how hard it was for the university to flourish when almost surrounded by decaying neighborhoods nearby.[2]

Yet a do-nothing policy had much to be said for it. To act decisively in the absence of clear and widespread consensus within the university community would have been rash indeed; and there was no consensus between 1945 and 1950. Instead, by pretending not to notice neighborhood problems, faculty and students as well as the administration could go about the business of being themselves. This permitted important branches of the university to enter upon a brief but intense efflorescence that could scarcely have been sustained if attention had been focused on the grubby, nasty problems of the neighborhood. In some sense, perhaps, Hutchins' quip: "The greatness of the University of Chicago has always rested on the fact that Chicago is so boring that our professors have nothing to do except work,"[3] was true; but only if one substitutes "alien" or even "hostile" for "boring."

What *was* true is this: between 1946 and 1950 scores of professors and hundreds of students cultivated high thoughts about very abstract matters and did so with an enthusiasm and intensity that cut them off from the immediate neighborhood completely and distinguished them from what went on at other universities as well. It was, in short, an era of bloom amidst decay; and a more or less deliberately cultivated inattention allowed both to proceed at a time when the clashes and risks involved in the changing pattern of international alignments provided all the distraction from professional and intellectual pursuits that the university community could or would afford.

The College was the most obvious seat of a new intellectual efflorescence; but the physical sciences and mathematics also flourished, as did the Law School, Oriental Institute, and some social science departments. By comparison, biological science languished, along with the humanities division and the Divinity School; while both the Graduate Library School and the School of Social Service Administration lost their earlier uniqueness as similar, competing schools arose elsewhere.

For the university as a whole, a sudden influx of veterans, with tuition paid by federal funds, created a crush of numbers, as the following table shows:

Year	Veterans Enrolled[4]
1944–45	134
1945–46	2,687
1946–47	4,829
1947–48	4,392
1948–49	4,150
1949–50	3,044

The total number of registered students nearly doubled from the low point of 1943–44, rising to an all-time crest of 14,432 in 1946–47, thereby overshooting the previous maximum, attained in 1929, by 187.[5] Dormitory and classroom space were in short supply. Arrays of wooden barracks sprouted on vacant land and former playing fields to accommodate the veterans and their wives. The postwar baby boom soon populated these shanty towns with a swarm of infants, so that for a few years veterans' families constituted a distinctive element in the university community. To accommodate student numbers, classes were scheduled early and late, and on TThS as well as MWF, thus surrendering half of the customary weekend. Additional teachers, recruited in haste, raised faculty numbers from the prewar figure of 490 in 1939–40 to 748 in 1950–51.[6]

So it was a boom time, and a time of new beginnings. Like a butterfly emerging from its chrysalis, students and faculty emerged from their war experiences eager to range far and wide on the strength of winged words, aided by whatever calculations, experiments, and observations seemed appropriate. Wartime controversies, which had been so bitter, were largely forgotten. Newcomers knew little and cared less about old quarrels between College and divisional faculties. They simply took the new state of things for granted, and survivors from the wartime struggle over the governance of the university were pleased to get back to research and teaching.

When Hutchins returned from his leave of absence in July 1947, he, too, was disinclined to renew the fray, even though his projected reform of higher education was far from complete, since the university had not acted on his proposals for making M.A. and Ph.D. programs coherent and liberal rather than narrowly departmental. Perhaps he was deterred by the fact that his divorce proceedings dragged on for another year (until July 1948); more likely, he had abandoned hope of prevailing against the entrenched departmentalism that pervaded the divisional faculties. The proportional system of election assured a preponderance of divisional faculty in the new Council; and the Council's statutory powers made it impossible for Hutchins to override their opposition.

In addition, Hutchins may have been aware of the precariousness of the College reform he had achieved with so much difficulty during the war years. The College of his dreams, the authentic Hutchins College, devoted to general studies and designed to attract students at the beginning of their junior year in high school, was indeed a going concern; but it did not work as expected. Relatively few students entered when they were supposed to, and the College accommodated high school graduates only by fudging placement examination results so as to excuse them from some of the required courses. Even so, most students who entered with a high school certificate took three years to finish and then faced difficulties in getting their B.A. degrees accepted for entry into graduate and professional schools.

Moreover, the College never played the role of pacesetter for American education that Hutchins had anticipated. Its new model of general education courses did not spread to other institutions as had happened with the New Plan of the 1930s, and its graduates were flocking into graduate and professional schools instead of going out into the world as ordinary citizens whose formal education had been completed. There was a great irony in the whole situation, for the secret and core of the College's success condemned Hutchins' hopes to frustration. What made the College so extraordinary was the concentration of high intellect and serious purpose that prevailed among students, supported and sustained by a comparable concentration of talent and commitment among a very youthful faculty. Such a conjunction was in its nature transitory, if only because the faculty could not remain young and enthusiastic forever. And the exceptional morale and abilities of the students meant that other institutions could not match Chicago's level.[7] Moreover, they did not want to try since other colleges, committed to undergraduate majors, continued to pretend that the Chicago B.A. was inferior because it did not allow students to concentrate in a single departmental field.

The disdain that other institutions displayed for Chicago's new B.A. was fully reciprocated. College teachers and students, sure that they were pursuing the right goals, took great pride in their accomplishment, and were not bashful in saying so to anyone who would listen. Residual distrust of the College within the university's graduate departments also provoked assertive counterthrusts, for College spokesmen were always ready to ridicule narrow scholarship and claimed that general studies, as defined by the new College courses, offered a better, more adequate approach to truth than could ever be fitted inside arbitrary departmental boundaries.

The new courses emerged from their years of gestation, 1942–46, with quite diverse characteristics. Their principal common denominator was that passive learning was everywhere discounted. Lecturing had been almost banished. Instead, discussion—endless discussion, in and out of class—was the preferred vehicle for active learning. Everyone—students and teachers alike—took part. Because prescribed readings were the same for every student in each of the courses designed to prepare for the required comprehensive examinations, students met the same authors and the same ideas at the same time, even though they attended different discussion sections. And since nearly all of the students were anxious to do well in school, they commonly talked about what they were reading at meals and in other spare time during the day—and late, late into the night. Old hands who had survived from the year before could exhibit their superiority by telling newcomers what they needed to concentrate on in each new assignment; and because of the theoretical richness of the readings, what began as practical tips often took wing, turning into vigorous debates about all sorts of abstract questions.

No one could come away from two or three years of such talk without achieving a superior level of verbal agility and acquiring an aptitude for taking on big questions and encountering unfamiliar data (or at least assertions) with complete aplomb. Chicago's students came to bear a common mark, which still survives. Even now, after more than forty years, veterans of the blizzard of words that the Hutchins College provoked among its faculty and students can often recognize one another by the assurance with which they are ready to discourse on almost anything and everything.

Writing received less emphasis. Papers were prescribed in English, and some other courses, but, like attendance at class, such exercises were not required. The comprehensive examinations did sometimes resort to essay questions. But essays were difficult to grade objectively, so, for the most part, the all-important examinations consisted of machine-scored multiple-choice questions. This was convenient and meant that grades were assigned on a genuinely impersonal basis. No one could curry favor with a teacher in hope of a better grade; and conversely, no one could be penalized for disagreeing or disliking a particular instructor, or for cutting his classes. Easy and open relations between students and teachers resulted. This was one of the great charms of the Hutchins college.

On the other hand, the examinations rewarded a special skill for taking multiple-choice tests that had little or no applicability in the world at large. Simply by eliminating answers with "always" and "never," and using a few other rules of thumb, a shrewd student could guess enough correct answers to get a passing grade without having precise knowledge or ever doing the exercises assigned in the preparatory course. But since nearly all of the students in the College were not content with a passing grade and wished vehemently to excel, this defect of the examinations did not do much to diminish the intensity of study and debate that pervaded most students' waking hours. The examinations did, however, reinforce the primacy of reading and talking and minimize the role of writing in the College—a feature which, in retrospect, I regard as its greatest weakness.

A second common denominator of the Hutchins college was the intensity of interaction among teachers. A basic assumption behind each course was that it addressed a body of knowledge that every citizen ought to command. This required the teaching staff to define what that body of knowledge was in precise detail. Teachers had to decide which passages of which books everyone should struggle through to attain a general education. Obviously, there was enormous room for difference of opinion; yet because each student was destined to take the same examination, each discussion section was supposed to treat the same material with, at least approximately, the same emphasis and level of insight.

Given the diversity of the teaching staff, which was unusually great owing to the rapidity (and emancipation from departmental standards) with which the College had recruited its teachers, uniformity was plainly impossible. But great efforts were made to minimize personal idiosyncrasy in the classroom, which, unchecked, would have made classes irrelevant to the examinations. The way to avoid that absurdity and injustice was to agree ahead of time on exactly what ought to be tested; and, at the examiners' insistence, much time was therefore spent trying to define the skills and knowledge students were supposed to acquire from each and every course. This sort of abstract agreement about course goals became operational through weekly staff meetings where the teaching staff talked over the next week's classwork. Commonly, a designated instructor would lead off by saying what he or she proposed to do. New recruits to the staff listened, more or less reverently, but everyone was free to set forth personal notions about how the readings for the week ahead really ought to be understood and explored in class.

Among an initially diverse group of teachers the effect was a good deal more powerful than most graduate seminars, for everyone present had to run the gauntlet of student reaction to what happened in the class he or she presided over. Students were ruthless in migrating away from some teachers' classes and swarming into those taught by persons whose performance won their approval. (There were rules about transferring, and ceilings were set on the size of each class; but taking class time to identify unauthorized visitors was awkward at best, and some of the most popular teachers did not try to do so.) Students, by thus voting with their feet, kept instructors very much on the *qui vive*, eager to pick up tricks of the trade from those whose success was attested by positive student response.

Tricks of the trade involved a good deal more than jokes and rhetorical mannerisms. Students wanted serious, competent discussion of the assigned texts, and the teaching staff worked hard to meet their expectation. No one thought teaching was part-time work. No one tried to find time to finish a Ph.D. dissertation—or write a book—by strolling into class scantily prepared. Students would simply have abandoned such a teacher, and the ever present threat of an empty classroom was a very powerful incentive for learning everything one could before having to stand in front of the next class and ask those really penetrating and illuminating questions about the current assignment that students expected and hoped for.

Teaching is always the best way to learn. But the discussion method, together with the vivacity and unforgiving expectations of Chicago undergraduates, made teaching in the Hutchins college a far more rigorous, demanding experience than reliance on more one-sided styles of classroom discourse could ever be. In this way, students and staff acted on and reacted to each other to make the College what it was: a truly extraordinary experience for anyone who cared about ideas or wanted to understand things in general, and human achievement in particular.

The College instructors were in an unusual position to learn from one another because the staffs brought together a number of refugees from Europe with (mostly younger) American-trained personnel. In social science and history, this provoked an especially fertile, mind-stretching interaction since the prewar German intellectual tradition in these fields had diverged from, and in some respects excelled, Anglo-American habits of thought. Less diversity of cultural background prevailed among the other course staffs, so that the energy and fruitfulness of interaction in humanities and natural science was less pronounced. But there too, and in mathematics, differences of personality and backgrounds made the process of coming to at least approximate agreement week by week about how best to organize class discussion into a valuable learning experience for all concerned.

Those who sat through lengthy staff meetings at which consensus was regularly hammered out sometimes bridled at being constrained by a party line. This was particularly apparent in the humanities sequence, where the imprint of McKeon's critical method was especially strong, and in the terminal course, "Observation, Interpretation, and Integration," that McKeon had designed as a philosophical cap for all the other courses. Under Joseph Schwab's energetic lead, an even more controversial party line developed in the natural science sequence as well. Spontaneity and consensus were greater in the social science courses, where Redfield's leadership, though real, was exercised much more gently, and where the interpenetration of European and Anglo-American intellectual traditions had a liberating effect. But even those who felt most constrained by the pressure to agree on how to teach materials others had chosen recognized that participation in weekly staff meetings sharpened their own ideas and clarified the grounds for their dissent from prevailing course doctrines.

It is impossible to reconstruct in detail how each course evolved. By autumn 1947, when for the first time the full array of fourteen required examinations was matched by fourteen staff-taught courses, the curriculum was finally in place. I joined the faculty at that time, and in the next few years taught Humanities II and Social Science III, and had the good fortune to take part in the genesis of a new History of Western Civilization course, which in 1947 was offered only on a pilot basis. By way of contrast, Humanities II was then in its fifth year, and the old hands inducted newcomers like myself into its mysteries with a distinctly dogmatic mien. The right way to analyze each text was precisely set forth; and we were expected to conform.

The experience was like putting on someone else's clothes. I had never before tried to look carefully at historical texts to see how their authors had put them together; and this we did for an entire quarter. It taught me a good deal about the writing of history, because I had previously tended to treat historical texts as (presumably) transparent windows offering vistas upon the human past whose dynamic I wanted to try to comprehend. Similar efforts to analyze rhetoric, drama, fiction, and philosophy followed; and these I found less rewarding. Social Science III, which I taught the next year, was less firmly structured and had no single viewpoint. Instead, we explored the meaning of political, economic, and social freedom in successive quarters, and the diverse viewpoints of different authors, most of whom reflected standard departmental divergences among political scientists, economists, and sociologists, never came together in any clear fashion. Nor did the staff even try to have a definite doctrine in the way that the Humanities II staff did.

Published materials, in particular *The Idea and Practice of General Education: An Account of the College of the University of Chicago by Present and Former Members of the Faculty*,[8] were designed to advertise the College, and therefore offer too much of an apologist's view to capture the authentic character of the separate courses and staffs. Nevertheless, the reading lists and carefully modulated descriptions of each course provided in this book make the reality at least partially recoverable. The archives add little, save for a thoughtful and well-informed account of the diverse ways in which the College had handled the physical sciences between 1930 and 1950.[9]

Even on this imperfect basis, it is easy to see that some course staffs deliberately repudiated older traditions, while others merely modified the survey courses of the 1930s. In the humanities, natural science and mathematics, revolution prevailed, whereas in social science, English, and foreign languages basic continuity was maintained. The history course was unique inasmuch as it had first been banished from the curriculum by the revolution in humanities and was then shoehorned back in as part of a deal, concluded in 1946, between the College and the divisions for abolishing alternative paths to the bachelor's degree.

I know too little to estimate the success of the three-year sequence in natural science, and of the alternate programs for high school graduates in physical and biological science that had been perpetuated by the compromise of 1946. Mutual interaction, and a few transfers back and forth from one staff to another, narrowed the distrust that initially prevailed between the rival courses and staffs. On the one hand, the natural science sequence diluted its diet of original scientific works by admitting some textbook materials of the sort that remained central to the other two courses. They, in turn, supplemented textbook-style introduction to the biological and physical sciences with some original scientific papers.[10]

Behind this discrepancy lay an acute difference of opinion about how science should be taught. Joseph Schwab and a few followers held that textbooks merely stuffed students' minds with slightly out-of-date ideas and formulae, thereby dogmatically (and inadvertently) disguising the reality of science as open-ended inquiry into the enormous complexity of living and inanimate nature. They preferred to explore science firsthand by studying how famous scientists had asked and answered a few important questions. But since strictly contemporary scientific papers were too difficult as a rule, because of highly specialized vocabularies and abstruse mathematical symbolisms, the science they explored firsthand came mostly from an older time.

This seemed outrageous to most scientists in the graduate departments, for they wanted the College to prepare students for their classes and seminars by acquainting them with as much of the vocabulary and conclusions of up-to-date science as possible and did not care in the least whether they understood how Archimedes, Galileo, or some other scientific innovator had once tried to make sense of the world. Nowhere else in the university was the collision between general education and professional preparation for graduate study so direct and uncompromising. For this reason, and despite the sophistication and dedication of a small band of teachers, the three natural science courses had no future at the university and exerted little influence elsewhere.[11] The fact was that even when the ideal of general education for citizens, not specialists, was burning brightest on the Midway, many high school graduates continued to prefer the more conventional alternative courses. Everyone who expected to become a scientist was required to do so by the graduate departments.

On the other hand, the Mathematics I course, which was also revolutionary inasmuch as it emphasized sets and number theory and bypassed calculus completely, may have been a progenitor of the "new math" that spread from MIT through a great many American high schools, beginning in the late 1950s. If so, it was the only course of the Hutchins-McKeon college that did have progeny elsewhere, but I do not know what connection, if any, actually existed between the College course of the 1940s and the MIT program of the 1950s. What is clear is that the new mathematics never aroused the hostility that beset the natural science sequence.[12] Yet an alternative Mathematics II course, that did teach calculus, was always available for students who placed out of Math I and planned on pursuing graduate work in science; so here, too, the discrepancy between general education and professional training was not successfully bridged.

No such difficulty existed in the areas of foreign language, social science, and humanities. The verbal agility and general knowledge, cultivated so lovingly in the College, served the graduate departments and professional schools in these areas very well. Dogmatism about analytical method was not so strong, even in Humanities II and O.I.I. (Observation, Interpretation and Integration), as to hinder students from fitting into graduate programs with distinguished success. And in the social sciences, the way Soc II mingled

European with American traditions and escaped the conventional limitations of departmentalization, proved to be an excellent preparation for more specialized studies at the graduate level. Edward Shils was a leading spirit in bringing European thinking into this course during its earliest phases. Later, the most influential member was probably David Riesman, who brought in Freud and helped to refocus the course around the theme of personality and culture.

Riesman's role in this course was symptomatic of another characteristic of the College in those years, for he had been trained as a lawyer and engaged in war work before coming to Chicago. As such, he lacked standard academic qualification for teaching social science. A good many other College teachers were in a similar position. Two or three had backgrounds in journalism, some were artists and poets; others were recruited from secondary schools or had begun teaching careers in Europe at sub-university levels. But nearly all of the recruits to the College teaching staff, whether or not they possessed the standard academic union card of a Ph.D., were exceptionally bright, open, and cultivated persons. The College gained greatly from the presence of academic interlopers and so did those who, emerging from traditional graduate programs, suddenly were asked to teach things they had never dreamed of when writing their Ph.D. dissertations. Some awkwardness arose from the fact that a few of the teachers from University High School, who had been assigned to the College in its early days, were not of the same intellectual caliber as the rest of the faculty. But with this exception, the unusual variety of backgrounds was an enormous strength, for, as we have seen, intense staff interaction assured the sharpening of insights and information brought to the subject by persons with widely differing experiences.

A related feature of the College was its public commitment to teaching. Recruits to the staff were promised that their careers at the University of Chicago would not depend on research and publication in the way that was expected of the graduate faculty. Instead, in return for a heavier class load (three courses per quarter instead of two as was common elsewhere in the university), College faculty members were to be retained and promoted solely on the basis of their teaching. Older members of the faculty were therefore under no pressure to write; and new-fledged Ph.D.'s, like myself, were under no pressure to polish up the dissertation and turn it into a first book. Quite the contrary, in some quarters writing scholarly books and articles was taken as a sign that the individual in question had betrayed the College and the ideal of general education by spending time on irrelevancies.

At the time, when everything was new and courses were still in rapid evolution, being freed from pressure to publish was a great boon. It allowed youthful teachers to continue to expand their mental horizons by interacting with diverse colleagues and with the very rich materials of different College courses. In 1947 most of the courses were still undergoing far-reaching revision. Finding something new to replace a reading judged unsatisfactory, persuading colleagues of its worth, and, like as not, editing or translating it for special publication by the College was almost as engrossing a task as getting ready for classes. It required the faculty continually to explore new possibilities. Rejection was far more common than acceptance; but that required initial exploration and an effort at appraisal by committee members charged with the job of making choices.

Altogether, it would have been difficult to contrive a situation more conducive to intellectual growth. The roster of distinguished professors who started in the College is considerable, especially in the social sciences, where the gap with the graduate departments was least. In addition to Riesman, it includes such figures as Daniel Bell, Bert Hoselitz, Barrington Moore, Edward Morgan, Edward Shils, Alan Simpson, Milton Singer, Sylvia Thrupp, and Meredith Wilson, among others.

Its limitations also deserve to be recognized. First of all, the initial freshness of the years 1943–48, when the Hutchins college took form and attained its apogee, was, in the nature of things, evanescent. As the College faculty grew older, those who got tenure for teaching inevitably found themselves repeating the same courses, year after year; and as more and more of the instructors turned into old hands, the courses they taught settled into nearly fixed routines. Within a few years staff members had learned all they were willing and able to learn from one another and from the texts they taught each year. Under these circumstances, those who "betrayed" the teaching ideal by writing books found it easier to retain intellectual vigor and live up to the promise of their youth than did those who did nothing but teach. Such persons usually left the College; those who stayed on found it impossible to maintain the elan and commitment that had prevailed so generally when everything was new.

Like all things human, the bloom of the Hutchins college was therefore inherently transitory, resulting from the youth and inexperience of the faculty interacting with the youth and inexperience of the students. Only by dismissing the faculty and starting anew after, say, ten years, could the original character of the enterprise have been renewed;[13] and even that would not work, for members of the second faculty generation, forewarned by the fate of their predecessors and looking ahead to their own dismissal, would have had to dilute their dedication to the College accordingly. In the 1940s we had no such anxieties. The academic world was expanding; so was the College; and Hutchins' distant but benevolent patronage within the university promised us as much security as a young academic could ask for or expect. The situation was unique and unrenewable. No one foresaw how intrinsically short-lived it was or anticipated the difficulty of maintaining intellectual vigor throughout a lifetime of teaching in lockstep with colleagues who had become too familiar to be stimulating any longer.

A second defect of the Hutchins college was its exclusive attention to a rationalized version of the European cultural heritage. Almost no attention was paid to the non-Western world, or to the ancient Orient, or to Judaism. Inattention to Judaism and to the role of Jews in European society may seem odd in retrospect, now that the loving cultivation of distinctive ethnic pasts has become widespread. But when the Hutchins college was in full flower, the assimilationist ideal that had prevailed in the 1930s still pervaded the consciousness of students and faculty alike. Reasonable people were interested in what united, not what divided, humankind. In practice this principle meant enthusiastic exploration of the riches of a rational, liberal version of the Western heritage, starting with the ancient Greeks. The unspoken but heartfelt assumption was that everyone would rally to that tradition, if given the chance, shedding the prejudices and disregarding the differences of physical appearance that in the unenlightened past had been used to pit peoples and groups against each other. It was a noble dream, and one that ought not to be lightly discarded, since no alternative basis for ethnic peace within American society has yet been devised. But its affirmation and embodiment in the College also meant exclusion of all the aspects of human belief and behavior that did not illustrate and accord with such ideals. That was a heavy price to pay, as the subsequent opening up of the College to non-Western studies and to courses in black and Jewish history attests.

Chicago ceased to be unique among prestigious private institutions when other leading colleges began to dismantle their barriers against Jews after World War II. But even after the Nazi death camps had shown what horrors anti-Semitism could lead to, change was gradual, with the result that Jewish students remained numerous at Chicago, and Jews were more prominent on the College faculty than before the war. This assured a continuity of the prewar assimilationist ideal that sought a common basis for public and private life in the exercise of human reason and deliberately refused to pay attention to religious differences.

Yet this faith and hope was already becoming old-fashioned. If the Jews of Germany, who had gone further than any other Jewish population toward assimilation into the nation around them, could be so savagely attacked, and if irrational motives were as fundamental to human behavior as Freud and others taught, what hope was there that ancient barriers between Jew and gentile would permanently dissolve as a result of reading Aristotle and arguing (more or less) rationally about everything under the sun? To be sure, the hope faded more slowly at Chicago than elsewhere. It was only as identification with the new state of Israel gained force in the American Jewish community after 1947, and as rejection of the assimilationist ideal became more explicit among blacks in the 1950s, that the liberal faith in reason as solvent and solution for ancient patterns of social discrimination wore thin. Hence, a new climate of opinion with respect to ethnic relations and individual identity emerged on campus only after Hutchins had departed. Seeds of subsequent disarray were present before 1950 and are easy to recognize in retrospect, but they were effectively hidden at the time because the liberal European tradition, to which the College adhered, was so genuinely attractive, with so many books to read and so many ideas to explore.

Asian, African, and Latin American studies were also beyond the pale. Like all American colleges of the time, Chicago paid next to no attention to the four-fifths of humankind that was just beginning to assert itself on the political stage as European colonial empires broke up after the war. One can therefore justly complain that Chicago's students were not being well prepared for effective citizenship in a world where peoples of diverse cultural backgrounds matter as much as Europeans and their heirs. Robert Redfield was beginning to address this issue by undertaking to study China (until the Communist victory of 1949 closed the door) and India from the bottom up, starting with village studies of an anthropological bent like those he had made in the 1920s and 1930s in Yucatan. But, beginning in 1944, this took him away from campus and from the supervision of the emerging social science sequence courses that he had exercised up to that time. Those he left behind were not yet ready to think in global terms. Melding Anglo-American with German thought was quite enough to keep them busy without trying to bring the diverse traditions of social science to bear upon non-Western civilizations and societies.[14]

A final deficiency of the Hutchins college was a defect of its strength. A passion for understanding the world rationally in order to shape practical judgments about public and private conduct was at the heart of Hutchins' personal commitment to general education. His vision filtered down to those who actually designed the new courses in variously diffracted fashions. Many agreed with Hutchins in distrusting history because it interfered with attaining timeless truth. Indeed the main thrust of the Hutchins' college (at least in the humanities courses) looks like a reaction against the central intellectual achievement of the nineteenth century, when notions of evolutionary development—biological, geological, sociological and, not least, theological—had carried all before them, discrediting philosophical and religious systems of thought that had attempted to set forth the truth in timeless, univocal fashion.

Hutchins and many of his generation yearned for intellectual certainty and moral guidance of the sort that his father's Presbyterian faith and the tight-knit Oberlin community had provided in his youth. Since faith in revealed truth had become impossible, a reified and all but deified Reason was called upon to take its place. The notion of temporal flux—fundamental, universal, and inescapable—appalled those who shared this moral and intellectual posture. They desperately needed to escape uncertainty, and study of history was no way to escape uncertainty. Only philosophical and, as Hutchins had said as early as 1936, metaphysical arguments offered the prospect of escape into a realm of permanence, justice, and truth—or so they hoped and believed.

Plato had felt a similar urgency to find a transcendental anchor for morals and politics; and Aristotle had turned Plato's philosophical flights—physical and metaphysical alike—into a professionally complete system with ready answers for every question. It was no accident, therefore, that Aristotle became something of a cult figure in the Hutchins college. Hutchins' quest, however sporadic and superficial it remained, resembled Plato's sustained and lifelong effort to impose a rational order on the world. McKeon's critical method, which actually dominated a large part of the College curriculum, resembled Aristotle's professionalization of philosophy, not by providing handy answers, as Aristotle had done, but by providing a handy way of classifying everybody else's answers. Adepts in McKeon's method delighted in their own cleverness and felt no responsibility for answering philosophical questions directly and unequivocally. Instead of ordering the world of men and of things, they were content to dissect and classify what others had said about the world of men and things. Mastery of such a skill kept College faculty and students content and busy. Yet it fell short of Hutchins' ideal, leaving all the great questions of philosophy unanswered and dropping them into a cleverly contrived methodological limbo instead.

Yet McKeon's ingenuity and Hutchins' yearning for certainty did not really make the historical, evolutionary angle of vision on the world any less cogent. The evidences that had led nineteenth-century thinkers to abandon timeless truths for truths evolving indefinitely across time were undiminished. In fact the rapid evolution of natural science steadily reinforced that view. With the development of atomic theory, the once eternal stars became celestial bodies with births and deaths, clustered into distinct generations. Soon after World War II, as evidence for the Big Bang accumulated, the universe itself, and all its parts, came to be viewed as an unstable, evolving flux of matter and energy.

In an odd way the Hutchins college recognized this change in the character of science, for, as we saw, beginning in 1943, Joseph Schwab had the effrontery to challenge "truths of modern science" that many professors in the graduate departments still deemed to be true forever, needing only to be memorized by undergraduates in their final, perfected form. Yet Schwab challenged this static view of science by analyzing texts in a fashion influenced by McKeon, thus all but squaring the circle, since the charm of McKeonism was that it reduced history to a minuet in which basic terms of discourse altered their relationship from time to time and text to text according to rules of logic that were themselves universal and outside of time.

The segments of the university where historical and evolutionary forms of thought were at home had taken little notice of what was going on in the College before 1946. But when the scientists looked about for allies in their struggle against making Schwab's sequence of courses the only way undergraduates could study science, they found support among previously disengaged faculty members who treasured, or at least respected, the historical vision and felt that its deliberate exclusion from the College was unacceptable. As we saw in the preceding chapter, this coalition prevailed in 1946, with additional support from those who wanted more language study in the College. The result was the preservation of the old-fashioned one-year survey courses in biological and physical science, the remodeling of Humanities III to permit "language variants," and, what was intellectually much more significant, the reintroduction of history into the curriculum.

The resulting course in the History of Western Civilization purported to be an integration of the entire curriculum, twinned with a philosophical synthesis aimed at in the course familiarly called O.I.I. (Observation, Interpretation, and Integration). In fact, it presented a quite different vision of the world from that which prevailed elsewhere in the College, for its pervasive assumptions were very close to those that had inspired Schevill's prewar humanities course. Its central notion was that time mattered because things changed, sometimes in spurts, sometimes more slowly, but always and ineluctably. In addition, the Western Civilization course assumed that all aspects of human activity tended to fit together in a given time and place, so that each age had a character of its own that could only be loosely described in words, but which nonetheless pervaded thought, art, politics, and everything else. As a result, eternal truths were not evident in history. Instead, unending change, cumulating power over nature, and clashing ideals provoked, or at least were used to justify, unending struggles among rival human groups.

Yet withal the tone was optimistic. Western, liberal nations had prevailed in modern times, thanks to the industrial and democratic revolutions; and those who taught the course subscribed with varying degrees of warmth to the liberal faith. History had made the United States a world power and leader of what we liked to call the free world. Fascism had been defeated; communism was seriously discredited by Stalin's strong-arm police methods in Eastern Europe. The idea that human wants were best served by a free marketplace in ideas, as well as by a free (or almost free) marketplace for goods and services, seemed far more convincing than it had in the 1930s.

Yet this thoroughly traditional endorsement of Western liberal traditions aroused intense opposition among McKeon's most ardent followers, whose dearest aspirations were contradicted by the obvious implications of such views. For if opinions changed and notions of truth evolved across the centuries, as the historians stubbornly insisted, it followed that McKeon's critical sophistication as expounded by the College's philosophically minded teachers was not necessarily and universally valid. Historical relativism, even when wedded to affirmation of existing American institutions, was unacceptable to wielders of a critical method that claimed universal applicability. The whole object of a general education was to know the truth, even if McKeon's truth no longer embraced the world directly and restricted its domain to the analysis of written texts.

Historians justly doubted the validity of such claims; but they were themselves vulnerable to the charge of using words loosely. In particular, their critics charged that historians merely skimmed texts in search of vague common denominators, picking evidence almost at random to back up preconceived (or at least impressionistic) notions about the character of an age. They therefore bypassed truth by failing to address texts on their own terms and as objects in and of themselves. Instead, they abused their sources by trying to make them into windows upon a mythical, or perhaps merely unknowable, social context.

Debate over this issue was prolonged, for the pilot History of Western

Civilization course existed only on sufferance in 1947 and needed approval from the entire College faculty before becoming a requirement for the B.A. degree. This was hard to get because, as initially constructed, the course failed to satisfy McKeon's followers. The great man himself entered the fray. To correct historians' sloppy use of terms, McKeon invented a new genre of "disciplinary history," meaning the study of how a particular technique or idea developed across the centuries. He claimed that from a careful examination of texts in which, for example, space and time were discussed, a precise and accurate history might emerge, purged of contamination from unprovable assertions about how extraneous events and circumstances affected the ideas in question.

Purists held that this was the only intellectually respectable form of history while defenders of traditional, sloppily inclusive historical thinking argued that even such abstract ideas as the conception of time and space evolved in a social context and could not be properly understood in isolation. Compromise eventually prevailed in the hope that the defects of each kind of history would perhaps cancel out if combined into a single course. Accordingly, in 1949 the College faculty approved a course devoting a minimum of seven weeks to disciplinary history as a proper preparation for an appropriately proportioned comprehensive examination. But since the champions of disciplinary history distrusted historians' bad habits, the staff was not declared "mature" and accorded full and final authority over the course until two more years had passed.

As chairman of the College history staff at the time, I was in the thick of this controversy. Its intensity was extraordinary. The meeting of the College faculty where the compromise decision was eventually reached lasted through three afternoon and evening sessions on successive days. Speeches were lengthy, abstract, and sometimes passionate. I have never experienced such a torrent of words about matters of immediate concern to me. No real meeting of minds resulted, but the experience was certainly well calculated to awaken historians from dogmatic slumber induced by traditional departmentalized training. Having to defend ourselves, we were forced to become conscious of habits of mind that had mostly been acquired by unthinking apprenticeship in graduate school. For College historians, at least, the sort of interaction that prevailed within each staff therefore extended across the College faculty as a whole, embracing with special intensity those most hostile to history as conventionally practiced. Learning to hold one's own in such an environment was equivalent to a rigorous postdoctoral examination, even if the rhetoric expended on both sides sometimes verged on the absurd.

Perhaps it is fair to say that just because it was so wonderful and vibrant, Hutchins college always hovered on the edge of the absurd, even at its apogee. The initial mix of veterans and youngsters, some of them without high school diplomas, was unusual. Both groups were eager to climb the educational ladder as rapidly as possible, but the veterans' age and experience diluted and did something to check the intellectual pride and emotional immaturity of those who had entered the College without completing high school. When the veterans left, the undergraduate body became distressingly lopsided. Prewar extracurricular activities had suffered serious erosion during the war. Such organizations as Blackfriars and Mirror disappeared; and College students were forbidden to join fraternities. Many fraternities and women's clubs failed to survive the war; those that did had to confine membership to divisional students, who were more interested in a cheap place to sleep than in anything else. The very real social pressure that ambitious fraternities had exercised before the war to get their members to engage in extracurricular activities therefore disappeared, along with most of the impetus for maintaining the lighthearted expressions of student life that had loomed so large in the 1920s. The loss was real. The Hutchins college became a collection of idiosyncratic individuals who badly needed an effective way of expressing their collective identity in an emotionally satisfying way. Arguing was not enough. It tended to isolate, not unite.

Despite the decline of Chicago's athletic successes, intercollegiate team sports had continued to serve as a basic cement of the undergraduate community before the war. But when Chicago left the Big Ten in 1946, most forms of intercollegiate competition ceased. Continued success in a few individual sports, such as fencing, was irrelevant for the College as a whole. Intramurals were no substitute. Instead, disdain for jocks and even for physical exercise became almost obligatory, since making mockery of muscular prowess allowed Chicago students to defend themselves and their school against the equation between athletic success and educational excellence that prevailed among the general public.

Intellectual prowess was what gave the College its identity, and since success in the pursuit of knowledge was measured exclusively by individual performance, rivalry tended to prevail over community. In particular, the comprehensive examinations, by pitting individuals against each other in an anonymous setting, were divisive and isolating. Students soon noticed the unfortunate result. In June 1950, fifteen of them expressed their dissatisfaction in a memorandum sent to F. Champion Ward, the youthful dean of the College who had succeeded Faust in 1947. "Sharp minds," they wrote, "by themselves are insufficient to promote communal and intellectual progress: intellectual bigotry, impatience, insensitivity to subtle factors in social and hence intellectual activity frequently co-exist with brilliant minds." Further-more, they remarked, the College atmosphere reinforced "aggressive criti-cism" and "alienation from creative activity." Instead, "increased feeling of community on campus" and a more "active interest in the students' non-academic problems" was what the College needed.[15]

Dean Ward took this manifesto seriously and forwarded it to Hutchins in September, with the suggestion that perhaps the College ought to imitate the pattern of Oxford and Cambridge by playing one intercollegiate match in each sport, including football, at the end of the intramural season. He pro-posed trying to persuade Johns Hopkins to become Chicago's athletic part-ner and rival on this basis. Hutchins scoffed, proposing instead an annual conference on the existence of God and control of the atomic bomb. On Saturday afternoon, during the conference, students wishing to play football "might adjourn for the purpose, and others could go boating or take in a Hopalong Cassidy movie." Dean Ward responded wistfully, wishing that "our students became festive en masse over some event which had no social sig-nificance whatsoever, over which they couldn't possibly picket each other, and which might reduce the 'humorlessness' so humorously complained of by . . . our best students."[16]

Shrill and humorless factional dispute often pervaded the *Maroon*. In-stead of appearing daily, as before the war, the paper came out only twice a week and no longer tried seriously to cover all the events on campus. The prewar recruitment, training, and promotion system, modeled on downtown newspaper practice, could not be restored. Because schoolwork came first for nearly everyone, staff was chronically in short supply. Reporters worked when and as they chose, with the result that the editorial staff varied mark-edly with the seasons and from year to year. Consequently, the paper was perpetually in danger of becoming a vehicle for a handful of incandescent leftists who were eager to thrust their views upon the public.

Not surprisingly, College authorities were sometimes dismayed by the distorted image of campus life that the *Maroon* offered to the world. Thus, for example, after considerable provocation, the Dean of Students banished a leftist editor from the paper in 1946 without provoking any reaction among campus defenders of free speech; and in 1950, Laird Bell, then newly ap-pointed as chairman of the Board of Trustees, complained to Hutchins: "If the *Maroon* represents our product something should be done about the classrooms."[17] Yet the political storms on the *Maroon* staff were unrepresentative of student opinion. Extracurricular political debates, so pervasive in the 1930s, engaged relatively few.

Musical performances, dormitory receptions and parties, together with frequent visiting lecturers did provide relief from the academic grind; and when sports audiences disappeared, a few students actually turned cheerleading practice into a new sort of theatrical performance with the help of a particularly energetic and imaginative gymnastics coach. The result, a show christened "Acrotheater," appeared in Mandel Hall for several years. But such inventiveness was exceptional. Except for "Acrotheater," student dramatics, which had engaged a great deal of extracurricular energy before the war, sank to a very low ebb, and so did dances and other traditional occasions for social enjoyment.

By contrast, amateur theatricals among the faculty flourished, reaching a particularly notorious high point in the Quadrangle Club Revels of 1949, when Hutchins appeared in a show, titled "The Rose Bowl Blues," dressed in the full regalia of a football hero. His physique made jest of the jest, for he quite looked the part. Lending himself to such lightheartedness aroused general amazement and (judging by Hutchins' expression as caught by the camera) cost him some wry embarrassment, but by then his second marriage to a warm and supportive wife was only two months away and the domestic storms that had shadowed his life almost from the day of his arrival on the Midway were safely behind him.

Yet solving his private difficulties did not bring Hutchins back to full engagement with the university. He must have realized that the College curriculum fell short of making general education into the guide for life he had expected. His hope of reforming society was not dead; but the university no longer seemed the most appropriate instrument for the purpose, partly because time was too short,[18] and partly because the new statutes made it impossible for him to overcome faculty opposition to further radical departures.

Hutchins therefore continued to devote considerable personal effort to extracurricular ventures, such as the Goethe Bicentennial celebration, staged in Aspen, Colorado, in July 1949 and the Aspen Institute for Humanistic Studies that emerged from that occasion.[19] He continued to spend a great deal of effort on the Great Books program, in collaboration with his long-time friend and confidant, Mortimer Adler. Between 1944 and 1946, the Downtown College of the University of Chicago had served as the vehicle for organizing Great Books discussion classes; but despite its quite extraordinary success in reaching out to new clienteles, Adler felt constrained by the musty academic atmosphere of conventional adult education. He and

Hutchins shared a flair for attracting attention; and since the task was to reform minds and hearts in a hurry, they mobilized their public relations skills to secure rapid results.

Accordingly, they helped to set up a new corporation, the Great Books Foundation, in July 1947 for the purpose of bringing the message more effectively to the whole nation. In September 1948 the foundation kicked off the campaign by staging a public meeting at Orchestra Hall where Hutchins and Adler conducted a demonstration discussion of Plato's *Apology* before a capacity audience. Stimulated by intense publicity and the political blessing of the mayor of Chicago and the governor of Illinois, who proclaimed a "Great Books Week" for the occasion, response was such that several hundred persons actually had to be turned away from the doors. After this spectacular launch, Adler undertook an evangelistic tour to get Great Books classes started across the nation. *Time* magazine cooperated by carrying a cover story on Hutchins in November, praising the College and the Great Books, which, it declared, constituted 75 percent of the curriculum. Helped by such publicity, Great Books classes did indeed begin to sprout luxuriantly in middle-class suburbs all across the country, just as they had previously done in and around Chicago.[20]

It is impossible to tell whether Adler and Hutchins really believed that they could precipitate the sort of moral transformation that Hutchins had often proclaimed necessary if humanity were to escape atomic destruction simply by getting the generation of adults who were actually in charge of affairs to participate in Great Books discussion classes. But it seemed worth a try, since educating youths was sure to take too long. In addition, Adler, and perhaps Hutchins too, found consorting with rich and powerful men of affairs more attractive than trying to awaken the minds of the young.

Even though Hutchins had abandoned hope of making the university over along rational lines as he understood them, he still could proclaim that Chicago was "not a very good university, simply the best there is."[21] His postwar efforts to make it live up to such a billing concentrated very largely on professorial appointments, for, as he explained to the *Time* correspondent, "The reason Chicago is as good as it is, is that the faculty is of high quality and they are talking to one another."[22]

The most conspicuous example of Hutchins' readiness to take financial risks was the establishment of the three new Institutes in Physical Science, described in the preceding chapter. Financial support from industrial corporations never matched expenses; and, in general, the development of peacetime uses of atomic energy never lived up to the rosy expectations that had prevailed in 1945. We can see now that the university in effect bet on the wrong horse by neglecting computers, another offspring of wartime research. A perhaps apocryphal story may explain why, for it is said that Fermi, when he heard of efforts to build the new machines, declared roundly that they could never work because the vacuum tubes upon which they then depended had too short a life. At the time, he may have been right; but his negative judgment failed to allow for the invention of dependable silicon chips, while his optimism about peacetime applications of atomic energy failed to antici- pate the problems of safety and waste disposal.[23]

Nevertheless, in the years after the war Chicago's physicists and chemists were in the forefront of a very active field of atomic research. Fermi became the acknowledged leader of a brilliant group of colleagues and graduate stu- dents who were attracted by his well-deserved reputation. The heroic days of atomic science were already fading into the past, but there were important and unexpected side effects from the physicists' and chemists' expanding mastery of nuclear processes. For example, the use of radioactive trace ele- ments in medicine allowed doctors in Billings Hospital and elsewhere to at- tain a new precision in understanding physiological chemistry, and archae- ology was profoundly affected by the discovery that radioactive Carbon 14 could be used to indicate absolute dates. Willard F. Libby turned to the Ori- ental Institute for help in testing this remarkable technique on accurately dated bits of wood from ancient Egypt and was able to announce positive results with usefully narrow margins of error on 6 May 1948. It was a notable new archaeological tool and Libby won a Nobel Prize in 1960 for his dis- covery.

Mathematics was another field in which the university renewed its excel- lence after the war. In this case, Hutchins was able to attract Marshall H. Stone from Harvard by promising him a free hand in rebuilding the Depart- ment of Mathematics. Accordingly, as chairman of the department from 1946 to 1952, Stone appointed a galaxy of young men who soon attracted a cluster of brilliant students. It was an international gathering, with André Weil from France, Antoni Zygmund from Poland, and S. S. Chern from China supplementing American talent. According to Saunders MacLane, one of the bright young men Stone attracted to Chicago, the result "was without doubt the leading department of mathematics in the country." He describes it thus: "In this period at Chicago, there was a ferment of ideas, stimulated by the newly assembled faculty and reflected in the development of the remarkable group of students who came to Chicago to study. Reports of this excitement came to other universities; often students came after hearing such reports. (I can name several such cases.) This serves to emphasize the observation that a great department develops in some part because of the presence of outstanding students there."[24]

In the social sciences the rise and fall of graduate departments did not occur so abruptly as in mathematics. But anthropology, economics, and political science all enjoyed periods of renewal after the war. Under Redfield's leadership, Chicago's anthropologists began to extend the dominion of their discipline by considering how peasant societies fitted into the larger context of urban civilizations, while Sherwood Washburn pushed backwards in time by studying human evolution and Robert Braidwood brought newly refined archaeological methods to bear on the transition to agriculture in the ancient Near East. More than other social science departments, Chicago's anthropologists therefore cultivated a vision of the entire human adventure on earth. This presumably appealed to Hutchins, but the department's apogee lay still in the future when Hutchins left the university in 1950, and he never backed Redfield as unrestrainedly as he backed Stone in mathematics.

The same observation applies to economics and political science. Hutchins was influential in bringing Leo Strauss to Chicago in 1949;[25] and he, together with Hans Morgenthau in international relations, brought a more theoretical, Germanic tradition into the department than had reigned in Charles Merriam's day. Strauss, in particular, eventually developed a coterie of admiring students whose impact upon American political science was similar to that of McKeon in philosophy. As for the economics department, it had been distinguished for the rigor of its theory long before the war. Even though one of its most distinguished members, Jacob Viner, resigned to go to Princeton in 1946, its doyen, Frank Knight, remained active until (and after) his retirement in 1951, while younger men, of whom Theodore Schultz and Milton Friedman became the most famous, continued to defend and explore the ramifications of the market as their predecessors had done since before the war.

Like the anthropologists, Chicago's economists tended to expand the domain of their science. They did so, for instance, by applying economic calculus to the formation of human capital, or, as it is more commonly called, to training and education. Eventually, military service and family relations were brought under the economists' scrutiny as well. But in polar opposition to the anthropologists, Chicago's economists paid little or no attention to cultural differences and concentrated attention on industrialized societies where statistics were most abundant and reliable. A rather narrow view of human behavior resulted, but mathematically minded economists and verbally inclined anthropologists did not often talk to one another.

In the humanities division, the Department of English continued to harbor a distinctive school of criticism, though the reformers' energy began to fade as hope of discovering (and agreeing upon) clear criteria of literary excellence slackened among them. In philosophy, McKeon's personal influence within the department and within the university at large far outweighed the influence of anything he wrote. His colleagues so disagreed among themselves that nothing like a school of philosophy emerged from the babble of tongues McKeon provoked. Most of the other humanities departments were running down, clinging to historical and philological traditions of scholarship by applying them to more and more trivial texts.

The Oriental Institute was an exception, partly because of an influx of German refugees, like Benno Landsberger, and partly because, under the leadership of Henri Frankfort, Egyptologists and Assyriologists began to talk seriously to one another for the first time. In the 1940s, Frankfort organized a very fruitful faculty seminar to bring the two traditions of learning together. As a consequence, even Egyptologists were eventually persuaded that Mesopotamian civilization antedated and influenced that of Egypt—thus reversing a longstanding belief in Egypt's superior antiquity.[26]

In the biological sciences no comparable burst of intellectual innovation manifested itself. Perhaps Sewall Wright's lifelong study of genetics, in the course of which he worked out a mathematical theory of genetic drift and the mechanics of species differentiation, ought to count; but he worked by himself and founded no school. Much the same may be said of Charles Huggins, whose studies of cancer later won him a Nobel Prize. But in general and overall, the biological sciences did not flourish at Chicago after the war, and the perennial problems of hospital finance and staffing continued to strain the university's resources severely.

Among the professional schools, the Law School experienced the strongest postwar recovery. The broadened curriculum developed in the late 1930s really caught on, allowing the Law School to give its graduates better training in jurisprudence, economics, and psychology than before the war. In 1949, when Hutchins chose Edward Levi to succeed Wilber Katz as dean, they made a deal similar to the deal that had brought Marshall Stone to the mathematics department, for Levi accepted only on condition that he be allowed to make at least three distinguished new appointments. By appointing Allison Dunham, Karl Llewellyn and his wife Soia Mentschikoff, Levi was therefore able to assure the Law School of continuing distinction.

The Divinity School, under Dean Bernard Loomer (1945–50), attempted the sort of curricular transformation that had revivified the Law School. It was easy to repudiate the historical outlook upon the study of religion that had dominated the Divinity School curriculum before the war, but finding a satisfactory new basis proved to be impossible. Loomer, who had taught "Philosophy of Religion" before becoming dean, backed systematic theology as the obvious alternative. But he was no diplomat, and his effort to erect a new curriculum upon theology and philosophy at once collided with another serious difficulty troubling the theological schools that had federated in 1943. The fundamental problem was that students preparing to enter the ministry found the training offered by the Federated Theological Faculties unattractive. As a result, the Congregationalist Chicago Theological Seminary saw candidates for the B.D. degree diminish from 101 in 1943 to 39 in 1948. Parallel but less drastic declines occurred in the other seminaries.[27] The issue thus became whether to train ministers, as aforetime, or drive them away by studying religion in some abstract, intellectual way. Loomer was quite unable to resolve the deadlock. Instead, rancorous quarrels broke out, leading to the break up of the federation in the 1950s.

Nothing so painful affected the Graduate Library School and the School of Social Service Administration, but their flow of students was also affected when similar programs started up on other campuses after the war. Under the circumstances, the national roles previously enjoyed by both of these schools could not be maintained. They therefore declined in eminence even while maintaining all of their former professional respectability. As for the School of Business, its postwar efflorescence began only in the 1950s under Lawrence Kimpton's kindlier aegis.

Hutchins' efforts to build up the faculty after the war meant disregarding other problems pressing in upon the university as a whole. In particular, the decay of the neighborhood was starting to affect all aspects of campus life, and in 1949 a new Red scare in the Illinois legislature targeted Chicago and (the newly established) Roosevelt University for special investigation. Investing in a corps of recruiters for the College, beginning in 1948, may have slowed but did not counteract the decline of student numbers that set in after 1946–47. Equally, Hutchins' testimony before a committee of the Illinois legislature could not head off a barrage of unfavorable publicity—directed this time against student radicals rather than against faculty members, as had been the case in the prewar Walgreen hearings. Hutchins' rebuttal: "It would not be in the public interest to exclude students of communistic leanings. If we did, how would they learn better?" won few hearts, however logically compelling it may have been.

Even more serious was the fact that inflation was upsetting university finances. Professors reacted by fretting over the 4E contracts most of them had signed. Higher salaries offered in return for surrendering all outside income to the university according to the 4E contracts no longer seemed just when inflation ate away the increment and handing over earned extra income began to hurt. Tuition increases, which became an annual feature of making up the budget, provoked rather halfhearted but predictable student protests. Another source of friction within the university community was the unionization of staff, beginning in the hospitals, with some accompanying strikes. Fund-raising efforts, though successful by prewar standards, nevertheless fell short of matching increasing expenditures. The result was a deficit, which reached really serious proportions by 1950.

Under these circumstances, it is not very surprising that Hutchins decided to accept an invitation to become an officer of the newly established Ford Foundation. Paul Hoffman, a one-time student at Chicago and member of the Board of Trustees, headed the new foundation. Its enormous resources were certain to give it a great influence on American academic life and, indeed, on American society at large. Hutchins could therefore hope and expect that by giving money away for good causes, instead of seeking it as he had done so persistently for twenty years and more, he would be able to advance the reform of education and society more effectually than he could do by remaining at Chicago.

Hutchins' long-standing restlessness at the university was not exactly a secret, yet when he announced his decision to leave, on 19 December 1950, it came as a shock. The Council immediately passed a resolution, declaring that "no greater tragedy could happen to the university than for Mr. Hutchins to persist in his decision to resign."[28] His farewell address to the faculty at the annual trustees' dinner on 19 January 1951 was an emotional occasion despite (or because of) the despairing tone of his remarks. His administration, he declared, had been a moral failure "without any notable progress being made towards the creation of a dedicated community." In departing, "I carry with me the accumulated sins of twenty years." In a farewell address to students in February he was rather more flattering, remarking that they "have been the inspiration of my life and have given it such meaning as it had." Yet he chided them as well for their "determined insistence that you are neurotic" when in fact an educated person's "mission here on earth is to change the environment, not to adjust to it." [29]

On that defiant note he departed from Rockefeller Chapel where he had been inaugurated, a conquering hero, a little more than twenty years before. He was fifty-one years of age, graying at the temples, but hopeful still that from his new position he could carry through the reform of education and of society that he had advocated for so many years at Chicago. Yet his later years turned into such a dismal anticlimax that shortly before his death, he declared: "My life has been an entire failure." [30]

That judgment disregards his imprint on the University of Chicago. He made it a lively seat of intellectual debate throughout his presidency, and, at the College level, implanted a tradition of caring about general education that still endures. He made the university different from other institutions of higher learning and allowed us to believe, with some plausibility, that what was being done at Chicago was purer, better, and more genuinely intellectual than anything done elsewhere. Smugness and self-delusion may have entered in; and, as I have been at pains to point out, there were limitations to the viewpoints propagated on campus in Hutchins' day. But when all appropriate reservations have been weighed, a residue of truth remains. Chicago was unique. It was vibrant. It was serious. And it was energetic in the pursuit of truth.

The aspiration for intellectual excellence that Hutchins expressed and embodied still remains alive, along with his specific heritage of emphasis upon general education. Consequently, Hutchins has the right to stand beside Harper as symbolic of all that makes the University of Chicago important in the nation and in the world. Such a role ought not to be reckoned as "failure."

Still, Hutchins' failure was real enough. It arose from having impossibly high expectations, of himself and of those around him. In a secular, urban environment he wanted to build a cohesive moral community like that in which he had grown up at Oberlin before World War I on the basis of intellect alone. By the time he left Chicago for the Ford Foundation that ideal had lost most of its resonance within the university community, and beyond it as well. In that sense, Hutchins was a quixotic character, even in the splendor of his youth. Yet nearly everyone associated with the university he praised so extravagantly and goaded so persistently remembered him with awe, admiration, and indeed with love. He was that kind of man: and the university he presided over came to occupy a distinctive niche among the institutions of higher learning in the United States in large part because of his public presence and private influence upon those around him.

For a few years, it became Hutchins' University almost as much as it had once been Harper's; but as I hope I have shown, institutional inertia, together with the university's urban, national, and international settings, limited the impact even of so charismatic a figure as Robert Maynard Hutchins. Interaction of the man, the place, and the times is the stuff of history everywhere and always. What was unusual about Hutchins' University was the quality of mind and character that pervaded the community, the seriousness and energy of debate, and the intellectual stimulation it provided for thousands of students and hundreds of faculty members. Therein lay the greatness of the Hutchins era at the University of Chicago. His success ought to be measured by the remarkable way he provoked and sustained the cacophony of voices that constituted the university under his administration. His failure to prevail in all disputed matters (however large it loomed for him in retrospect) was the condition of his success, for what he strove for was a glorious, gleaming, glittering—and unattainable—ideal.

EPILOGUE

When Lawrence Kimpton was inaugurated as chancellor of the University of Chicago on 13 April 1951, he inherited a very difficult situation. An unbalanced budget had somehow to be balanced at a time when shrinking enrollments meant diminished tuition income and when a deteriorating neighborhood threatened the survival of a middle-class style of life in Hyde Park. Desperate circumstances generated desperate suggestions, such as the transfer of undergraduate instruction to Aspen, Colorado, or perhaps only to Mt. Carroll, Illinois, where, in 1950, Shimer College had revivified a long-standing affiliation with Chicago, dating back to Harper's time, by becoming the first and only other institution to model itself on the Hutchins' college. But the experiment at Shimer was never a real success, and flight to some suburban or small-town environment was a cowardly answer to the problems of black-white relations on Chicago's South Side.

Instead the trustees and Chancellor Kimpton decided to change priorities from those that had prevailed under Hutchins. First of all, the budget had to be brought back into balance. This required severe cutbacks. Tenured faculty, invited elsewhere, were often encouraged to depart; and since the University of California system was then beginning to expand very rapidly, a massive migration from the Midway set in. At a more junior level, most assistant professors were dismissed when their contracts expired. This had the effect of dispersing a majority of the College faculty. Since the number of students in the College was also shrinking at an annual rate of between 12 and 15 percent, drastic cutbacks in the College made budgetary sense, however costly to the morale and elan of those who remained behind.

Balancing the budget certainly hurt, but the purpose was to permit the university to survive and, eventually, to flourish anew on Chicago's South Side. To make that future possible, Kimpton and the trustees decided to

166

invest substantial sums from the endowment in local real estate. The university then sought to manage such holdings in a way that would maintain the existing middle-class patterns of life in Hyde Park-Kenwood and check the encroachment of slums. Additional measures were clearly called for, including the mobilization of Block Groups to maintain local morale and report violations of housing-code regulations to appropriate enforcement authorities. In 1952, the South East Chicago Commission was established to combat crime in the university community, sustained both by private contributions and by a subvention from the university. Finally, federal funds were secured for urban renewal. This meant, in practice, the destruction of substandard housing and its replacement with new and rather expensive townhouses.

The aim of allowing a racially mixed neighborhood to retain middle-class standards and patterns of life was in fact achieved. Often, enforcing housing-code provisions did mean depriving a black landlord of income derived from multiple occupancies of a single-family dwelling; and efforts to combat crime also tended to pit whites against black offenders. But middle-class black families also wanted safe streets, and whites tried hard to prevent their defense of the neighborhood from turning into a crusade against blacks. I think it is true that no other urban community in the United States managed to fend off an expanding black ghetto by mingling blacks and whites in roughly equal proportions while also maintaining a middle-class style of life. It took something like ten years, after which the frontier of black expansion within the city moved to other neighborhoods and the extraordinary pressures of the fifties on Hyde Park-Kenwood diminished. As a result, the university community stabilized on a racially mixed basis that survived with only minor perturbations into the 1990s. The outcome was a genuine triumph, unmatched elsewhere in the United States so far as I know. Kimpton and those who helped him manage community relations during these years deserve full credit for the upshot.

Costs, financial and psychological, were nonetheless substantial; and for a long time, the problems of the neighborhood made recruitment of faculty and of students much more difficult than would otherwise have been the case. Under the circumstances, Kimpton concluded that the early entrance program for the College would have to be abandoned. Parents were unwilling to send youngsters to Chicago at so tender an age; and the fact that the College B.A. was unacceptable at other institutions was a serious handicap as well. Accordingly, after months of deliberation by faculty committees, the issue came before the Council on 8 May 1953, and by a vote of 29 to 16 the

Council restored a standard pattern for undergraduate study, aimed exclusively at high school graduates and allocating two years to general education followed by two years for more advanced work under departmental jurisdiction. The trustees ratified the action at once, so that the university's undergraduate program no longer differed from the norm as had been the case since 1943.

Dean Ward resigned in protest, and, thanks to Hutchins, made a new career with the Ford Foundation. The College faculty, which had resisted alteration of the Hutchins college almost unanimously, now had to try to fit a four-year curriculum into a mere two years. Instead of rising to the challenge by designing new courses to fit the new circumstances, each staff dug in its heels, trying to defend the claim of existing courses to a place in the reduced general studies curriculum as best it could. Since there were fourteen courses vying for eight slots, the jostling that resulted was undignified to say the least. But jobs were at stake, and self-interest, narrowly construed, prevailed over any serious effort to rethink and renew the pattern of general studies.

Eventually, strenuous recruitment restored student numbers, and the College faculty began to adjust the fractured curriculum that survived the initial struggle by taking more cognizance of the non-Western world. And throughout the most difficult period of retrenchment, the university's commitment to general education remained firmly in place and continues still. In that sense, Hutchins' legacy was never repudiated and remains characteristic of the campus today as much as in the 1930s.

For the university as a whole, Kimpton's policies meant survival, but only at a lower level. By 1957, a more or less objective rating of graduate departments placed Chicago sixth in the nation, behind Harvard, California, Yale, Columbia, and Michigan. In 1925, the same method of comparison had put Chicago second only to Harvard. Slippage was greatest in biology, where Chicago rated fifteenth in the nation in 1957; least in social science where Chicago came in still at the head of the pack.[1]

In retrospect it is clear that Chicago's decline began long before Kimpton took charge of the university. The most important turning point, perhaps, was the failure of Hutchins' plan for creating a genuinely comprehensive private university for the city of Chicago by merging with Northwestern University and the Lewis Institute, setting up a series of junior colleges and technical institutes on the north, south, and west sides, and thus identifying the university with a broad spectrum of Chicago's needs and aspirations. Instead, after negotiations for the merger collapsed in 1934, Hutchins turned more and more toward trying the make the university over into a dedicated community of scholars, whose shared intellectual life, by its very intensity and abstraction from practical matters, meant isolation from the urban setting and from the mainstream of American society.

To be sure, geographical and social circumstances made it improbable that the University of Chicago could have remained ahead of other institutions indefinitely. As Americans came to recognize that academic research was worth paying for, other universities were bound to catch up with Harper's pioneering. As other parts of the country experienced sustained economic growth, the boom atmosphere that had prevailed in Chicago and the Middle West before World War I shifted elsewhere and was soon harnessed to support the rise of great universities in California and Texas just as Harper had been able to connect Chicago's boom mentality with the rise of his university. In addition, the University of Chicago was severely handicapped in trying to keep up with leading schools of the Ivy League because the sons and daughters of wealthy families from all over the country flocked to those institutions in such numbers after World War I that fund-raising became comparatively easy for them. In sharp contrast, Chicago played a significant national role as a social escalator, being wide open to talent regardless of ethnic origin or economic class in a way no other private university quite equalled. This was, and is, a noble role, but it did not produce very many wealthy alumni and made fund-raising as well as the recruitment of students of merely average intellect and ambition rather difficult.

Given these circumstances, it certainly seems that the University of Chicago was destined to lose its initial primacy in research and graduate study, regardless of what its presidents did. Hutchins postponed rather than hastened the university's decline, for his personal charm and the publicity he attracted kept the university very much in the public eye throughout his tenure of office. Certainly, he generated a sense of excitement on campus. The College community, students and teachers alike, really believed that Chicago's curriculum was the best there was anywhere in the world. For them, and for a good many others whom Hutchins attracted to the university in one capacity or another, the university was a very special place. Their presence helped to make it so; but so did Hutchins, with his lofty manner, electric wit, and rhetorical extravagances.

He also made it a very special time, remembered by those who lived through it with awe. Greatness, or something very much like it, walked among us then; and, in due course, when expansion again became possible under Presidents George W. Beadle (1960–69) and Edward H. Levi (1968–75), Hutchins' heritage renewed itself, and, with Harper's, haunts and inspires the campus still.

NOTES

1. The University of Chicago in 1929

1. Harold S. Wechsler, *The Qualified Student: A History of Selective Admission in America* (New York, 1977), pp. 131ff., gives details.

2. In 1928 the comptroller estimated that closure of the Junior College (i.e., freshmen and sophomore years) and foregoing the annual tuition income of $520,800 would save only half that amount in reduced expenses, thus involving a net loss of about $260,400 per annum for the university (Regenstein Library, University Archives, Presidential Papers, 1925–45, Box 21, folder 9).

3. Martin Bulmer, *The Chicago School of Sociology: Institutionalization, Diversity, and the Rise of Sociological Research* (Chicago, 1984), gives a workmanlike account of the subject.

4. Cf. George W. Stocking, Jr.'s incisive pamphlet, published by the Regenstein Library in connection with the fiftieth anniversary of the Department of Anthropology in 1979, entitled *Anthropology at Chicago: Tradition, Discipline, Department.*

2. Honeymoon on the Midway, 1929–1931

1. A private, domestic scandal was the occasion and perhaps the real reason for Mason's resignation; but it is also possible that fundraising had lost its charms for him. At any rate, he crossed to the other side of the street and started to give money away as head of the Rockefeller Foundation (1929–36).

2. Barry Karl, *Charles E. Merriam and the Study of Politics* (Chicago, 1974), pp. 157–62, provides an informed account of these events on the basis of the papers of two of the members of the faculty committee—Merriam and the historian William E. Dodd. Cf. also Benjamin McArthur, "Taking a Chance on Youth," *University of Chicago Magazine* 82 (Fall 1989): 28–31.

3. Harry S. Ashmore, *Unseasonable Truths: The Life of Robert Maynard Hutchins* (Boston, 1989), p. 59.

4. The elder became a missionary and teacher in China; the younger succeeded his father as president of Berea College. All three sons thus followed their father into education; and they all maintained cordial relations with their parents, despite divergences in religious views and observances.

5. Cf. Ashmore, *Unseasonable Truths*, pp. 4–5.

6. Ibid., p. 89.

7. Robert Maynard Hutchins, *Education for Freedom* (Baton Rouge, 1943), pp. 6–7.

8. Regenstein Library, University Archives, R. M. Hutchins Papers, Box 19, folder 1, speech entitled "The Yale Law School in 1928."

9. Hutchins' inaugural speech received extensive newspaper coverage, but these quotations come from a printed version that was distributed to Chicago alumni "not because it is an epoch-making document, but because it sets forth briefly some of the plans we now have in mind for the development of the University of Chicago."

10. Regenstein Library, University Archives, R. M. Hutchins Papers, Box 19, folder 1, speech at the Inauguration dinner.

11. Regenstein Library, University Archives, R. M. Hutchins Papers, Box 19, folder 1, speech to student assembly, 20 November 1929.

12. Regenstein Library, University Archives, R. M. Hutchins Papers, Box 19, folder 3, RMH speech, 20 November 1930, to secondary school administrators: "I have been asked to speak on the reorganization of the University of Chicago, apparently because it was felt that that at least was a subject I might know something about. Nothing of course is further from the truth. It is common knowledge that University presidents spend their time in addressing associations of high school principals, going to football games and taking credit for the things their associates do in their absence. To this rule I am no exception."

13. In our time, when economists have a near monopoly on public wisdom, it is interesting to remember that President Hoover turned to sociologists for guidance when the depression hit. The result was *Recent Social Trends*, a massive survey of American society, edited by William F. Ogburn, professor of sociology at Chicago, and published in 1933. The fact that empirical information, even when painstakingly accumulated, gave no hint of what to do became embarrassingly evident as the enterprise went forward. Sociology, as initially conceived by Thomas and Park, never recovered from this failure; and only during World War II, when a new style of macroeconomics showed how theory, information, and action could be united effectively, did a different branch of social science recover the prestige sociologists had lost.

14. Ruml soon left the university to become an officer of Macy's department store in New York, from which unlikely vantage point he attained national importance by persuading Congress (almost single-handedly) to collect income taxes by withholding from wages.

15. Mortimer J. Adler, *An Intellectual Autobiography: Philosopher at Large* (New York, 1977), pp. 107ff., gives a vivid account of their first encounter and its background. Much of what follows derives from this book, as well as from long-standing acquaintance and personal discussion with Mr. Adler. He, however, disagrees with many of the views I express about him, about Hutchins, and about their impact on the university.

16. Almost a decade after commencing his search, Hutchins wrote to Adler on 21 July 1939: "I have read the *Politics* and it leaves me just as confused as it did the first time I read it." Regenstein Library, University Archives, R. M. Hutchins Papers, Box 4, folder 7.

17. Adler did not become a self-professed Thomist until 1938 and parted com-

pany with Roman Catholic philosophers in 1943 when he discovered logical errors in Aquinas's proof of the existence of God. Adler was, however, a convinced Aristotelian when he arrived on campus in 1930 and had begun to explore St. Thomas's elaboration of Aristotelianism with lively and sympathetic interest. He was therefore condemned as a Thomist by Chicago's amazed and offended professors at a time when he had not yet identified himself as such.

18. Thomism was, of course, official doctrine for Catholic seminaries; but these institutions had almost no connection with American Protestant (or ex-Protestant) universities, since their function was to train priests to guard the faithful against the corruptions of American life, including not least the irreligion of American higher education. Departments of philosophy and religion in Catholic universities were equally, or almost equally, isolated from secular philosophy, and for the same reason: they were charged with the defense of an official doctrine against corruption coming from outside and therefore kept very much to themselves.

19. Regenstein Library, University Archives, R. M. Hutchins Papers, Box 4, folder 7, letter, 27 March 1929. The letter concluded: "P.S. I passed all the exams and am now MJA, Ph.D."

20. Adler had in mind the creation of a center of philosophical studies that would correct the errors of the various disciplines independently of the Department of Philosophy—which itself was a prime candidate for correction. But when opposition to the appointment of his two friends became vehement, this project was a first casualty, and I do not know how firmly Hutchins had ever endorsed it.

21. Hutchins sought outside advice and circulated a list of candidates among a number of well-known philosophers in the United States and abroad. Adler's two young friends did not get high marks, and McKeon was angered at having his reputation thus put on the block surreptitiously. The whole procedure had the effect of advertising the dispute at Chicago to the academic profession at large. Cf. Adler, *Philosopher at Large*, pp. 145–47.

22. Ibid., pp. 134–35.

23. Edward Shils, "Robert Maynard Hutchins," *American Scholar* (Winter 1990): pp. 214–16, records his hostile personal reaction to Adler's performance on this occasion and his frustration at the incapacity of those who argued against him. This seminar took place during the 1933–34 academic year.

24. This lecture was part of a series of public lectures on the social sciences organized by Dean Ruml. In March 1990, Mr. Adler kindly sent me a copy of the notes he used on this occasion.

25. Regenstein Library, University Archives, R. M. Hutchins Papers, Addenda, Box 72, folder 1, letter, 30 September 1936. Redfield was reacting to Hutchins' recently published book, *The Higher Learning in America*, when he wrote these words.

26. Regenstein Library, University Archives, R. M. Hutchins Papers, Box 19, folder 1.

3. Chiaroscuro of the Depression Years, 1931–1936

1. Regenstein Library, University Archives, Presidential Papers, 1925–45, Box 87, folder 4.

2. Otto Struve, "The Story of an Observatory (The Fiftieth Anniversary of the

Yerkes Observatory)," *Popular Astronomy* 55, nos. 5 and 6 (May and June 1947): pp. 18–21, provides many vivid details.

3. Regenstein Library, University Archives, Presidential Papers, 1925–45, Box 74, folder 6.

4. Fifty-seven professors retired between 1930 and 1936, according to the *President's Report to the Board of Trustees, 1935–36.* I have not found any comparable general index of new professorial appointments, but the total was assuredly much smaller.

5. In 1936, likewise, a straw poll of the faculty conducted by the student newspaper favored Landon over Roosevelt, though this time only by 3.6 percent. The Socialist candidate got just 1.1 percent of the faculty vote.

6. Regenstein Library, University Archives, R. M. Hutchins Papers, Box 20, folder 2.

7. According to the Registrar's Report for 1944–45, student enrollments were as follows:

	College	Divisions	Prof. Schools	At Large	Downtown	Total
1929–30	2,017	6,466	3,161	338	3,824	14,245
1930–31	1,999	6,300	2,964	383	3,654	13,646
1931–32	1,911	5,662	2,125	516	3,425	12,359
1932–33	1,782	5,056	2,284	379	3,760	11,960
1933–34	1,738	5,063	2,660	535	3,894	13,118
1934–35	1,833	5,324	3,087	504	3,206	13,050
1935–36	1,894	5,120	3,103	529	3,106	12,847
1936–37	1,901	5,228	2,955	598	2,734	12,788

8. Regenstein Library, University Archives, Presidential Papers, 1925–45, Box 19a, folder 2.

9. Regenstein Library, University Archives, *Report of the President to the Board of Trustees, Academic Years 1930–34,* mimeographed report, 1 February 1935.

10. Regenstein Library, University Archives, Presidential Papers, 1925–45, Box 75, folder 4.

11. Regenstein Library, University Archives, Presidential Papers, 1925–45, Box 67, folder 1. W. F. Cramer to Vice President Filbey, 24 March 1933.

12. Regenstein Library, University Archives, Presidential Papers, Box 60a, folder 3, memo to Hutchins, 16 December 1933. This memorandum was stimulated by an inquiry from Northwestern. President Scott scrawled at the bottom of the letter in which he asked Hutchins for the information: "Your percentage is supposed to be 99%." Obviously, anti-Semitic feeling in Evanston was fueling criticism of the proposed merger between Northwestern and Chicago.

13. Harold S. Wechsler, *The Qualified Student: A History of Selective Admission in America* (New York, 1977), pp. 131ff.

14. Chicago did discriminate against Jews but far less so than other institutions. An undated study prepared for Vice President Filbey showed 115 gentile students refused admission out of an applicant pool of 1,048, and 115 rejections of Jews, out of an applicant pool of 465. The average aptitude test score for rejected Jews was 57

as against an average of 32 for gentiles rejected (Regenstein Library, University Archives, Presidential Papers, 1925–45, Box 75, folder 4).

15. Regenstein Library, University Archives, Presidential Papers, 1925–45, Box 57, folder 4. There was one exception. When the City of Chicago set up four new junior colleges in the early 1930s they instituted exact carbon copies of the Chicago surveys. For a year or two, Chicago lecturers were regularly invited to appear at each junior college for a fee of $20 per lecture.

16. Regenstein Library, University Archives, *Report of the President to the Board of Trustees for the Academic Years 1930–34.*

17. The university's lead was largely due to the enthusiasm of Judith Weller, a young woman who, on graduating from Chicago, became a powerful figure at radio station WMAQ. She invented the Roundtable, helped to promote other broadcasts from the Midway, and, more generally, became a leading advocate of serious programming within NBC. She remained a special patron (and critic) of the Roundtable throughout its long career.

18. Adler, *Philosopher at Large*, pp. 163–67, offers a vivacious account of the affair, which may also be followed in the pages of the *Maroon* as microfilmed in Regenstein Library.

19. Regenstein Library, University Archives, Presidential Papers, 1925–45, Box 30, folder 9. These surprising figures were collected in connection with the abolition of intercollegiate football in 1939. They show Michigan with eighteen Big Ten Championships, Chicago with eleven, Illinois with six, Indiana with five, Minnesota and Northwestern with three, Iowa with two, Ohio State with one, and both Purdue and Wisconsin with none! According to these same figures, in 1938–39 Chicago offered eighty-two athletic scholarships to Michigan's seventeen; but much had already gone undercover, at Chicago as well as elsewhere. Harold Swift, chairman of the Board of Trustees, for example, had a friend in California who recruited football players for Chicago, mostly from among graduates of California's junior colleges; and Swift exhibited persistent care and concern for his "California boys" after they got to campus (cf. Presidential Papers, 1925–45, Box 78, folder 7). Just what financial inducements Swift may have arranged are not recorded, but suitably private gifts to deserving athletes probably played a part in sustaining a regular migration of football players from California to the Midway.

20. On 24 February 1934, Hutchins was called "advisor to Moscow" in a story whose headline read: "U of C Prof Attacks US at Communist Rally."

21. The text of Hutchins' speech on this occasion was published in the *Daily Maroon* (19 April 1935, p. 2), from which these quotes are taken.

22. Sidney Hyman, *The Lives of William Benton* (Chicago, 1969), pp. 3–6, 160ff., describes how Benton came to Chicago.

23. Reprinted in R. M. Hutchins, *No Friendly Voice* (Chicago, 1936). He rated this his best speech in an oral interview near the end of his life. Transcript of this interview by George W. Dell, 6 January 1975, is available in Regenstein Library, Special Collections.

24. R. M. Hutchins, *The Higher Learning in America*, pp. 97, 105.

25. Ibid., pp. 66, 95.

26. R. M. Hutchins, "University Education," *Yale Review* (Summer 1936): pp. 665–82.

27. Harry D. Gideonse, *The Higher Learning in a Democracy: A Reply to President Hutchins' Critique of the American University* (New York, 1937), p. 33.

28. Ibid., pp. 1, 25.

29. M. J. Adler, *Philosopher at Large,* pp. 173–76, gives a restrained, rather self-serving account of this episode. For a more colorful version, written largely from Buchanan's point of view, see Ashmore, *Unseasonable Truths,* pp. 136–41.

4. The Drift toward War, 1937–1941

1. Regenstein Library, University Archives, R. M. Hutchins Papers, Box 18.

2. Otto Struve, "The Story of an Observatory, Presented at a Staff Meeting of the Yerkes Observatory, 25 March 1947," pp. 23–24, describes how Hutchins approached him in 1935, asking him to nominate suitably young (under 35) astronomers of world-class ability.

3. With the grace of an accomplished man of letters, David Daiches, *A Third World* (Sussex, 1971), pp. 12–13, describes how Hutchins recruited him and his arrival in Chicago.

4. For sidelights on Shils's personal connections with Hutchins, see his essay "Robert Maynard Hutchins," *American Scholar* (January 1990): 211–35.

5. Regenstein Library, University Archives, R. M. Hutchins Papers, Box 4, letter, Adler to Hutchins, 1 July 1938. In the same letter, Adler accused McKeon of fearing Catholicism. Obviously, Adler still felt that disagreement with his own views could only be attributed to stupidity or to a moral defect.

6. Adler, *Philosopher at Large,* pp. 185–90; *The Daily Maroon,* 14 November 1940.

7. Regenstein Library, University of Chicago Archives, Reports of the President to the Board of Trustees.

8. Ibid.

9. Average attendance was 37 out of the 200 eligible full professors according to Hutchins' report to the trustees. The Senate Committee on University Policy, which was an elected body, allowed persons whom Hutchins described as "poor representatives" of their schools and departments to block his initiatives routinely.

10. Regenstein Library, University Archives, Presidential Papers, 1925–45, Box 36, folder 13, memorandum on "The Province of a Department of History." Crane concluded that historians should confine themselves to past politics, though why he felt historians rather than politicians (or political scientists) were qualified for that role was left unclear.

11. Daiches, *A Third World,* p. 12.

12. Ibid., pp. 43, 45.

13. Listener statistics were indeed impressive. In July 1938 a survey found that 12 percent of all congressmen listened to the Roundtable habitually; 8.5 percent of all radios were tuned to the program across the entire country in June 1938; eighty-one stations carried the Roundtable in December 1939, more than twice as many as eighteen months before. These statistics come from Regenstein Library, University Archives, Presidential Papers, 1925–45, Box 69, folder 20.

14. Cf. Hyman, *The Lives of William Benton,* pp. 202–4, 241–42.

15. Such departments were set up in every Big Ten school except Chicago between 1910, when Wisconsin led the way, and 1929, when Purdue followed suit. Most of them were founded in the early 1920s. Cf. Robin Lester, "The Rise, Decline and Fall of Intercollegiate Football at the University of Chicago, 1890–1940," Ph.D. diss., University of Chicago, Department of History, 1974, p. 310.

16. Ibid., p. 261.

17. Ibid., p. 234.

18. Ibid., p. 270.

19. *The Daily Maroon,* 29 November 1938. The Bears were having trouble negotiating for use of Wrigley Field at the time.

20. Cf. Ashmore, *Unseasonable Truths,* pp. 191–99.

21. Texts of both speeches are available in Regenstein Library, University Archives, R. M. Hutchins Papers, Box 23, folder 1. The second speech was broadcast by The Town Meeting of the Air, 26 May 1941. For an account of Hutchins' rather reluctant entry into this controversy see Ashmore, *Unseasonable Truths,* pp. 210–19.

22. These quotes come from the same two speeches; a "Committee for Humanity First" being affirmed in the Town Meeting of the Air, whereas the second sentence appeared in his earlier radio address.

23. Harold Ickes, *The Secret Diaries of Harold L. Ickes, III: The Lowering Clouds 1939–41* (New York, 1954), p. 472, attributed Hutchins' intervention in the national debate to "just resentment over the manner in which the Administration has treated him, plus political ambition." On p. 256 of this same volume, Ickes recorded how Hutchins called on him in July 1940 at the time of the Democratic convention in Chicago, trying to promote himself as candidate for the vice presidency. Ickes therefore had good reason to think that Hutchins had political ambitions. Moreover, Hutchins had been publicly touted for the presidency in 1940 before Roosevelt made it clear that he would run for a third term. Many of his intimates, mesmerized by his remarkable personal charisma, had long believed that the presidency of the United States was the only role fit for such a man. In 1990, as wise and experienced a person as Edward Levi affirmed that if he had not been handicapped by his wife's irresponsible conduct, Hutchins would surely have become a viable candidate for U.S. President.

5. The War Years, 1941–1946

1. Ashmore, *Unseasonable Truths,* pp. 222–23.

2. Robert M. Hutchins, "State of the University 1944," 19 October 1944, in *State of the University, 1938–1946, 1949* (Public Relations Office), University Archives.

3. Regenstein Library, University Archives, Presidential Papers, 1925–45, Box 92, folder 6.

4. Regenstein Library, University Archives, Presidential Papers, 1925–45, Box 92, folder 5.

5. This was decided on 18 December 1941 in the immediate aftermath of Pearl Harbor. Cf. Henry De Wolf Smyth, *Atomic Energy for Military Purposes: The Official*

Report on the Development of the Atom Bomb under the Auspices of the United States Government, 1940–1945 (Princeton, 1946), p. 78. I have relied on this official document, prepared by a veteran of the enterprise, both for dates and details and for a sense of the way participants felt when the wartime effort first became public knowledge.

6. Ibid., pp. 76–77.

7. Regenstein Library, University Archives, Presidential Papers, 1925–45, Box 92, folder 5.

8. Ibid.

9. Reproduced in Smyth, *Atomic Energy for Military Purposes,* p. 254.

10. Alfred DeGrazia, *The Student,* unpublished autobiographical manuscript, pp. 374ff.

11. Reuben Frodin, "Very Simple but Thoroughgoing," in *The Idea and Practice of General Education: An Account of the College of the University of Chicago by Present and Former Members of the Faculty* (Chicago, 1950), p. 67. Frodin's account of the tumultuous political process that generated the Hutchins Four-year College is by far the most accurate and accessible record available, though he deliberately glosses over the bitterness of controversy among the faculty, which was intense.

12. Regenstein Library, University Archives, Presidential Papers, 1925–45, Box 86, folder 11. One historian, three scientists, and one language teacher voted to retain the existing surveys. One biologist and one economist joined the three teachers of English (plus one faculty member whose field I do not know) to tip the balance within the committee.

13. Regenstein Library, University Archives, Presidential Papers, 1925–45, Box 86, folder 11. Hutchins got some sort of encouragement from the presidents of Stanford, Cornell, and Texas in this matter, but when the storm of criticism broke, none of them made a move to follow suit.

14. Regenstein Library, University Archives, Presidential Papers, 1925–45, Box 22, folders 8–13 contain abundant materials about the public reaction to the new B.A. degree. Charles H. Judd was the only person of standing among educationists who supported the move, but his arguments were easily discounted since he was a professor at Chicago.

15. Vote counting ahead of time, in so amorphous a body as the University Senate, was almost impossible, and Hutchins may not have realized in advance how quickly the majority tallied in January had eroded away.

16. As a lawyer, Hutchins knew his rights. Because the vote was by written ballot, he was entitled to vote; but most of the faculty were not familiar with this technicality of Roberts' Rules of Order, and when the news spread, the defeated party felt that he had cheated them in still another way in order to prevail.

17. Undated carbon copy in my possession, but written in July 1944 as shown by Hutchins' letter of acknowledgment, dated 19 July 1944.

18. Robert M. Hutchins, *Freedom, Education and the Fund: Essays and Addresses, 1946–56* (New York, 1956), pp. 185–86.

19. Regenstein Library, University Archives, Presidential Papers, 1925–45, Box 87, folder 8.

20. Regenstein Library, University Archives, Presidential Papers, 1925–45, Box

86, folder 12. This memorandum is a striking example of Hutchins' ability to write a powerful legal brief, being remarkably concise and rhetorically persuasive.

21. Regenstein Library, University Archives, Presidential Papers, 1925–45, Box 41, folder 7.

22. Regenstein Library, University Archives, Presidential Papers, 1925–45, Box 19, folder 1. The occasion was the annual trustees' dinner for the faculty.

23. Regenstein Library, University Archives, Presidential Papers, 1925–45, Box 41, folder 2.

24. Ibid.

25. John U. Nef, *The Search for Meaning* (Washington, D.C., 1973), a confused and confusing autobiographical essay written in his old age, opens a (perhaps distorting) window on Nef's personality and interests.

26. Regenstein Library, University Archives, Addenda to Hutchins' Papers, Box 72, folder 2. This document carries no date and was never acted on; but Nef's reaction to the faculty memorial of February 1944 denouncing a putative scheme for an Institute of Liberal Studies suggests that it ought to date from about the same time—or perhaps a bit earlier.

27. Hutchins often had to cancel scheduled evening appearances downtown because his wife objected to letting him out of her sight after the end of ordinary office hours. In this and other ways Maude deliberately hampered her husband's career. Cf. Ashmore, *Unseasonable Truths*, pp. 287–92.

28. Herman Kogan, *The Great EB: The Story of the Encyclopedia Britannica* (Chicago, 1958), pp. 254–59; and Sidney Hyman, *The Lives of William Benton*, pp. 245–62, give details of this rather complicated negotiation and its resolution.

29. Hyman, *The Lives of William Benton*, pp. 286–89; Kogan, *The Great EB*, pp. 260–67. By 1990, 763,316 sets of the Great Books had been sold, according to Mortimer Adler's records, making it a publisher's dream.

30. Regenstein Library, University Archives, R. M. Hutchins Papers, Box 7, folder 6 contains details. Hutchins chose the members of the commission himself, yet had difficulty in getting them to agree on anything.

31. Regenstein Library, University Archives, R. M. Hutchins Papers, Box 12, folder 1 has details. Characteristically, Adler, who was among those who helped draft this document, created the major controversy when during a speech in Cleveland he declared that "we must do everything we can to abolish the United States." See *The Congressional Record*, 1 November 1945, speech by John E. Rankin.

32. Regenstein Library, University Archives, Presidential Papers, 1925–45, Box 92, folder 5.

33. Regenstein Library, University Archives, Presidential Papers, 1925–45, Box 1, folder 8. Adler was thinking of the new physics institutes, for he explicitly claimed that he and Scott Buchanan were "as good in philosophy as Fermi and von Neumann etc. are good in physics and math," and deserved the same vote of confidence from Hutchins.

34. Regenstein Library, University Archives, Presidential Papers, 1945–50, Box 32, folder 7. In 1948, Probst suggested that the university ought to move into TV—but by then Benton had departed and with him the real sparkplug behind Chicago's

remarkable role in educational broadcasting disappeared. Consequently, nothing was done, even after a public TV channel started up in the city.

35. Alice Kimball Smith, "The Politics of Control—The Role of Chicago Scientists," in *The Nuclear Chain Reaction—Forty Years Later,* edited by Robert G. Sachs, pp. 54–65 (Chicago, 1984), p. 60.

36. Cf. Edward Levi, "Memories about the McMahon Act," in *The Nuclear Chain Reaction—Forty Years Later,* edited by Robert G. Sachs, pp. 65–67. The most active political leaders among the atomic scientists were refugees from Europe who knew little of American public life. Men like Szilard and Franck, with their memories of German fascism, were far more distrustful of the U.S. government and of the U.S. military than men like Compton. Unlike Szilard, Fermi never put much stock in international control. As an old-fashioned American, eager to get back to his normal, peacetime work, Allison objected vehemently and publicly to military efforts at maintaining secrecy, which he saw as a hindrance to further research. Differences of opinion were very intense within the circle of atomic scientists as well as among laymen and politicians, nearly all of whom wanted to keep the bomb an American monopoly, but were unsure how to do so.

37. Regenstein Library, University Archives, Presidential Papers, 1925–45, Box 26, folder 3. This remarkable and inflammatory speech is also quoted from *in extenso* in Ashmore, *Unseasonable Truths,* pp. 236–40.

38. Regenstein Library, University Archives, R. M. Hutchins Papers, Box 16, folder 7. This memorial passed the Senate, nonetheless, only after an amendment which read: "This Memorial should not be construed to indicate confidence or lack of confidence in the President."

39. Regenstein Library, University Archives, Presidential Papers, 1925–45, Box 41, folder 2. In this memorial, Nef explicitly shifted the blame from Hutchins to "certain members of the faculty" (i.e., McKeon), for the fault of trying to impose a single philosophy on others.

Rival memorials, circulated in advance to gain a maximum number of signatures, produced acute polarization among the faculty. There were odd bedfellows: McKeon went along with Crane. His clash with Nef, in effect, put him in the anti-Hutchins camp despite the fact that he, too, had once disliked departmental sovereignty and was a principal architect of the new College curriculum. Cf. Ashmore, *Unseasonable Truths,* pp. 240–42.

40. Regenstein Library, University Archives, Presidential Papers, 1925–45, Box 41, folder 2.

41. Quoted from "The Organization and Purpose of the University: An Address by Robert M. Hutchins to the Faculty and Students of the Summer Quarter," a published pamphlet, pp. 11–12. The pamphlet can be found in Regenstein Library, University Archives, Robert M. Hutchins Papers, Addenda, Box 10.

42. Hutchins' deteriorating relation with Maude must also have contributed to his agitated state of mind. After unending provocation, he stormed out of the house one morning in 1946 and never returned. Divorce proceedings dragged on until 1948.

43. Frodin, "Very Simple but Thoroughgoing," in *The Idea and Practice of General Education,* p. 79. This vote was itself controversial, for Dean Faust had pruned the

roster of College faculty of several professors from the divisions who taught only part time in the College and whose central loyalty was to their departments. This sort of gerrymandering provoked vigorous protest, especially from some of the biological science departments. Cf. Regenstein Library, University Archives, Presidential Papers, 1925–45, Box 13, folder 3.

44. Lawrence Kimpton reported to Hutchins on 22 August 1946 that Faust was "in a very curious state of mind. He is still very tired. His wife is not well and hates Chicago, and he indicated he might want to leave the institution altogether." Regenstein Library, University Archives, Presidential Papers, 1925–45, Box 12, folder 7.

6. Bloom and Decay: The End of an Era, 1946–1950

1. The Quadrangle Club was private, though most of its members were also members of the faculty, and the club provided a setting for many official and quasi-official university receptions.

Lunchtime conversation at three large "roundtables" in the dining room constituted a key factor in creating and propagating public opinion among the faculty on issues of general concern. The intensity of universitywide politics, described in the preceding chapter, and the general cohesion of the university community depended in some degree on the communications system arising from the informal seating pattern at Quadrangle Club lunches.

2. Edward Shils, "Robert Maynard Hutchins," *The American Scholar* (Spring 1990), pp. 232–33, reports how he tried to alert Hutchins to neighborhood problems, but in vain.

3. Ibid.

4. Regenstein Library, University Archives, Presidential Papers, 1945–50, Box 41, folder 8.

5. These figures come from Robert M. Hutchins, *The State of the University, 1929–49, Covering the Twenty Years of His Administration,* and may be inflated, since a Registrar's *Report to the President* on deposit in Regenstein Library, University Archives, Presidential Papers, 1925–45, Box 67, folder 1, gives a total figure for 1946–47 of only 12,366. The discrepancy perhaps arose from counting—and not counting—Great Books classes.

6. Regenstein Library, University Archives, Presidential Papers, 1945–50, Box 12, folder 5. Cf. ibid., Box 17, folder 8, where another calculation shows that Chicago increased its faculty size, at least proportionately, more than Columbia, Wisconsin, Michigan, or Illinois did between 1940 and 1948.

7. Regenstein Library, University Archives, Presidential Papers, 1945–50, Box 12, folder 3, records the result of an effort to validate the new B.A. degree by having all students graduating from the new program take the standardized Graduate Record Examination in the spring of 1947. On the general education section of the exam, Chicago's average student came in at the 92d percentile; and in specialized fields, 14 percent of Chicago's graduates attained or exceeded the average score despite having taken no specialized courses and being, in most cases, two years younger than those with whom they were being compared.

8. This text was published in 1950.

9. Regenstein Library, University Archives, Presidential Papers, 1945–50, Box 12, folder 5, T. W. Page, "The Two Year Program in Physical Science, 1950."

10. *The Idea and Practice of General Education*, pp. 193–98, reproduces assigned readings lists for these courses as of 1949–50.

11. Joseph J. Schwab's lengthy essay, "The Natural Sciences," in *The Idea and Practice of General Education*, pp. 149–98, by its excessive complexity, illustrates both the strength and weakness of these courses.

12. Eugene Northrup, its creator, refers to "favorable reactions from colleagues at Chicago and elsewhere." See *The Idea and Practice of General Education*, p. 203.

13. Hutchins once said that universities ought to be burnt down once every twenty-five years "lest they get in a rut" (Regenstein Library, University Archives, Papers of R. M. Hutchins, Box 16, folder 5).

14. Redfield returned to campus in 1946–47 and became a member of the Soc II staff. From this position, he began to induce Milton Singer and other members of the staff to take non-Western studies seriously; but effective curricular changes only came about a decade later, with the creation of separate courses in non-Western civilizations that were entirely independent of the social science course that then survived in the core curriculum.

15. Regenstein Library, University Archives, Presidential Papers, 1945–50, Box 12, folder 5. Donald Levine, a future dean of the College and professor of sociology, was leader of the group.

16. Ibid.

17. Regenstein Library, University Archives, Presidential Papers, 1945–50, Box 25, folder 15. It is worth noting, perhaps, that David Broder, who later became a distinguished Washington journalist, was editor of the *Maroon* in 1948–49.

18. In January 1946 at the annual trustees dinner for the faculty, Hutchins announced that there were "only five more years to live" before atomic disaster should be expected. In September 1950, when the five years were almost up he declared to students entering the College, "We are closer to war now than we have been in the last five years . . . Cities and houses in America will be destroyed." Texts of almost all of Hutchins' speeches, arranged chronologically, are available in Regenstein Library, University Archives, Papers of R. M. Hutchins. These citations come thence.

19. James S. Allen, *The Romance of Commerce and Culture: Capitalism, Modernism, and the Chicago-Aspen Crusade for Cultural Reform* (Chicago, 1983), describes this enterprise, and the high hopes surrounding it, with sympathy and penetration.

20. Allen comments: "It looked as though, having left the university through the corridors of adult education and mass publicity . . . the Chicago Bildungsideal might renovate culture after all." Ibid., p. 106.

21. *Time Magazine* cover, 21 November 1949. The story inside, pp. 58–64, identified the quote as something he had said "recently." This famous phrase, completely characteristic of his deprecating wit, does not appear in any other context that I could find.

22. Ibid.

23. Fermi wrote to Hutchins on 14 September 1945: "There is little doubt that the applications [of atomic science] both to medicine and to sciences other than phys-

ics will develop rapidly" (Regenstein Library, University Archives, Papers of R. M. Hutchins, Box 6, folder 3).

24. Saunders MacLane, "Mathematics at the University of Chicago: A Brief History," *A Century of Mathematics in America,* part II (Providence, RI), p. 148. According to MacLane, "The department continued in similar activity until about 1959 when it suddenly came apart."

25. Edward Shils, "Robert Maynard Hutchins," *The American Scholar* (January 1990), p. 223.

26. Another result of this seminar was an exceptionally elegant book by H. and H. A. Frankfort, John A. Wilson, and Thorkild Jacobsen, *The Intellectual Adventure of Ancient Man* (Chicago, 1946).

27. Regenstein Library, University Archives, Presidential Papers, 1945–50, Box 17, folder 1.

28. Regenstein Library, University Archives, Papers of R. M. Hutchins, Box 16, folder 6.

29. Regenstein Library, University Archives, Papers of R. M. Hutchins, speeches.

30. Regenstein Library, University Archives, George W. Dell interview with R. M. Hutchins, 6 January 1975.

Epilogue

1. George W. Pierson, *The Education of American Leaders: Comparative Contributions of United States Colleges and Universities* (New York, 1969), pp. 199–203. These ratings were based on tabulated personal estimates made by academic administrators and leading professors in each departmental field.

INDEX

Abbott, Grace, 43
Acrotheater, 157
Adler, Mortimer J., 50–51, 61, 82, 91; arrival at university, 34; conflicts with faculty, 39, 58–59, 67–71, 77–79, 81; and Great Books, 34–36, 66–67, 121–23, 157–58; Hutchins' relationship with, 34–40, 66–67, 79; McKeon contrasted with, 79–80; Philosophical Institute proposal of, 124; resignation from university, 132; and World War II, 100
Alamagordo, New Mexico, 107–9
Allison, Samuel, 43, 104, 107
"America First" movement, 100
American Association of University Professors, 83
American Council on Education, 43
American Men of Science, 43
American Student Union, 73, 74
Anselm, St., 55
Anthropology, 124, 160–61
Anthropology, Department of, 11, 160–61
Apology (Plato), 158
Aquinas, St. Thomas, 34, 36–39, 61. *See also* Thomism
Archaeology, 9, 76, 159, 160. *See also* Oriental Institute
Argonne National Laboratory, 106–7
Aristotelianism, 34, 36–39, 58, 59, 80
Aristotle, 150; and Adler, 34, 36–39; cult of, 151; on history, 113
Art, Department of, 75–76, 81–82, 119, 120
Assimilationism, 149–50
Assyriology, 161
Astronomy, Department of, 42, 76

Athletics, 14, 52; in Great Depression, 62; under Harper, 4; in postwar period, 155, 156; in prewar years, 95. *See also* Football
Atomic bomb, 123, 128–29, 133, 156; development of, 102–9; issue of civilian control, 125
Atomic energy, 102–3, 107, 125, 158–59
Atomic Energy Commission, 107, 125
Atomic research: Manhattan Project, 102–9; postwar, 123–24, 158–59

Bachhofer, Ludwig, 75
Baptists, 3, 6, 14, 18
Barden, John, 58–59
Barr, Stringfellow, 70–71
Basketball, 62, 95, 96
Beadle, George W., 169
Bell, Daniel, 148
Bell, Laird, 117–18, 129, 156
Beloit College, 96
Benton, William: arrival at university, 66; Broadcast Center idea of, 124–25; and *Encyclopaedia Britannica*, 122, 123; isolationism of, 100; public relations efforts by, 91–94, 97; withdrawal from campus affairs, 129, 132
Berwanger, Jay, 62, 95
Biblical studies, 3, 4, 46, 69
Big Ten. *See* Football
Billings Hospital, 159
Biological Sciences Division, 31–33, 131
Biology, 57, 91, 112; in Great Depression, 43; under New Plan, 31–33, 56; in postwar period, 139, 145, 161, 168; refugees' impact on, 82

185

Fraternities, 7, 61, 95, 155
Freud, Sigmund, 56, 147, 150
Freund, Ernst, 14
Friedman, Milton, 160
Funding and fund-raising, 94; at 50th anniversary, 100–101; in Great Depression, 41–42, 65; in 1920s, 8–9, 12; in postwar period, 163; in World War II, 103, 106, 108–10

Germany, 5, 41, 54; biblical criticism, 3; events leading to World War II, 72–75, 81; intellectual tradition, 81, 87–88, 143; refugees from, 75–76, 81–82, 161; in World War II, 99–100, 102, 108, 149–50
G. I. Bill, 126
Gideonse, Harry D., 32, 55–56, 69–70, 83–85
"God and the Professors" (address by Adler), 78–79
Goldsmith, Oliver, 46
Goliath: The March of Fascism (Borgese), 81
Gosnell, Harold, 110
Grades, 28, 141–42
Graduate departments, University of Chicago: dissatisfaction with College natural sciences courses, 146; in Great Depression, 42–44; growth of, 7, 10–13; Hutchins' attempts to restructure, 67, 90, 126; New Plan reorganization, 30–33; postwar developments, 152–54. *See also individual schools, departments, and subject areas*
Graduate education: growth of, 5; Harper on goals of, 26
Graduate Library School, 14, 139, 162
Graduate Record Examination, 181n.7
Grants. *See* Funding and fund-raising
Great Books, 32, 112; classes in, 34–36, 66, 91, 121–23, 157–58; publication of set of, 122
Great Books Foundation, 158
Great Britain, 99–100
Great Depression, 13–14, 41–71, 72, 135, 136; and descriptive social science, 34; impact on university, 26, 27, 41–47; Marxism during, 59–66; success of College reforms during, 47, 49–57; tenure issue during, 83; and World War II, 74, 99
Greek, Department of, 76, 77, 80, 120

Grene, David, 77, 120
Groves, Leslie, 106, 108

Haarlow, Bill, 95
Halas, George, 97–98
Hall, James Parker, 14
Hanford, Washington, 105–6, 125
Harper, William Rainey, 26, 30, 43, 46, 166, 169; and football, 4, 97, 98; Hutchins compared with, 17, 27, 164, 165; plans for university expansion, 47, 49; as president, 3–7, 13
Harvard University, 76, 159; Chicago compared with, 13, 43, 168; development of, 4–5; football, 5, 62
Hearst, William Randolph, 63, 65, 71
Heirens, William, 136
Herald Examiner, 63
"Higher Learning in a Democracy, The" (Gideonse), 69–70
Higher Learning in America, The (Hutchins), 66, 68, 83
High School, University of Chicago, 147; and four-year liberal arts curriculum, 111, 114; honors course, 66–67, 91
High schools, 146, 155; and four-year liberal arts curriculum, 114–15, 140; relation between college and, issue of, 26, 28–29, 66
Hiroshima bombing, 107, 109, 126, 128
History, 11, 81; exclusion of, 87, 113–14, 130–31, 150–52; in postwar period, 143–45, 152–54
History of Western Civilization (course), 152–54
Hitler, Adolf, 41, 68, 72–74, 79, 82, 108
Hobbes, Thomas, 91
Hoffman, Paul, 163
Hoover, Herbert, 41, 47, 172n.13
Hoselitz, Bert, 148
Hospitals, University of Chicago, 10, 12, 44; admission of blacks, 85–86, 137
Huggins, Charles, 45, 161
"Human Adventure, The" (radio series), 93
Humanities, Division of: and four-year liberal arts curriculum, 110–14, 131; in Great Depression, 43, 46; under McKeon, 78–80, 87–90, 119–21, 130; origin, 31–33; in postwar period, 139, 143–45, 161; refugees' impact on, 82

Rockefeller family, 9, 10
Rockefeller Foundation, 25, 86
Roman Catholicism, 2, 6, 37, 45, 173n.18
Romance Languages, Department of, 80–81
Roosevelt, Franklin D., 41, 68, 99–101
Roosevelt University, 162
"Rose Bowl Blues, The" (show), 157
Rothfels, Hans, 81
Roundtable, 57, 62, 91–93
Rubin, Arthur, 70
Ruml, Beardsley, 12, 33–34, 39
Rush Medical School, 9–10, 13, 44, 85
Russia. *See* Soviet Union

St. John's College, 36, 71
Salaries, 14, 41–42, 44, 86, 126–27, 163
Sandburg, Carl, 4
Saturday Evening Post, 93
Schevill, Ferdinand, 32, 54–55, 87–88, 91,
    113–14, 152
Schultz, Theodore, 160
Schuman, Frederick L., 64–65
Schwab, Joseph, 144, 145, 152
Scott, Arthur, 88, 91
Scott, Walter Dill, 47, 49
Sears Roebuck Company, 121–22
Securities and Exchange Commission, 99
Semiotics, 78
Senate, University of Chicago; conflict over
    tenure, 83, 84; and curriculum restructur-
    ing, 30, 111–17; and governance issue,
    117–19; and Hutchins' appointment, 16;
    replacement by Council, 129
Sharp, Malcolm, 79
Shaughnessy, Clark, 62, 98
Shils, Edward, 77, 125, 147, 148
Shimer College, 166
Simpson, Alan, 148
Simson, Otto von, 76
Singer, Milton, 148
Sloan Foundation, 91–92
Smith, Leon, 110
Smith, T. V., 57, 78, 92
Socialism, 60–64, 80
Socialist Club, 60, 63
Social sciences: development of, 10–12; in
    four-year liberal arts curriculum, 113; in
    Great Depression, 43, 45–46; under New

Plan, 31–34; in postwar period, 139, 143–
    48, 160–61, 168; role in law, for Hutchins,
    25; survey course in, 32, 55–56
Social Sciences, Division of: Adler's criticism
    of, 39, 59; Committee on Social Thought,
    119–21, 124; origin, 31–34; Redfield's at-
    tempt to restructure, 89–90
Social Sciences Research Building, 12
"Social Scientist's Misconception of Science,
    The" (address by Adler), 39
Social Service Administration, School of, 14,
    43, 139, 162
Sociology, 32, 56; black community studies,
    135; Chicago school of, 10–11, 13, 33–34;
    in Great Depression, 45–46
Sociology, Department of, 11, 15
South East Chicago Commission, 167
Soviet Union, 60, 64, 125; and Cold War,
    133; in World War II, 68, 72–74
Spelman Memorial Fund, 12
Sports. *See* Athletics
Stagg, Amos Alonzo, 4, 6, 62, 96–98
Stagg Field, 104, 105
Stalin, Joseph, 60, 64, 68, 72–74, 153
Stampf, Joe, 95
Stanford University, 115
Stone, Marshall H., 159–61
Story of Philosophy (Durant), 36
Strauss, Leo, 160
Stromgren, Bengt, 76
Struve, Otto, 42, 76
Students, University of Chicago: attrition
    rates, 52; demographic characteristics, 6,
    52–54; enrollment figures, 139, 174n.7;
    faculty relations with, 141–44, 147–48;
    and football, loss of, 98; intellectual char-
    acteristics, 50–52, 54, 58, 91, 94–95,
    140–41, 155–56; numbers in 1950s, 166,
    168; radical politics, 72–74; veterans, 126,
    139, 155
Summa Theologica (Aquinas), 34, 37, 39
Summer Quarter, 13–14
Supreme Court, U.S., 68, 99
Survey courses: athletes in, 95–96; conflicts
    with curriculum changes in 1940s, 112;
    Hutchins' dissatisfaction with, 33, 47, 49,
    58; New Plan, 28–33; postwar develop-
    ment, 144–48, 152–54; success of, 50,
    54–58